THE NEW DEAL

Problems in American History

Series editor: Jack P. Greene

Each volume focuses on a central theme in American history and provides greater analytical depth and historiographic coverage than standard textbook discussions normally allow. The intent of the series is to present in highly interpretive texts the unresolved questions of American history that are central to current debates and concerns. The texts will be concise enough to be supplemented with primary readings or core textbooks and are intended to provide brief syntheses to large subjects.

Already published

Jacqueline Jones	*A Social History of the Laboring Classes*
Robert Buzzanco	*Vietnam and the Transformation of American Life*
Ronald Edsforth	*The New Deal*

In preparation

Tom Purvis	*Causes of the American Revolution*
Norrece T. Jones	*Slavery and Antislavery*
Jack Rakove	*The American Constitution*
Frank Ninkovich	*American Imperialism*
Robert Westbrook	*America and World War II*
Amy Turner Bushnell	*The Indian Wars*
Fraser Harbutt	*The Cold War Era*
Peter Onuf	*Jeffersonian America*
J. William Harris	*The American South*
Anne Butler	*The American West*
Richard Ellis	*The Jacksonian Era*
David Hamilton	*The American State*
Lacy K. Ford, Jr	*Journey to Civil War*
Donna Gabaccia	*Migration and the Making of America*

THE NEW DEAL

America's Response to the Great Depression

Ronald Edsforth

Dartmouth College

First published 2000

2 4 6 8 10 9 7 5 3 1

Blackwell Publishers Inc.
350 Main Street
Malden, Massachusetts 02148
USA

Blackwell Publishers Ltd
108 Cowley Road
Oxford OX4 1JF
UK

Library of Congress Cataloging-in-Publication Data
Edsforth, Ronald, 1948–
    The New Deal : America's response to the Great Depression / Ronald Edsforth.
        p.   cm. — (Problems in American History)
    Includes bibliographical references (p.) and index.
    ISBN 1-57718-142-5 (hb : alk. paper) — ISBN 1-57718-143-3 (pb : alk. paper)
    1. United States—History—1933–1945.   2. United States—Economic conditions—1918–1945.   3. United States—Social conditions—1933–1945.
    4. New Deal, 1933–1939.   5. Depressions—1929—United States.   I. Title.
    II. Series.
    E806.E456 2000
    973.917—dc21   99-043955
                                                                                CIP

British Library Cataloguing in Publication Data
A CIP catalogue record for this book is available from the British Library.

Typeset in 11 on 13 pt Sabon by Ace Filmsetting Ltd, Frome, Somerset
Printed in Great Britain by MPG Books, Bodmin, Cornwall

This book is printed on acid-free paper.

Contents

To my sons, Nick and Oliver

Figures

Acknowledgments

This book distills more than a dozen years of reading, research, and teaching about the Great Depression. I take full responsibility for the ideas and whatever errors the book may contain. Travel grants from the Franklin D. Roosevelt Four Freedoms Foundation, American Historical Association, Henry J. Kaiser Family Foundation, and National Endowment for the Humanities enabled me to keep up my research during a long period of uncertain employment. In recent years students in my seminar on the Great Depression helped me sort out the massive disorders of the early 1930s through their diligent work in Dartmouth's Baker Library. Students who went on to write senior theses with me deserve special thanks. What I learned from Brandon Miller's work on racial violence, Andrew Weinberg's thesis on the Glass–Steagall Act, and Marissa Piropato's study of FDR's failed court reform made this a more meaningful book. I also want to thank Robert Asher, Alex Bontemps, Jere Daniell, Mickey Maloney, and an anonymous reader for their critical responses to drafts of various chapters. My wife Joanne Devine provided me with editorial assistance and invaluable psychological support during a stressful period when we were juggling serious health problems, the task of raising two children, and this book project. Finally I want to thank Susan Rabinowitz and Ken Provencher of Blackwell Publishers for their patience with an author who had trouble meeting every deadline.

Ronald Edsforth
June 30, 1999

Franklin D. Roosevelt, Eleanor Roosevelt, and Senate Majority Leader
Joseph Robinson at the Inauguration ceremony, March 4, 1933.

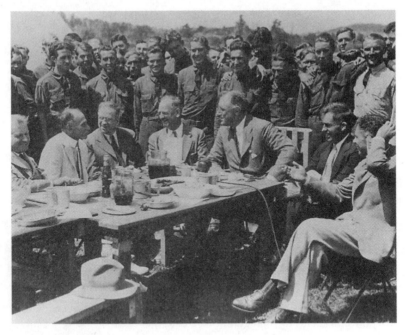

President Roosevelt visiting a Civilian Conservation Corps camp in Big Meadows, Virginia, August 12, 1933. Seated at the table (left to right) are General Malone, Louis Howe, Harold Ickes, CCC director Robert Fechner, FDR, Henry Wallace, and Rexford Tugwell.

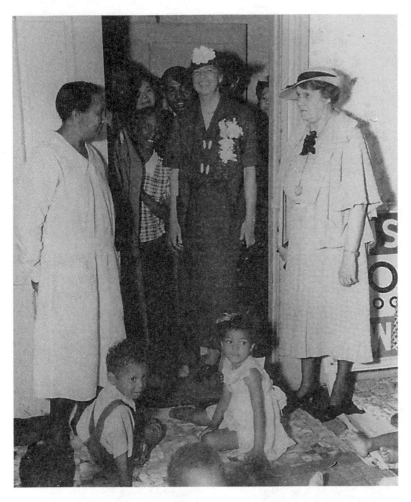

Eleanor Roosevelt visiting a WPA Negro Nursery School in Des Moines, Iowa, June 8, 1936.

Portrait of a healthy President Roosevelt taken by Leon Perskie in 1938. The photograph was used as the official campaign portrait of FDR in 1944 when he actually looked much older and was seriously ill.

Introduction: The New Deal in Historical Perspective

"I pledge you, I pledge myself, to a New Deal for the American people."
Franklin D. Roosevelt, accepting the Democratic
nomination for President, July 2, 1932

"A New Deal" is what Franklin Delano Roosevelt (FDR), the Democratic Party's candidate for President, promised voters in the fall of 1932, three years after the crash of stock prices on Wall Street had signaled the onset of the Great Depression. "The New Deal" is what the new President, the press, and everyone else in the country called the laws Congress began enacting just days after FDR took office in the first week of March 1933. This New Deal, an unprecedented expansion of federal government programs during Franklin Roosevelt's first two administrations, was America's national response to the Great Depression. It dramatically reshaped politics, presidential power, and the role of the federal government in the economy of the United States of America.

By 1936 most Americans recognized the New Deal as a tremendously important turning point in their nation's history. The public held very strong opinions about Franklin D. Roosevelt and his New Deal. Many millions of Americans loved FDR and vehemently defended the New Deal. Other Americans, far less numerous but usually better heeled, hated the President and his New Deal reforms. This impassioned political division over the New Deal established new meanings for the terms "liberal" and "conservative;" meanings Americans still use today to identify a person's politics.

For a majority of Americans who lived through the Great

Depression and a majority of their children, the New Deal was understood as a great national achievement, something akin to establishing the Republic or abolishing slavery. This New Deal adapted the powers of the federal government to an America that had become a great urban industrial nation in the twentieth century. At the heart of the New Deal reform program was a liberal commitment to make federally guaranteed economic security a political right for every American citizen. This ideological commitment was expressed in a host of New Deal programs such as social security pensions, federal unemployment benefits, federal deposit insurance, and federal farm price supports. Supporters believed these New Deal programs and others like them were both necessary and inviolable.

Franklin Roosevelt tried to make the New Deal permanent during his last years as President during World War II. As the nation's war leader, and a candidate for an unprecedented fourth term, Roosevelt defined a new "Economic Bill of Rights" that would set an agenda for politics after the war. In one of his famous fireside radio addresses on January 11, 1944, the President explained that "true individual freedom cannot exist without economic security and independence." He claimed the American people "have accepted . . . a second Bill of Rights under which a new basis of security and prosperity can be established for all – regardless of station or race or creed." FDR's universal Economic Bill of Rights included rights to "a useful and remunerative job;" to "adequate food and clothing and recreation;" to "a decent home;" to "adequate medical care;" and "a good education." It promised farmers prices for their crops "that will give them and their families a decent living;" and businessmen "freedom from unfair competition and domination by monopolies." Finally, it pledged to all "the right to adequate protection from the economic fears of old age and sickness and accident and unemployment." As Franklin Roosevelt aptly noted, "All these rights spell security."

In 1944, and for three decades after the war, a majority of American voters supported government efforts to guarantee this kind of economic security. Most of them recognized that the actual achievement of the goals set forth in the Economic Bill of Rights required a great expansion of the federal government's power, and they approved the goal and the methods. Voters approved of income security programs for individuals and farmers, regulation of financial institutions and industrial corporations, spending programs to build infrastructure and create jobs, and many other federal initiatives to foster economic growth. Carrying the scars of the Great Depression into the Cold War era, the majority of Americans expected the rich to be more heavily taxed than working people, and the benefits of government programs to be shared more or less equally by all citizens. These basic assumptions had guided the New Deal, and they continued to give direction to the dominant Democratic Party after World War II.

White Americans, including many farmers and working people who admired FDR and the New Deal, were actually deeply and often bitterly divided over the goal of achieving true racial equality. In 1948 white Southern Democrats led by South Carolina governor Strom Thurmond bolted from the Democratic national convention protesting the party's platform commitment to racial equality. After this incident Democratic leaders tried to avoid disturbing questions about the racial distribution of jobs, income, wealth, and power implicit in the New Deal's linking of economic security to racial equality. Many Cold War Democrats such as John F. Kennedy hoped that economic growth alone would guarantee economic security for all. In the early 1960s, however, civil rights marches and demonstrations organized by black Americans forced two Democratic administrations and the Democratic majorities in Congress to take strong actions, including the Civil Rights Act of 1964 and Voting Rights Act of 1965, to end racial segregation and economic inequality.

Black America's political victories were increasingly resented among white Americans as working-class and lower-middle-class living standards deteriorated and crime rates soared in the 1970s. Respect for the work of the federal government, a key attribute of the New Deal majority also crumbled in those years as people tried to make sense of both the atrocities and military defeat in Southeast Asia, and the crimes committed by high officials in the Watergate affair. Turning the discontent about "the imperial presidency" into attacks on "big government," anti-New Deal conservatives made the most of the moment. With Ronald Reagan acting as a very effective standard bearer, conservatives presented their attack on New Deal government as a restoration of individualism, family values, states rights, and patriotic pride. They easily took control of the Republican Party after the party's defeat in the presidential election of 1976. By 1980, when Ronald Reagan first won the presidency, conservative Republicans had put together a cross-class national majority of mostly white voters.

That conservative majority has more or less persisted down to the time of this writing. During Bill Clinton's first four years as President it could count among its victories the scrapping of New Deal agriculture policy in 1995 and the momentous abandonment of federal guaranteed economic assistance to the poor in 1996. The current conservative majority can trace its roots directly back to the anti-New Deal alliance between Republicans and white Southern Democrats that first emerged in Congress in 1937. Like their predecessors, today's conservatives deny that federally guaranteed economic security is a political right, and they oppose federal efforts to apply its standards everywhere equally "regardless of station or race or creed."

Since the mid-1970s, Republican conservatives have been extremely successful in undermining popular confidence in core New Deal beliefs. These conservatives dismissed the New Deal and Democratic liberalism as an outdated mish-mash of programs that undermined free markets and wasted the taxpayers' hard-earned money. The conservatives of today, like those of the 1930s, want to return the power to make decisions affecting economic security from the federal government back to the states and to the marketplace of privately owned corporations. They still view federal subsidies to private corporations as proper and necessary, but see labor unions as either anachronisms or anathema. Conservatives also want to abolish progressive taxes of all kinds. But unlike their Depression predecessors, today's conservatives have renounced protective tariffs (a traditional Republican Party policy favored by many industries in the 1930s) in favor of global free trade (a policy favored by big corporations in recent decades).

In the 1980s, Ronald Reagan hammered away at "tax-and-spend liberals" and "big government" and twice won the White House. Self-proclaimed "New Democrats" led by Arkansas governor Bill Clinton thought they saw the handwriting on the wall, so they too openly renounced the "big government" liberalism of their own party, the party of Franklin Roosevelt and the New Deal. Clinton and his cohorts won the battle for control of the Democratic Party. Since Bill Clinton's election to the presidency in 1992, bi-partisan cooperation has clearly sped up the work of dismantling the New Deal.

Today most Democratic Party leaders run from the word "liberal" and praise the rationality and fairness of "free markets." Today politicians in both major parties run over each other in a competition for contributions from the burgeoning class of millionaires, the greatest beneficiaries of recent tax cuts and federal subsidies. Reports of scandals and how individual politicians handle them fill the void left in the news by the simultaneous end of the Cold War and the collapse of New Deal liberalism within the Democratic Party.

In these circumstances, most Americans have lost touch with the New Deal. Those who took part and those who remember it well are few, and getting fewer. And it's not just a matter of who is left to tell their stories. Twenty years of politicians and political reporters who are publicly cynical about politics have cut us off from the spirit of the New Deal. Americans have been bludgeoned with the companion ideas that all Washington politicians are corrupt and that government is what's wrong with the economy and just about everything else. We have been told over and over to depend on the marketplace not government, that free markets will provide wealth for some and well-paying jobs for everyone else. Conservatives insist that the new global economy dominated by a few hundred corporations is natural and inevitable, and that resistance to it is futile. Conservative ideas such as these now thoroughly inform the way political news is framed and public issues are discussed. Simply put, New Deal liberalism has lost its legitimacy. It's almost as if the Great Depression and the New Deal never happened.

At the outset of this book then, the question arises, what were the circumstances that brought the New Deal to power? Those days were so very different from our own. In the early 1930s, as the world economy sunk deeper and deeper into depression, capitalism in the United States collapsed. In those days, the collapsing free market economy was impoverishing most of the American people. They simply could not fend for themselves and their families. Even millionaires felt the pinch. Confidence in the self-correcting rational marketplace, so widely in evidence in the 1920s, was hard to find. Businessmen, bankers, and plantation owners were among the throng in Washington on Inauguration Day, March 4, 1933, hoping to persuade the new President and new Democratic Congress to lend them a hand. Like the homeless and the destitute, the cold and the hungry, they had nowhere else to turn.

To begin to recover the extraordinary ways the New Deal transformed American government and political culture we have to begin by somehow stepping out of our own times into the depths of the Great Depression. That long national crisis seems almost unimaginable to us today. Yet we must try to imagine it. We must suspend what we think we know today about politics and economics in order to be, as Americans were in the winter of 1932–33, in desperate anticipation of something called a New Deal. If we can somehow accomplish this feat of historical imagination, we may be able to feel, if only for just a moment, the uncanny thrill of recognition most people must have felt as they leaned toward the radio on March 4, 1933 to hear their new President Franklin D. Roosevelt exclaim, "the only thing we have to fear is fear itself – nameless, unreasoning, unjustified terror which paralyzes needed efforts to convert retreat into advance."

From our point of view, located as we are in our own peculiar present, it is very difficult for us to really grasp what

Roosevelt was talking about, to feel the terrifying possibilities that confronted Americans in early 1933. The tens of millions of Americans listening to the radio voice of their new President on March 4, 1933 could not be sure how, or even if, the Great Depression could be ended. But we know what happened next. We know that the downward economic spiral was reversed later that year, and that Franklin Roosevelt and his New Deal restored the confidence of most Americans in capitalism and democracy. We know that the problem of mass unemployment was not fully resolved until 1942 when the United States was engaged in a terrible war against Nazi Germany, Fascist Italy, and Imperial Japan. We also know that for a generation after World War II the American economy created the highest average material living standards in the history of the world. All of this accumulated knowledge makes it very difficult to approach the New Deal, as its contemporaries did, with no certainty about what might arise from the wreckage of their free enterprise economy.

For us to truly understand the New Deal, we must first take some time to examine the long downward economic spiral that was only slowly recognized as the "Great Depression." The particular way America's free enterprise economy collapsed, the failure of President Herbert Hoover's recovery program, and especially the great fears that gripped the nation during the winter of 1932–33 were the most important forces shaping the New Deal. These fears have sometimes been overlooked, and more often been dismissed, by historians. Within long scholarly discussions of the "interregnum" – the uneasy four months between Herbert Hoover's defeat and Franklin Roosevelt's inauguration – the great fears of 1932–33 have been typically presented as merely a fleeting episode of mass irrationality in the run up to the New Deal. Franklin Roosevelt himself was a principal source of this error. His famous first inaugural words about fearing "only fear itself," and his description of that fear as "nameless, unreasoning, unjustified terror" have been cues for historians ever since to discount widespread contemporary apprehension about the survival of law and order, capitalism, and democracy as unfounded and

very short-lived. Roosevelt contributed to the error in another
way too. He and the Congress so quickly restored public confidence in basic institutions – it took just those legendary Hundred Days in the spring of 1933 – that it has been all too easy
to assume the preceding winter's fears of revolution, or anarchy, or race war, or some awful combination of these things
were actually of little consequence.

The interpretative issue here is of the first importance. If we
assume the "fear itself" of which Roosevelt spoke was just a
kind of temporary insanity, then subsequent New Deal reforms that addressed problems as if those fears were justified
would have been flawed from the outset. If free enterprise
hadn't really failed, but most Americans including their elected
leaders just got swept up in a panic, then once confidence was
restored, there would have been no need for basic institutional
reforms aimed at providing universal economic security. In
other words, the New Deal would have been unnecessary, and
by implication "bad" because it impeded the "natural" evolu-
tion of American capitalism. Since Herbert Hoover's defeat in
1932 this interpretative leap has been a favorite among conservatives, especially free market fundamentalists who believe
that capitalism can never fail, and therefore could not have
not failed in the Great Depression.

This belief in a failure-free American capitalism cannot be
squared with historical evidence from the Great Depression.
That evidence tells us, just as it told most Americans at the
time, that the country's free enterprise economy did fail in
1932–33. Subsequent chapters of this book present some of
this evidence, and find in it rational bases for the great fears
that then gripped the nation. When we go back to those four
months between Roosevelt's election victory in November
1932 and his first actions as President in March 1933, we
discover terrible human suffering, bewilderment, and much
despair. And we also find a very widespread breakdown of
respect for law and deference toward legal authority. Daily
theft and looting of stores for food, farm strikes, anti-eviction
and anti-foreclosure riots, Communist-led hunger marches,
seizures of public buildings, police gassing and shooting of

unemployed workers, attempted assassinations of public officials, lynch mobs and vigilante violence; these were the kind
of disturbing events that emanated from the failure of American capitalism in 1932–33. So in that fourth winter of the
long downward economic spiral, when the American banking
system finally crumbled, who could really say what might come
next?

That same awful winter, events overseas suggested chilling
possibilities. In early 1933, Americans read in their newspapers about Japan's assault on China and the collapse of
democracy and consolidation of Nazi power in depression-
ravaged Germany. They saw Adolph Hitler's image in photographs and newsreels almost as often as they saw the image of
their President-elect. Militarism and fascism were not hard to
imagine. Neither were revolution, race war, or anarchy; all
seemed possible when the economic system underpinning everyday life failed to provide so many people with the means of
existence. At such an extraordinary historical moment, most
Americans rightly feared for the survival of not just capitalism, but for the survival of democracy and social order too.

The New Deal was how a democratic America responded
to the Great Depression and the great fears of 1932–33. During the spring of 1933, in just a few months of tremendously
creative political activity, President Franklin Roosevelt and
the newly elected Congress reversed the long downward economic spiral that had culminated in the collapse of the nation's banking system. For this reason alone, the New Deal
was experienced as a salvation by most Americans. But the
New Deal did much more. By 1941, the first two Roosevelt
administrations had built up a set of federal institutions and
programs designed to provide security to all citizens regardless of their economic function in society, no matter what their
age, sex, or race. Using workers who had been made redundant by the collapse of private enterprise, the New Deal had
also built up the infrastructure – including water projects, hydroelectric dams, national forests, airports, roads, bridges, and
tunnels – that would permit the whole nation, and especially
the West and the South, to grow and prosper during and after

World War II. These were new roles for the federal government, roles that conservatives have never been able to accept
as legitimate. Yet in its own time, in the decade of the Great
Depression and fascist aggression, the New Deal was viewed
as a triumph of democracy by people all around the world.
This book seeks to make this view of the New Deal once again
comprehensible.

FURTHER READING

Primary Sources

Buhite, Russell D. and Levy, David W. eds. *FDR's Fireside Chats*. Norman:
University of Oklahoma Press, 1992.
Geddes, David Porter ed. *Franklin Delano Roosevelt: A Memorial*. New
York: Pocket Books, 1945.
Roosevelt, Franklin Delano. *The Public Papers and Addresses of Franklin
D. Roosevelt, Volume Two: The Year of Crisis 1933*. New York: Ran-
dom House, 1938.

Secondary Sources

Fraser, Steve and Gerstle, Gary eds. *The Rise and Fall of the New Deal
Order 1930–1980*. Princeton: Princeton University Press, 1989.
Gunther, John. *Roosevelt in Retrospect: A Profile in History*. New York:
Harper & Brothers, 1950.
Alonzo L. Hamby. *Liberalism and Its Challengers: From FDR to Bush*.
New York: Oxford University Press, 1992.
Kuklick, Bruce. *The Good Ruler: From Herbert Hoover to Richard Nixon*.
New Brunswick: Rutgers University Press, 1988.
Leuchtenburg, William E. *In the Shadow of FDR: From Harry Truman to
Bill Clinton*. Ithaca: Cornell University Press, 1993.
Leuchtenburg, William E. *The FDR Years: On Roosevelt and His Legacy*.
New York: Columbia University Press, 1995.
Maney, Patrick J. *The Roosevelt Presence: A Biography of Franklin Delano
Roosevelt*. New York: Twayne, 1992.

1

From New Era Prosperity to a World in Depression

"It is high time to admit with courage that we are in the midst of an emergency at least equal to that of war."

Franklin Roosevelt, April 7, 1932

Herbert Hoover's Fate

Herbert Hoover had never held elective office before he ran for President of the United States in 1928. Yet Republican leaders and most of the nation's editorial writers believed he was perfect for the position. Hoover had succeeded fabulously at everything he had ever tried: as an engineer and international businessman before World War I, as director of the United States Food Administration during the war, as the organizer of food relief for Europe after the war, and as Secretary of Commerce since 1921. Herbert Hoover was expected to be a most successful President. All Hoover really had to do, it seemed to most observers, was to continue the policies of the Harding and Coolidge administrations in which he had served. Stress efficiency in government, lower taxes, and business-government cooperation not regulation, and America's booming industrial economy would do the rest. True, prohibition had developed into a serious political problem as urban ethnic workers started to vote in larger numbers. Nonetheless Hoover believed the nation's Protestant majority still shared his commitment to "the noble experiment."

Herbert Hoover also had a few progressive ideas that put him in the center of his mostly conservative Republican party.[1] He wanted the federal government to encourage cooperative marketing among farmers hard hit by falling world prices for grain and cotton. He also wanted federal regulation of the new radio broadcasting and air travel businesses. However, on most economic questions, Herbert Hoover was conservative. He believed strongly in unfettered individualism, the efficiency of markets, the international gold standard, and the necessity of balanced government budgets.

By 1928 most Americans shared Herbert Hoover's confidence that private investors and unregulated markets would produce continuously rising living standards and increased leisure time. Although we know this economic confidence was mistaken, at the time people had good reasons to believe they were living in what was often called the "New Era." Per capita disposable income had increased nearly 50 percent since 1922; and a seemingly endless array of new things – streamlined automobiles, electric appliances, radio entertainment, Hollywood spectacles, film stars, and sports heroes – dazzled most Americans. Big business propagated a wonderful new dreamscape of goods and pleasurable activities that transformed what most people expected from life. The United States became the first (and at the time, the world's only) true mass-consumer society, and there was no shortage of corporate advertisers, business leaders, and Republican politicians willing to claim responsibility for this achievement.

Mass marketing of new consumer goods and reductions in work time that permitted many people to enjoy new commercialized forms of recreation were the most visible signs of the New Era. But the most important underlying cause of New Era optimism was the near doubling of industrial productivity in the 1920s. Companies that produced machines such as automobiles, radios, and home appliances for consumers led the way, but there were significant productivity gains made in other industries too. The greatest beneficiaries of increasing output per worker were the relatively few rich Americans who shared ownership of leading companies. Nonetheless, when Herbert Hoover first ran for President the average annual wages of working Americans were the highest in human history.

America's remarkable economic performance clearly influenced Herbert Hoover's acceptance of the 1928 Republican nomination. "We in America today are nearer to the final triumph over poverty than ever before in the history of any land," he proclaimed,

> The poorhouse is vanishing from among us. We have not yet reached the goal but, given a chance to go forward with the policies of the last eight years, we shall soon, with the help of God, be in sight of the day when poverty will be banished from this nation. There is no guarantee against poverty equal to a job for every man. That is the primary purpose of the policy we advocate.

Unfortunately for Herbert Hoover, the collapse of America's economy would soon make this vision of an emerging free enterprise utopia seem naive, and even tragic.

Yet Herbert Hoover's ideas did not disappear in the Great Depression; in fact they are still very much alive today. His assumption that economic plenty for all would result when the federal government assists, instead of regulates, privately owned corporations remains a cornerstone of modern conservative politics. Moreover the insistence on individual responsibility for economic outcomes expressed in Hoover's belief that "a job for every man" is the only necessary anti-poverty program also remains an article of conservative faith, although it has been modified to include single mothers and working wives in recent years.

Today we call Hoover's political-economic ideas "conservative" because they acquired that label when set in opposition to Franklin D. Roosevelt's "liberal" New Deal. In 1928, however, Hoover's Republicanism was widely identified with what was new and modern, especially the new things that defined America's unique mass consumer culture. Like Hoover, most Americans accepted the constantly advertised message that the New Era economy would eventually bring almost everyone better homes and health, as well as cars, electricity, frozen foods, mass entertainment, and annual vacations. By the late 1920s, this vision of the future amounted to the modern "American Dream" that leading figures in both major political parties embraced as the proper goal of federal government policies.

In November 1928, Herbert Hoover won 444 electoral votes for President, easily defeating Al Smith, the Catholic governor of New York who wanted to repeal prohibition. Smith won just 87 electoral votes and only one state outside the Deep South. Smith's religion, support for repeal of prohibition, and strong Manhattan working-class accent split his party, leading many Protestant Democrats to vote Republican for the first time in their lives. Smith outpolled Hoover in the ethnically diverse big cities, but lost nearly everywhere else including Upper South states that had not produced a Republican majority since Reconstruction. Al Smith even lost to Hoover in his home state of New York, while his handpicked candidate, Franklin Roosevelt, eked out a narrow victory to hold the governor's office for the Democrats.

During the next four years, America's New Era economy failed Herbert Hoover and the nation. Gross domestic investment fell from $16,000,000,000 in 1929 to just $1,000,000,000 in 1932. Private construction, automobile production, and steel output each fell to less than one-quarter their 1929 levels. By autumn 1932, the new American Dream of a home full of electrical gadgets and new car was still widely advertised, but it had receded from the practical reach of most families with frightening speed. As Hoover and Roosevelt campaigned for the White House, the majority of voters worried about putting enough food on the table and other matters of basic survival. President Hoover nevertheless held fast to his optimistic New Era ideas, even when the words he had used so successfully four years earlier were turned against him by his Democratic opponent. Instead of moving America closer to the abolition of poverty, Hoover had presided over what Franklin Roosevelt correctly described at the outset of the campaign as "a depression so deep it is without precedent in modern history." Roosevelt continued,

> The people will not forget the claim ... that prosperity was only a domestic product manufactured by a Republican President and a Republican Congress. If they claim paternity for the one they cannot deny paternity for the other [the ongoing depression].

As election day approached, Hoover campaigned frantically, making as many as 23 short speeches in 15 hours. Over and over, he blamed the depression on events overseas, while defending his administration's austerity budgets, maintenance of the gold standard, and high tariffs. Hoover described Franklin Roosevelt as a dangerous radical who would ruin America with "the same philosophy of government which has poisoned all Europe." This charge was a gross parody of Roosevelt's actual reform proposals, but it hardly mattered. In November 1932, Hoover's real opponent was the Great Depression. For three long years he had insisted the American economy was sound while it was actually collapsing. In the end, Franklin Roosevelt easily won the election of 1932 because Herbert Hoover could not disassociate himself from the Great Depression and its brutal effects on the everyday lives of most Americans.

The Limits of New Era Prosperity

During the presidential campaign of 1932, the Great Depression had not yet reached its nadir, but already more than one in five workers were unemployed. As orders for goods declined, many companies laid off their oldest and youngest workers while reducing hours for their most productive workers. For example, the United States Steel Corporation had nearly a quarter of a million full-time workers on its payroll in 1929; three years later only 19,000 full-time workers remained. By March 1933, all of United States Steel's remaining workforce were part-timers. As unemployment and underemployment soared to record levels, America's traditional system of locally controlled poor relief collapsed. Private charities and local governments went bankrupt trying to provide even minimal subsistence to the new armies of the poor. At the same time millions of rural families faced the loss of their farms as prices for the harvest of 1932 collapsed to their lowest levels of the twentieth century.

What were the origins of this economic catastrophe, the

worst ever depression in the United States' history? How and why had the American economic system collapsed? By 1932, most Americans realized that their free enterprise economy was unsound, but they could not understand why it was breaking down so completely. Explanations of the Great Depression have multiplied over the years, and still there is no expert consensus on the exact nature of the process that shattered the American economy in the early 1930s. Yet many of the facts are not in dispute.

One thing is certain; when Herbert Hoover began his presidency in March 1929 not a single prominent economist, businessman, or political leader predicted the disastrous depression that lay ahead. Most of them were confident that the New Era would continue indefinitely. By 1929, the American economy was very different from what it had been at the turn of the century. People realized that tremendous growth and transformation had occurred, but only a handful of experts spoke of the preceding three decades as a "second industrial revolution." Four major developments interacting on each other created this second industrial revolution. These developments included the institutionalization of scientific research and technological innovation in corporate laboratories and universities; an intense mechanization of industrial production; the growth of huge bureaucratically managed corporations that decreased competition in their national markets; and the relentless selling of products to individual consumers by those corporations. Nineteenth-century economics, derived from the study of agriculture and of small highly competitive firms, was not adequate for explaining the way the mass consumer economy of the New Era functioned. Yet when the Great Depression began, virtually all of America's political leaders including Herbert Hoover and Franklin Roosevelt had a nineteenth-century understanding of economics. This gap between the economic understanding of the political leadership and the actual functioning of the new mass consumer economy contributed greatly to the ineffectiveness of America's initial responses to the Great Depression.

The automobile industry epitomized the second industrial

revolution and its impact on American society. By 1929 General Motors, Ford, and Chrysler formed an oligopoly that systematically developed new products to be manufactured on assembly lines and sold everywhere in the United States via non-stop advertising and an unprecedented extension of credit to consumers. By 1929, the daily use of 30,000,000 automobiles and trucks had brought about especially dramatic changes in the way everyday life was organized. That year, 60 percent of America's households owned at least one motor vehicle, and perhaps as many as one in every nine non-farm workers was employed either directly or indirectly in producing, selling, and servicing of motor vehicles. Local, state, and federal road-building programs had created an ever more tightly knit national marketplace, which in turn promoted increased urbanization and suburbanization. Rush-hour traffic jams and weekend congestion on roads leading to popular recreation areas were a new source of stress by the late 1920s. In less than one generation, the American people's enthusiastic embrace of cars had made automobile-centered mass consumerism the dominant pattern of national economic development. For New Era prosperity to continue the expansion of automobility had to be sustained. Instead automobile production collapsed during the early 1930s.

The end of the New Era was signaled by the Great Crash, a precipitous decline of stock prices on the New York Exchange in October and November of 1929. The standard price index of all stocks traded on the New York Exchange had more than doubled in the late 1920s, and then it plunged over 25 percent in the Great Crash. On paper, losses to investors totaled more than $15,000,000,000. Stock prices spiraled down for another two years. By June 1932, common stocks traded in New York were worth just 15 percent of their September 1929 value. At the time, many Americans were quick to blame greedy speculators for the Great Crash, and the Crash for the Great Depression. "I say this whole panic was brought on by [a] dishonest group which I hope will be punished," a typically angry citizen wrote to President Hoover in 1930. New Dealers both promoted and exploited this view of the Great

Depression, using it to build popular support for banking reform and federal regulation of financial markets. The "rulers of the exchange of mankind's goods have failed through their own stubbornness and their own incompetence," Franklin Roosevelt explained in his first inaugural address. He continued, "Practices of the unscrupulous money changers stand indicted in the court of opinion, rejected by the hearts and minds of men." It was time, Roosevelt went on to proclaim, to make the nation's financial institutions act according to "social values more noble than mere monetary profit." Subsequent New Deal measures that imposed federally enforced standards of behavior on banks and securities markets – including the Banking Acts of 1933 and 1935, the Securities Act of 1933, and Securities Exchange Act of 1934 – all resulted from this popular interpretation of the origins of the Great Depression.

The absence of regulation of companies issuing stocks and of the way stock market transactions were financed created a situation ripe for speculation and the bursting of the speculative bubble in 1929. However, the Great Crash itself was more a catalyst than a cause of the Great Depression. The million or so Americans who suffered losses in the Great Crash certainly limited their consumption and investment expenditures. But the more important effect of the Crash was psychological. The collapse of stock prices in late 1929 brought about a swift alteration in the attitudes of lenders and investors from supreme confidence to deep uncertainty about the future.

In the late 1920s, the uncritical confidence of investors in the rising stock market and their eagerness to speculate with borrowed money were actually symptoms of weaknesses in both America's domestic economy and in the international economy that had been accumulating since World War I. The billions of dollars that poured into New York's call loan market feeding the rapid rise in stock in 1928–29 indicated a dearth of highly profitable investment opportunities in production at home and abroad.[2] Fears of excessive speculation with borrowed money led the Federal Reserve in New York to raise its discount rate (the interest rate it charged member banks) in

August 1929, but prices on the New York Exchange continued to rise into September. Central banks in Europe followed
New York's lead, establishing higher interest rates abroad on
the eve of the Great Crash. At this time, many financial experts expected a sharp correction on Wall Street and a slowing down of economic growth, but no one predicted a Great
Depression.

Hindsight enables us to bring the serious underlying economic problems of the New Era into focus. The United States
had suffered a significant economic slowdown after World
War I; however, by 1922 the economy as a whole was expanding rapidly. Investment in electric power, new types of
factories and equipment, and in the assembly line methods
pioneered by the automobile industry created increases in productivity that raised incomes and generated widespread economic optimism. Nonetheless, by the late 1920s serious
impediments to future expansion of the new mass-consumer
economy had emerged. Three of these problems were especially important: agricultural prices declined sharply; income
and wealth were very unequally distributed; and other nations
were unable to provide strong demand for American exports.

Prices of crops sold on international markets that had never
fully recovered from postwar deflation began moving down
again in 1926. World agricultural prices fell about 30 percent
from the harvest of 1925 to the harvest of 1929. The Soviet
Union's decision to sell wheat on the world market beginning
in 1926 may have contributed to American farmers' economic
difficulties. But the larger problem resulted from millions of
individual decisions made around the globe. Since farmers
everywhere tended to respond to lower prices by increasing
production, and demand for their crops was not growing as
rapidly as supply, agricultural prices declined in the late 1920s.

At the time, some experts in the United States defined the
root cause of declining farm incomes as overproduction. These
experts included Henry A. Wallace, a developer of hybrid corn
and editor of a leading Midwestern farm journal who became
Franklin Roosevelt's first Secretary of Agriculture; and Rexford
Tugwell, a Columbia University economist who was one of

Roosevelt's closest advisors during the campaign of 1932. What Wallace and Tugwell learned about agricultural markets in the late 1920s convinced them that the federal government had to take actions to prevent surpluses from holding down commodity prices. As New Dealers, they would implement this idea under the authority of a series of Agricultural Adjustment Acts. These laws, passed by large majorities in Congress between 1933 and 1938, authorized federal payments to farmers who limited production, as well as federal purchases and storage of crop surpluses that had a depressing effect on markets.

The world agricultural depression that began in 1926 had an enormous impact in the United States because huge regions of the country remained primarily rural and agricultural. In 1929, fully two-fifths of all Americans still lived in rural places.[3] That year, agriculture created one-quarter of all American jobs, and export sales comprised 28 percent of the nation's farm income. Cotton and wheat were America's biggest exports. The world agricultural depression sharply reduced farm incomes. As a result large segments of the American population were excluded from the New Era's prosperity. Furthermore, by reducing the incomes of less-developed nations that were far more dependent on agriculture than the United States, the world agricultural depression also severely limited export opportunities for American industry.

Two huge regions – the cotton belt that stretched west from South Carolina to Texas, and the wheat belt that ran south from Minnesota and North Dakota to Kansas and Oklahoma – were especially hard hit by low world prices in the late 1920s. Tenants and sharecroppers in those regions saw their cash incomes disappear after they had paid their rents and what they owed local storeowners for supplies and foodstuffs. Owner operators who had borrowed to buy more land, new tractors, farm machinery, and cars also found themselves strapped as their incomes were reduced by falling prices. Farm foreclosures and the numbers of tenant farmers both began to rise in 1926 as a result of the agricultural depression. Already in difficult straits by 1929, and about to face catastrophic price declines, American agriculture was simply in no condition to sustain the nation's economic transformation when the financial and industrial sectors of the economy weakened at the end of the decade.

In the late 1920s, there were at least two other signs that all was not well in the American economy. First, construction expenditures which had more than doubled in five years, declined from a peak of $10,700,000 in 1926 to just $8,700,000 in 1929. Secondly, 1926 turned out to be the last year that Henry Ford could profitably manufacture his famous Model T. New car sales increased slowly during the next three years, but for the first time in the industry's 30-year history replacement car buyers outnumbered Americans purchasing their first automobile. This change in the composition of the automobile market greatly benefited the Ford Motor Company's major rivals because they sold a variety of stylish and colorful new models more attractive to buyers who were turning in their first or second car for something new. But the change in automobile market, like the decline in new construction, also indicated that the practical limits of those able to buy into the new American Dream were fast being approached.

These limits were primarily defined by the distribution of national income and wealth. Although the new American dreamscape of universal mass consumption was widely disseminated via newspapers, magazines, movies, and radio, the actual material benefits of New Era prosperity were very unevenly distributed. In 1929, a Brookings Institution study revealed that the wealthiest 27,500 families had combined incomes equal to all the income earned by of the poorest 11,450,000 families. That year less than 30 percent of all families had incomes over $2,500, an amount widely identified as the threshold of an "American Standard of Living" that included home and automobile ownership; more than an adequate diet, clothing, and health care; as well as disposable income for regular recreation and purchases of non-essential goods. A tiny fraction of these comfortable families earned most of their income from investments or the ownership of very large farms. The rest had primary wage earners in business or the professions, or they were headed by the skilled craftsmen and machinists that social historians call "the aristocracy of labor." Together, these 7,967,000 families sustained the mass-consumer prosperity of the New Era. But even many of them were not financially secure. The same Brookings study showed that nearly 80 percent of all families had no savings whatsoever in 1929. They all would be especially vulnerable when the Great Depression began to drastically lower employment and incomes.

New Era prosperity was actually concentrated in urban areas, especially in the Northeast, the Great Lakes states, and along the Pacific Coast. The oil-producing centers of Texas, Oklahoma, and other Western states also enjoyed considerable growth and prosperity during the automobile boom. But across the continent, rural Americans generally remained out of the mainstream of New Era prosperity. Farmers who supplied vegetables, fruits, meat, eggs, and dairy products to nearby urban markets did not immediately fall victim to declining world prices in the late 1920s, but their incomes fell further and further behind urban incomes. As the New Era ended, most farm owners and some tenant farmers owned motor vehicles, but very few could afford a new car or truck. In 1929, nine out of every ten farm families lived without electricity.

During the New Era and throughout the Great Depression the South remained the nation's poorest region. Cotton-mill towns in the Southeast were busy in the 1920s, but mainly because mill owners exploited the region's low wage labor market and its absence of industrial regulations. A few Southern cities such as Atlanta and Houston entered the automobile age, but on the whole the 13 states that had made up the Confederacy remained a separate regional economy distinguished by its rural character, its apartheid-like segregation laws, and huge disparities in income and wealth. In 1929, fewer than 500 individuals in the entire region had incomes over $100,000, while most of the South's five million white and three and a half million black tenant farmers were already desperately poor. Novelist Richard Wright later recalled that all the black families he visited on Mississippi plantations in the 1920s lived in "shacks, sleeping on shuck mattresses, eating salt pork and black-eyed peas for breakfast, dinner, and supper." Poor Americans like these tenant farmers would face total destitution in the Great Depression.

Although conditions were generally better in other regions, workers in older manufacturing and extractive industries also suffered from poverty during the 1920s. New England textile, shoe-making, and shipbuilding towns never fully recovered from the postwar recession. Nor did the coal-mining regions of Appalachia and the West. Even in the industrial and financial centers of the North and the Far West where the new mass-consumer culture flourished, unskilled workers in older heavy industries, as well as men and women employed in the needle trades, retail sales, and domestic service generally earned incomes well below the "American Standard of Living." Low hourly wages and frequent bouts of unemployment due to fluctuations in demand for products made the lives of most working-class Americans insecure. Three ongoing developments – migration, mechanization, and the collapse of unions – also contributed to low wages for most workers.

Despite severe restrictions placed on immigration from Europe and Asia after World War I, New Era employers found a steady stream of migrants from rural America, as well as many Canadians and Mexicans, eager to take jobs that would earn them more cash than they could make back home on the farm. On average in each year of the 1920s two million Americans moved from rural areas to the cities. Throughout the decade employers were also able to replace much work formerly done by skilled workers with mechanized processes that required less skilled and lower paid workers. One study of technological unemployment in manufacturing, railways, and coal mining estimated that more than three and a quarter million workers had their jobs replaced by machines during the 1920s, and that over a million of these displaced workers were still unemployed in 1929. Overall, there is no consensus of how many Americans were unemployed in each year of the 1920s, but it seems clear that local labor markets were never tight for long.

Throughout the decade, in cities and towns across the country, the continuous presence of men and women looking for jobs made it difficult for employed workers to protest low wages and harsh working conditions. So did the weakness of labor unions. Scorned by most politicians and the press, unions had not yet achieved a secure place in American law and society. In fact, since the Red Scare of 1919–21, when the combined forces of local, state, and federal governments had been used to crush a wave of postwar strikes, most unions in the American Federation of Labor had disintegrated. By the beginning of the Great Depression, reform-minded Senators such as New York Democrat Senator Robert F. Wagner and Wisconsin's independent Progressive Robert LaFollette Jr. were convinced that a healthy labor movement would prevent economic stagnation by raising workers' incomes, thus insuring the growth of mass-consumer purchasing power. Seemingly far outside the political mainstream in the late 1920s, this progressive idea about the economic importance of unions would gain many adherents during the Great Depression. After the election of 1932, Senators Wagner and LaFollette would discover they had enough support in the White House and the Congress to begin to write pro-union ideas into federal law.

By 1929, the low incomes of most industrial workers and farmers had become a major impediment to the development of a mass consumer society in the United States. Simply put, together these workers and farmers could produce far more than they could consume at current prices (the prices that sustained what were considered necessary profit margins). Farm surpluses were driving down commodity prices, and markets for industrial goods were growing slowly or not at all. Industrial production began slipping down from its pre-Depression peak in July 1929. By the time the stock market crashed, one-fifth of America's industrial capacity was not being used.

As this situation arose, it made little sense for investors to put more money into the creation of new productive capacity in the United States. Yet money available for investment was piling up as many banks and corporations reported record profits. Much of this "excess" capital found its way to Wall

Street in the form of direct purchases of stocks, or as funds directed into the call loan market. Fully eight-five percent of the $8,500,000,000 in broker loans in play on Wall Street in early October 1929 came from corporations and individuals.

Before the final rush to cash in on the stock market boom, considerable sums had been invested overseas. Between 1924 and 1928, American institutions loaned $5,800,000,000 to Europe, Latin America, and Canada. Although these loans were made for private profit, they had the effect of promoting international development and expanded American business activity abroad. Unfortunately, the volume of these loans was nowhere near enough to promote an "economic miracle" overseas. And to make matters worse, American lending abroad was sharply curtailed in 1929 as investors on both sides of the Atlantic got swept up in the rush to make easy money on Wall Street.

In retrospect we can see that if the United States had been able to find or create growing markets for American farm products and industrial goods overseas, the Great Depression might well have been avoided. In the late 1940s this is precisely the lesson that New Dealers turned postwar economic policy makers used to justify the Marshall Plan and other American foreign aid programs. But at the time, although the United States was far and away the richest country in the world, it was not politically ready to pursue a planned approach to global economic expansion. And neither was the rest of the world.

Most of Africa, as well most Asian countries except China and Japan, were still under the direct and indirect control of Western European governments, the Soviet Union, and the United States. These colonial economies provided cheap foodstuffs and raw materials to their industrialized mother countries, but the vast majority of their populations were far too poor to become modern consumers. The agricultural depression of the late 1920s further impoverished many of the colonial countries, just as it sharply diminished the ability of independent nations in Latin America to develop into significant markets for American exports. British dominions such as

Canada, Australia, and New Zealand also suffered from the world agricultural depression and a weakening of demand for raw materials. Protectionist policies designed to favor British goods and investors limited the expansion of American business in these English-speaking nations. Among Asia's few independent nations, China was poor and disordered by civil war, and the Japanese economy was relatively poor and weakened from extensive earthquake damage in 1923 and a severe banking panic in 1927.

In the 1920s, the industrialized nations of Western Europe remained the most likely markets for expanding exports of American foodstuffs and industrial goods. But all of them, including France and Britain, had been devastated by World War I. Ten years after the guns fell silent, not a single European nation had sufficiently recovered to create anything like an "American Standard of Living" for its people. We have already seen that low wage levels were inhibiting the development of America's mass-consumer economy. But compared to wages across Europe, American wages were very high. And higher wages meant higher material living standards. In 1928, an International Labor Office study reported real wages in New York were more than twice the real wages in every European capital except Britain's; and New York's real wages were 79 percent higher than real wages in London. Europe still had a long way to go before it would enter the mass-consumer era.

Reparations owed by Germany to France and Britain, and war debts owed to the United States by France, Britain, and most other European nations complicated international economic relations throughout the interwar period. Three aspects of this difficult subject are pertinent to this discussion. First, European recovery from the war was greatly retarded by the way that reparations and war debt payments pulled capital away from the places that needed it for recovery and development purposes. Secondly, the stability of the postwar transatlantic financial system depended on the willingness and ability of the United States to extend loans to Europe, and especially to Germany. Third, although British and French authorities were loathe to admit it, German recovery was the key to the growth and transformation of Western Europe. These three points, which later became the basis for American economic policy in Europe after World War II, were not well understood before the Great Depression. The result was growing instability and a series of international financial crises in the early 1930s.

The inflexibility of the international monetary system of the interwar years also contributed to the Great Depression. In the mid-1920s, hoping to restore what World War I had shattered, leading nations including the United States re-established a monetary system which required nations to balance their international accounts by shipping gold. In this gold standard system, the relative values of national currencies were set according to a schedule of fixed exchange rates that approximated pre-war parities. Most famously, the British pound sterling was valued at 4.86 American dollars. At the time, as a matter of faith, all international bankers and almost all economists were certain that this gold standard system would guarantee long-term financial stability, even though some argued the American dollar was undervalued. In 1925, while urging the Bank of England to resume the gold standard, the governor of New York's Federal Reserve Bank, Benjamin Strong, had warned that a failure to re-establish the gold standard would create "violent fluctuations in the exchanges . . . hardship and suffering, and possibly some social and political disorder." Strong's views were typical and very influential. Yet the kinds of disorder he predicted were exactly what resulted when nations tried to maintain the gold standard system in the early 1930s. What went wrong?

Although the leading financial minds of the era did not realize it, the international gold standard imparted a strong deflationary bias to the economic policies of all nations. Each country participating in the system was forced to protect its gold reserves. Moreover, since exchange rates were fixed, nations could not respond to serious deficits in their international accounts by devaluing their currency. So how could a country faced with significant international deficits protect its gold reserves while maintaining the gold standard? There was only one strategy; the appetite for foreign goods and services had to be curtailed. This was accomplished in two ways. Financial authorities would raise interest rates to slow economic activity and curb demand for imports; and often in concert, political authorities would cut government spending and/or raise taxes. In the late 1920s, several nations suffering international payments difficulties including Britain were forced to impose such deflationary policies on their people, but the system as a whole worked well because the entire world economy was growing. After 1929, however, that growth ceased, and world trade in industrial products, raw materials, and agricultural commodities all contracted sharply. In these new and unforeseen circumstances, the gold standard not only failed to provide stability, it actually became a force propagating the Great Depression.

From Economic Nationalism to Global Catastrophe

The Great Depression wreaked havoc upon people all around the world. As a global economic disaster, the Great Depression was terrible in its own right; but it also forged the crucial link between the two worst wars in human history. Economic dislocations that resulted from World War I helped prepare the way for the worldwide collapse of the early 1930s. Once it had begun, this Great Depression encouraged militant nationalists who were able to seize control of governments in several powerful nations. In Germany and Japan especially, these ultra-nationalists adopted policies that led to the catastrophic destruction of human lives and property in what we now know as World War II.

All industrial nations and less developed producers of primary products and foodstuffs suffered from severe price deflation and rising unemployment during the first four years of the Great Depression. The total volume of world trade shrunk by an astounding two-thirds from the last quarter of 1929 to the first quarter of 1933. This unprecedented collapse of global commerce reduced producer prices and wages in virtually all parts of the world. Industrial economies were especially hard hit as consumption of all but essential goods plummeted. Unemployment reached crisis proportions throughout the industrialized world, but was most severe in the United States and Germany. As nations were sucked into this frightening economic collapse, political leaders of all stripes found the pressure to protect one's own banks, businesses, farmers, and workers irresistible.

Britain, which had acted as a lender and market of last resort goods prior to the Great War, was no longer capable of performing these economic functions. And the United States which might have tried take over Britain's role, did not do so effectively. Between 1929 and 1933, as world trade relentlessly contracted, governments adopted economic policies designed to protect domestic producers from cheap imports. The movement towards greater economic protection had begun as a response to declines in agricultural prices in 1926. But prior to the Great Depression, collaborative efforts to maintain the gold standard, collect reparations, and establish war debt payment schedules had restrained protectionist politicians. A preliminary global agreement to freeze tariffs was actually worked out at a World Economic Conference in 1927. Unfortunately the final document was not ready for ratification until 1930, and by then it was too late. France, Italy, and Australia took the first steps away from tariff stabilization in 1929, but it was subsequent increases in American tariffs that seemed to trigger a global rush to protection.

In February 1930, the United States did not send any delegates to the meeting that tried to finalize the international moratorium on higher tariffs. Instead, the Republican majority in Congress went ahead and passed the now infamous Smoot-Hawley bill that raised tariffs on many U.S. imports. President Hoover signed Smoot-Hawley into law on June 17, 1930 despite his own reservations, and the public protest of 1,028 professional economists who predicted the new tariff schedules would result in retaliatory action by other nations. Historians still debate the precise impact of Smoot-Hawley on world trade, but there is no doubt about the message it sent to the rest of the world. Smoot-Hawley was interpreted as an American refusal to lead the way out of the depression by keeping its markets open to goods that could not find buyers elsewhere. By the end of 1930 Canada, Mexico, Cuba, France, Spain, Switzerland, Australia, and New Zealand had raised tariffs against American goods. And in the years that followed, many other nations adopted similar "beggar thy neighbor" trade policies adding momentum to the downward spiral in world trade.

One year after he approved the Smoot-Hawley tariffs, Herbert Hoover briefly appeared to abandon economic nationalism. Deeply concerned that a worsening financial crisis in central Europe would undermine the gold standard and bring down Germany's shaky democratic government, President Hoover worked out a one-year international moratorium on war debt and reparation payments that he announced on June 20, 1931. The Hoover moratorium was hailed in the press around world, but it did not end the financial crisis in Germany.[4] Rejecting the pleas of the French government and the advice of Secretary of State Henry Stimson, President Hoover refused to ask Congress to approve an emergency loan to Germany. Instead, the United States stood aside as financial panic spread from central Europe to Britain, where a coalition government was formed to deal with the crisis. The international gold standard crumbled as soon as this new British government rejected the costs of forcing more deflation upon their already depressed economy.

When the Bank of England suspended gold payments on September 20, 1931, the British pound lost nearly one-quarter of its value against the dollar in just a few days. By December it was valued at just 3.25 American dollars. This depreciation made British goods cheaper overseas; and since British industry was heavily dependent on exports, it helped to arrest the downward economic spiral in Britain. Twenty-five other nations followed Britain off the gold standard, hoping to also benefit from market adjustment in the value of their currencies against the pound. But the United States, France, Germany, Italy, South Africa, and a number of other nations continued gold payments. The resulting proliferation of monetary arrangements complicated, and further depressed, the world economy.

In the fall of 1931, the ongoing crisis spread to the United States when central banks in France and other gold bloc countries began to convert their dollar holdings into gold. In the month following Britain's suspension of gold payments, the Federal Reserve System lost $755,000,000 in gold. To stem what could have developed into a run on the dollar (a panicky conversion of dollars into gold in anticipation of devaluation) the Hoover administration proclaimed its commitment to the gold standard while the Federal Reserve Banks raised their discount rates two percentage points. This large interest rate hike protected American gold reserves by encouraging foreign depositors and discouraging imports, but it also discouraged domestic borrowing. In the United States, stock prices, commodity prices, and industrial production all began to decline more swiftly; and bank failures increased. In retrospect, it thus appears America's adherence to the gold standard in 1931 insured the downward spiral would continue into 1932.

Two years after British devaluation, France attempted to restore the universal gold standard and revive tariff stabilization at a World Economic Conference in London. On July 3, 1933, America's new President, Franklin Roosevelt, shocked the assembled delegates with a message that his new administration would pursue its own program for domestic economic recovery before considering any international agreements to stabilize currency values and tariffs. Roosevelt's nationalistic insistence that "the sound internal economic system of a nation is a far greater factor in its well being than the price of its currency" doomed cooperative efforts to end the Great Depression to failure.

The Smoot-Hawley tariff of 1930 and Franklin Roosevelt's "bombshell message" to the World Economic Conference of 1933 were typical expressions of depression-era economic nationalism. Indeed as the Great Depression persisted, protectionism gave way to a more radical form of economic nationalism, the kind of economic self-sufficiency known as *autarchy*. In the mid-1930s each of the world's major industrial nations looked to establish trading blocs in which their own currencies would be dominant and secure. Britain managed a sterling bloc made up of its colonies and the Commonwealth countries, and France headed a gold bloc which included its empire and other countries that retained a gold standard linked to the franc. After Franklin Roosevelt took the United States off the gold standard in late 1933, it formed a dollar bloc that eventually included American colonies and much of Latin America. Other industrial nations controlled by truly fanatical nationalists used threats of war, and war itself, to secure needed raw materials, markets, and the prestige of empire. Fascist Italy tried to establish a new Roman Empire in the Mediterranean basin, Nazi Germany a Third Reich in central Europe, and Japan a "Co-Prosperity Sphere" in East Asia.

Germany's attack on Poland in September 1939 is usually identified as the beginning of World War II; but in truth the worldwide conflagration had begun in September 1931 when the Japanese army invaded Manchuria. By the time the United States entered the war 10 years later, the New Dealers who still controlled the federal government had renounced the economic nationalism of the United States' early responses to the world depression. Franklin Roosevelt's wartime administration acted on a new belief that global conflict had grown out of "beggar thy neighbor" protectionism and the pursuit of autarchy. In the 1940s, New Dealers enshrined international collaboration in economic development, currency stabilization, and tariff reduction as the guiding principles of the foreign economic policy of the United States. In February 1945, when President Roosevelt asked the Congress to fund new international economic institutions to achieve these goals, he warned, "The world will either move toward unity and widely shared prosperity or it will move apart into necessarily competing economic blocs." As the twentieth century ends, the international institutions Roosevelt envisioned – the World Bank, International Monetary Fund, and General Agreement on Trade and Tariffs –

remain the most impressive reminders of the New Dealers' acquired conviction that depression-era economic nationalism had caused World War II.

FURTHER READING

Primary Sources

McElvaine, Robert S. ed. *Down and Out in the Great Depression: Letters from the Forgotten Man.* Chapel Hill: University of North Carolina Press, 1983.

Myers, William Starr and Newton, Walter eds. *The Hoover Administration: A Documented Narrative.* New York: Charles Scribner's Sons, 1936.

President's Research Committee on Social Trends. *Recent Social Trends in the United States.* New York: McGraw-Hill, 1933.

Roosevelt, Elliot ed. *F.D.R.: His Personal Letters, 1928-1945.* New York: Duell, Sloan and Pearce, 1950.

Roosevelt, Franklin Delano. *The Public Papers and Addresses of Franklin D. Roosevelt, Volume One: The Genesis of the New Deal 1928–1932.* New York: Random House, 1938.

Roosevelt, Franklin Delano. *The Public Papers and Addresses of Franklin D. Roosevelt, Volume Two: The Year of Crisis 1933.* New York: Random House, 1938.

Terkel, Studs. *Hard Times: An Oral History of the Great Depression.* New York: Random House, 1970.

Wright, Richard. *Black Boy.* New York: Harper and Row, 1945.

Secondary Sources

Bernstein, Irving. *The Lean Years: A History of the American Worker 1920–1933.* Boston: Houghton Mifflin, 1960.

Bordo, Michael D.; Goldin, Claudia; and White, Eugene N. eds. *The Defining Moment: The Great Depression and the American Economy in the Twentieth Century.* Chicago: University of Chicago Press, 1998.

Eichgreen, Barry J. *Golden Fetters: The Gold Standard and the Great Depression, 1919–1939.* New York: Oxford University Press, 1992.

Feis, Herbert. *1933: Characters in a Crisis.* Boston: Little, Brown and Company, 1966.

Galbraith, John Kenneth. *The Great Crash 1929.* Boston: Houghton Mifflin, 1954.

Green, Harvey. *The Uncertainty of Everyday Life 1915–1945.* New York: Harper Collins, 1992.

Kindleberger, Charles. *The World in Depression, 1929–1939*. Berkeley: University of California Press, 1986.

Parrish, Michael. *Anxious Decades: America in Prosperity and Depression, 1920–1941*. New York: W.W. Norton, 1992.

Temin, Peter. *Lessons from the Great Depression*. Cambridge, Massachusetts: MIT Press, 1989.

2

The Politics of the Great Depression

"Today, perhaps as never before, our very form of government is on trial in the eyes of millions of our citizens."
President Herbert Hoover, October 12, 1932

The Erosion of Confidence

The Great Depression was not a crash. Stock prices plummeted in the fall of 1929 but it was a long road to economic rock bottom – over three and half years to the utter collapse of early March 1933. Gross investment declined 35 percent in 1930, and again in 1931; but other indicators fell more slowly. Wholesale prices dropped 9 percent in 1930 and 16 percent in 1931, yet consumer prices declined only 3 percent in 1930 and 9 percent in 1931. The trend in output was more steeply downward; real gross national product fell 28 percent from 1929 to 1931. As a result, estimated unemployment rose from just 3 percent of the labor force in 1929 to 9 percent in 1930, and continued rising to 16 percent in 1931.[1] Today, economic trends like these would surely create a political crisis in the United States. However, there was no crisis atmosphere in the United States until late 1931.

In the immediate aftermath of the Wall Street crash most experts and editorial writers rightly recognized that America was the only mass-consumer society in the world, and that their nation had achieved this enviable status largely by using its own natural resources, capital, and labor. Surveying the national scene in early 1930, what still seemed most prominent were the accomplishments, not the problems, of the New

Era economy. Business leaders generally agreed that tumbling stock prices on the New York Exchange would not create a terrible depression. No major companies or large banks had failed, and the Federal Reserve seemed to be taking the appropriate steps to make money more available for those who wanted to invest it. New York's Federal Reserve Bank had responded to the stock market crash with increased purchases of securities, paying out several hundred million dollars directly to those still active in the market. Subsequently, the regional Federal Reserve Banks tried to stimulate investment by lowering their key rediscount interest rate from 6 percent to 2.5 percent between October 1929 and June 1930.

President Hoover's conviction, first stated on October 25, 1929, that "the fundamental business of the country, that is the production and distribution of commodities, is on a sound and prosperous basis" still seemed unquestionably correct a few months later. The belief that Wall Street was an infallible moneymaking machine had of course vanished, but the real assets of the American economy were still in place. In early 1930, both the Harvard Economic Service and the influential economist Irving Fisher of Yale University predicted the downturn would be shorter and less severe than the postwar depression 10 years earlier. Commerce Secretary Robert Lamont told reporters, "one may predict for the long run a continuance of prosperity and progress." Treasury Secretary Andrew Mellon concurred, "I see nothing in the situation that warrants pessimism." At the time, history seemed to be on the side of the optimists.

There had been five serious financial panics and related depressions in the United States since 1873, and each time the economy had rebounded strongly. The most recent depression of 1920–22 had begun with declines in prices, output, and employment even steeper than those of 1929–30, and it had been followed by the remarkable growth and transformation of the New Era. This remembered history was a most important reason for what looks to us like the misplaced optimism of America's economic elite during the early Great Depression. Men such as Andrew Mellon, whose family's

Pittsburgh bank had weathered every crisis since the Civil War, never questioned the assumption that financial panics and depressions were necessary parts of a "natural" business cycle. Panics, in this orthodox view, drove speculators out of markets while depressions pushed down prices from inflated levels, thus preparing the way for real economic growth through sound investment. Treasury Secretary Mellon's confidence in the self-correcting character of the American business cycle explains his now infamous advice to investors in late 1929, "Liquidate labor, liquidate stocks, liquidate farmers, liquidate real estate." To our ears, Mellon's language sounds incredibly brutal, but this advice was actually commonplace thinking among bankers and financiers. The man who put his assets into cash would not only survive panic selling and deflation; he would also be well positioned to make profitable investments when calm returned to the markets.

The optimism of America's business leaders was strongly colored by their class background. Men such as Andrew Mellon remembered depressions as periods of needed corrections in markets and prices, not as long bouts of unemployment and stressful poverty. In the early 1930s, many leading financiers and businessmen seemed incapable of empathy with working people and poor farmers. When Robert LaFollette's Senate Subcommittee on Manufacturing called leading bankers to Washington to testify about the disturbing rise in unemployment in the fall of 1931, they appeared extraordinarily callous in this regard. Albert Wiggin, the chairman of the giant Chase National Bank of New York, told Senator La Follette that nothing could be done to prevent economic depressions. The Senator responded,

> Your counsel is really one of despair, then. We are going to suffer these terrific dislocations and the suffering that goes with them on the part of the people generally?

Albert Wiggin replied, "Human nature is human nature. Lives go on." The New York banker continued,

> ... you are always going to have, once in so many years, difficulties in business, times that are prosperous and times that are not prosper-

ous. There is no commission or any brain in the world that can prevent it.

Senator LaFollette then asked the Chase National chairman
this rather remarkable question: "You think, then, that the
capacity for human suffering is unlimited?" Without hesitat-
ing, Wiggin answered, "I think so."

Herbert Hoover, like Andrew Mellon and Albert Wiggin,
did not believe that government could plan economic activity
so as to avoid human suffering. But Hoover did not endorse
the *laissez-faire* fatalism of the financiers that appeared before LaFollette's committee. He had enormous faith in the creativity and productivity of American business, but he also
insisted that government had to periodically intervene in the
economy to encourage voluntary cooperative actions beneficial to interested parties and the whole nation. "The economic
fatalist believes that these crises are inevitable and bound to
be recurrent," Herbert Hoover observed, "I would remind
these pessimists that exactly the same thing was once said of
typhoid, cholera, and smallpox."

As Secretary of Commerce throughout the 1920s, Hoover
had convened scores of business conferences in Washington,
bringing together corporate executives from particular industries, encouraging them to form trade associations and stand-
ardize business practices. He had also, in 1921, convinced
Warren Harding to convene a President's Conference on Unemployment. At this conference, the new Commerce Secretary persuaded businessmen to agree that increases in public
works and private construction would speed recovery from
the postwar depression. In the winter of 1929–30, Herbert
Hoover revived the idea of White House conferences to prevent deflation and mass unemployment.

From his chairman's seat at this latest series of White House
conferences, President Hoover constantly reminded gathered
businessmen and reporters that "there was no reason why
business should not be carried on as usual." Obviously the
President wanted to restore investor confidence and avoid
the creation of a crisis atmosphere. But these conferences were
not a public relations gambit. Hoover really believed that

voluntary coordinated private sector responses would prevent a panicky stampede to liquidity and mass unemployment. And at first, Hoover's method appeared successful. Business leaders left these winter conferences pledging themselves to maintain prices, wages, and employment, and to increase planned construction. The *New York Times* editorialized, "the patient at the end of January has begun to recover." As the spring of 1930 arrived, construction activity briefly picked up, and payrolls stabilized. There were few signs that the country was already sliding into its worst-ever economic depression. Charles M. Schwab, chairman of Bethlehem Steel, observed in March that "all present indications are that 1930, in broad perspective, will prove a year of normal business progress." Two months later President Hoover concluded, "we have passed the worst and with continued effort we shall rapidly recover."

For a year after the stock market crash there was little in the nation's urban newspapers to suggest an America that was already mired in the Great Depression. Shortened schedules, pay cuts, and layoffs were scattered events felt by small groups of people at different times all across a vast continental nation. In 1930–31, before economic conditions were widely acknowledged to be a national catastrophe, many Americans simply had no daily experience and no daily news of a "great depression." We must also recall that creative artists had not yet implanted in the national culture the images of the Great Depression which we take for granted – images of hopeless people waiting at unemployment offices, breadlines snaking down streets in New York and San Francisco, and soup kitchens in Chicago; images of urban shanty towns, sharecropper shacks, and migrant tent colonies. The art that continues to define the Great Depression as twentieth-century America's greatest human tragedy, the work of painters Ben Shahn and Raphael Soyer, photographers Dorothea Lange and Walker Evans, writers John Steinbeck and Richard Wright, and film makers William Wyler and John Ford was still to come.

What filled the newspapers and magazines of 1930–31 were spectacular stories of bootlegging gangsters such as Jack "Legs"

Diamond, Dutch Schultz, and Al Capone; the continuing sagas of sports heroes including football coach Knute Rockne, golfer Bobby Jones, and baseball's Babe Ruth; the latest buzz about "talking pictures" and new movies stars such as Jean Harlow, James Cagney, and the Marx brothers; as well as coverage of entertainment fads such as miniature golf and radio's *Amos and Andy*. Crime so dominated the daily headlines in 1930–31 that even the corporate executives, bankers, and economists who belonged to the National Economic League found "prohibition, the administration of justice, and lawlessness" to be the nation's most serious problems in both January 1930 and January 1931. Political and business leaders competed for space with gangsters and celebrities in the nation's most widely read newspapers and magazines, and more often than not, the gangsters and celebrities won the front pages.

Economic conditions were discussed regularly only on the daily business pages and in specialized business magazines. There, optimism about the underlying strength of America's free enterprise system prevailed throughout most of 1930–31. Ongoing declines in investment, commodity and stock prices, production, and employment were tracked with some precision, and yet rosy forecasts predominated. The president of U.S. Steel was just one of many voices in January 1931 when he confidently proclaimed, "The peak of the depression passed thirty days ago." For two years after the Wall Street debacle of 1929, the nation's economic elite assured Americans the downturn was an expected part of a "natural" business cycle. "The fact that we have to let nature take its course may augur well for the ultimate prosperity of the country," explained Richard Whitney, president of the New York Stock Exchange. "Let business alone," Henry Ford advised government leaders. This insistence that there was no need for special government recovery and relief programs would come back to haunt bankers, businessmen, and conservative politicians in 1932–33 when a vast majority of Americans concluded just the opposite.

Even when indications of depression were unmistakable, most of America's economic elite persisted in the belief that there were no serious flaws in American capitalism, and no need for reforms. Opinion-makers blamed events overseas for the nation's economic troubles, especially in the months following the European financial crisis of mid-1931. President Hoover summed up this influential view of the origins of the depression in his State of the Union address in December 1931 when he proclaimed, "Our self-contained national economy, with its matchless strength and resources, would have enabled us to recover long since, but for the continued dislocations, shocks, and setbacks from abroad."

As we have already seen, international problems certainly contributed to the severity and extent of America's Great Depression, and the economic nationalism of the United States exacerbated the global crisis. But just as the New Era's mass-consumer society was principally the result of domestic economic developments, so too was America's Great Depression. The long downward economic spiral developed in the early 1930s when further investment in the productive capacity of America's farms, factories, and mines became, from a business standpoint, irrational. In other words, when those people who had money to invest no longer saw the possibility of profitably investing in expanded production *anywhere in the economy*, the profit-oriented free enterprise system began seizing up, reducing nearly everyone's income and making millions of workers redundant. What so confounded contemporary observers was the fact that during the Great Depression, America was not suffering from a shortage of either land and resources, or skilled and unskilled labor, or capital to invest in plant and equipment. Eventually this situation led many observers to conclude that America in the 1930s had reached a historic turning point when neither westward expansion nor rapid population growth could be counted on as sources of economic progress. With only technical innovation left to spur expansion, what the influential president of the American Economic Association Alvin Hansen in 1939 called "a hard and seemingly immovable core of unemployment" seemed like a permanent condition.

Using hindsight, we now see clearly that the pessimism of

"stagnation theorists" of the late 1930s was not justified. So again the question arises, why did the American economy collapse when it did, in the years 1929–33? The general answer is that the financial and market mechanisms that sustained crucial economic circuits connecting investment in production with consumption of what was produced broke down. Most contemporaries believed that free markets would clear surpluses as prices fell, and that this process would encourage new investment and recovery. However, the market system did not function as expected. Critical breakdowns occurred when investment in construction and new mass-consumer industries (such as automobiles and home appliances) slowed and then ceased altogether in response to weakening demand. Declining production in these sectors forced reductions in industries that supplied raw materials, components, and energy as well as in the railroad and trucking industries. By 1931, the entire American industrial economy was contracting at the same time Europe experienced a series of financial panics and world agricultural prices were plunging. Deflation was synchronized across the domestic and global economies. Neither urban nor rural customers at home, or foreign buyers, were able to rescue America's mass-consumer economy in the year that followed.

At first, however, the optimists who believed the current business downturn would be no worse than that of the early 1920s seemed right. For more than a year big companies were for the most part able to keep the promises they had made at President Hoover's White House conferences during the previous winter. In 1930 more than 90 percent of America's workers stayed employed, while short time schedules reduced real weekly earnings in manufacturing just seven percent. That year the American economy was in what we would now call a significant "recession", but it did not appear to be collapsing. Both economic theory and past experiences led experts to expect that the downturn would not last long.

The Great Depression provides a sobering lesson for all who believe they can make accurate predictions about a constantly changing economy which is composed of tens of millions of participants who make billions of individual decisions. In 1930, businessmen and the business press believed the gold standard guaranteed financial stability and that markets were self-regulating. The most influential economic decision-makers had no doubts that lower prices would eventually stimulate demand and bring about not just the full re-employment of existing capital and labor but enough growth to warrant higher prices, new investment in production, and new hiring. Yet for next three years economic developments ran counter to what most informed observers were sure would happen.

In the winter of 1930–31, many companies reduced the hours, and thus the earnings, of their employees. At the same time, further declines in agricultural prices and poor crops in some areas forced more farm foreclosures and more bank failures. Western and southern banks were increasingly vulnerable as the agricultural depression worsened. On December 12, 1930, a large institution named the Bank of the United States failed. This bank had 57 branches and 440,000 depositors in the country's financial center, New York City; but it actually was neither one of the country's biggest banks nor was it connected to the federal government. Nonetheless its failure was an ominous sign that sent many panicky bank customers outside of New York to their withdrawal windows seeking to turn deposits into cash, and bank managers to their books looking for ways to trim risky loans from their asset columns. As 1931 began farm state Congressmen wanted to increase the money supply, but the banker-dominated Federal Reserve rejected inflationary policies. Big bankers still believed the system was sound (despite a doubling of bank failures in 1930), and that bank reserves were large enough and interest rates low enough to encourage borrowing and economic recovery. This judgment was very much in error.

By 1931 most banks had become much more cautious about lending reserves that might be needed to stem a run by anxious depositors. Banks now routinely rejected loan applicants that they would have approved in 1929. Just as importantly, far fewer businessmen and farmers tried to borrow available reserves because there were not enough customers either at home or abroad to buy up the surpluses that weighed so heavily on markets. In these circumstance low interest rates alone were insufficient to spur borrowing and new investment. Not until Congress established the Federal Deposit Insurance Corporation (FDIC) in the summer of 1933 could bankers begin to feel secure from the threat of massive withdrawals by depositors who feared their bank's insolvency. But long after FDIC made runs on banks much less likely, most banks continued to be very cautious about making new loans.

The failure of the Federal Reserve in 1931 was compounded by the failure of President Hoover's policy of limited government intervention in markets. The Agricultural Marketing Act of 1929 had established a Federal Farm Board in 1929. The Board used $500,000,000 in public funds to subsidize cooperatives and stabilization corporations that purchased and held commodities in the hope that "orderly" marketing over 12 months would smooth out the agricultural business cycle. Relentless agricultural deflation made it impossible to realize this hope. For example, the federally subsidized Grain Stabilization Corporation purchased massive quantities of wheat in early 1931 at 81 cents per bushel, about 20 cents above the prevailing world price. These purchases were a subsidy for American wheat farmers, but they were not supposed to cost the taxpayers anything. It was expected that world prices would move up as the harvest was sold off, allowing the stabilization corporation to recover its investment in wheat. But prices did not move as expected. By the end of the year, when the world price for wheat slid below 40 cents per bushel, the Grain Stabilization Corporation was bankrupt. It was storing over a quarter of a billion bushels of wheat that it had purchased for more than twice the prevailing world market price, an investment that it could not recoup.

The failure of the Hoover administration's cooperative marketing policy led to a Congressional investigation in which many witnesses testified that overproduction, not disorderly marketing was the root cause of the agricultural depression. These witnesses proposed domestic allotment; a plan to pay farmers to reduce cultivated acreage. In 1932, this approach was still too radical for the majority in Congress and President Hoover, who threatened to veto a domestic allotment bill sponsored by Senator Elmer Thomas of Oklahoma. Yet just one year later, after more deflation and the election of a new President and Congress, domestic allotment would be successfully implemented in the New Deal's first Agricultural Adjustment Act.

The downward economic spiral accelerated with frightening speed in the fall of 1931. On September 23rd U.S. Steel and Bethlehem Steel announced 10 percent across the board wage reductions that broke the promises they had made at a White House conference in early 1930. Most major industrial corporations followed the steel companies' lead. Industry publications were soon denouncing "cut-throat" and "suicidal" competition. Voluntary restraint, one of the foundations of the Hoover administration's economic program, was dead. During the next 18 months, market pressures would devastate America's corporate payrolls.

In the fall of 1931, the United States also had to deal with the effects of the collapse of the universal gold standard. At the time, President Hoover still believed that federally sponsored voluntary cooperation could create enough investor confidence to stimulate recovery. As remaining gold bloc nations began converting dollars to gold, and more American banks failed, Hoover convened a secret meeting at Andrew Mellon's house on October 4th. In this extraordinary Sunday night conclave, Hoover convinced banking and insurance industry leaders to create a privately funded credit association that could come to the rescue of failing institutions. Hoover's intervention resulted in the National Credit Corporation, a privately managed pool of $500,000,000 for use by member banks that needed assistance in meeting the demands of panicky depositors. The National Credit Association received the positive publicity Hoover intended when it was announced. A few months later George Harrison, governor of New York's Federal Reserve Bank, testified "The whole psychology of the bankers' mind, especially the smaller country banker. . .was immediately changed." Yet when pressed by members of the Senate Subcommittee on Banking and Currency to detail what positive steps the National Credit Association had taken, Harrison admitted that by year's end it had loaned just 2 percent of its funds to threatened banks. Other witnesses explained that the association's board, acting like the conservative bankers they were, had been unwilling to take "slow assets" of weak banks as collateral for loans.[2]

There had been nearly 25,000 banks in the United States in 1929. By the end of 1931, nearly 15 percent of those banks had disappeared after failing to meet the demands of depositors. The Hoover administration's policy of organizing a voluntary cooperative rescue for the banking system had come to naught. People remained anxious about the condition of their banks, and with good reason. The depression was undercutting the value of bank assets and increasing depositors' needs for cash. Moreover, as the National Credit Corporation fiasco showed, large banks holding ample reserves did not want to lend to weaker banks in crisis. Clearly, stronger measures were required to prevent new financial crises and reverse the downward economic spiral. In his year-ending 1931 State of the Union message, President Hoover finally asked Congress to intervene more directly in the economy to spur recovery. His proposals to establish a federally funded Reconstruction Finance Corporation and a Home Loan Bank Board were Hoover's admission that this depression could not be reversed by voluntary cooperative actions. The downward economic spiral was forcing momentous political-economic changes upon a Republican administration not anxious to take up the banner of reform.

Politics and Ideology

In 1932 the Great Depression engulfed urban as well as rural America. Since 1929 national income had declined more than 50 percent. Manufacturing output in 1932 was just over half of what it had been three years earlier. Business failures had increased each year since 1930. By mid-year nearly 12,000,000 workers were unemployed, and perhaps half that number were working reduced schedules. These involuntary part-timers were suffering doubly from shorter hours and deep cuts in wage rates. As a group American wage earners were paid 40 percent less in 1932 than 1929. Poverty and real destitution increased rapidly, especially among urban workers and their families.

In February 1931, Herbert Hoover had lectured the nation on poor relief. He insisted that, "The basis of successful relief in national distress is to mobilize and organize the infinite number of agencies of self-help in the community." Local responsibility for poor relief was a tradition dating back to the colonial era, but this tradition had never been tested in an urban mass-consumer society. The numbers of people seeking relief from charities and local governments overwhelmed local resources in the spring of 1932. By mid-year New Yorkers had seen 400 private charities, one-third the city's total, close their doors. Chicago's private relief agencies had carried about half that city's caseload in 1931. In the summer of 1932 private agencies could handle less than 5 percent of those in need, and the city was selling discounted tax warrants to finance public relief. That summer Atlanta's Central Relief Committee was forced to terminate all work relief projects even though nearly 100,000 of the city's workers were unemployed. Atlanta's local authorities could afford just $1.30 per week in direct assistance for families seeking relief. In Los Angeles unemployment doubled to at least one-fourth the labor force despite construction and business activity associated with the summer Olympics. Yet after 1,500 angry property owners stormed a meeting of the Los Angeles county supervisors and forced a reduction in assessments, the county was unable to offer any greater assistance to private relief agencies than it had in the previous year.

The executive secretary of Philadelphia's Community Council testified before a Senate committee in May 1932 that nearly 300,000 workers were unemployed in his city, and that since December 51,000 families had been added to the list approved for public assistance. Weekly relief payments to destitute families in Philadelphia had been reduced to a level that this official described as "an amount needed to provide two-thirds a health maintaining diet." Philadelphia's policy was not unusual. In mid-1932 only one-quarter of America's unemployed workers and their families were receiving public assistance. In most cities, only truly destitute families were eligible for relief, and starvation-level benefits were a common public policy. Looting for food and well-organized protests against insufficient relief became more frequent occurrences in urban America. By the third year of the Great Depression, poverty and poor relief had become politically explosive issues.

State and local governments were required by law to balance their annual budgets. In 1932, as private charities failed, this requirement constrained public efforts to meet the soaring demand for poor relief. Funding for relief was tied to available tax revenues, and revenues from established property, business, sales, and income taxes were all declining. Taxes could be raised to pay for relief, but as the incident in Los Angeles illustrates, this strategy was political dynamite. Moreover, funding relief out of additional taxes made local business depressions worse. Although raising taxes to pay for relief did not shrink aggregate demand for all goods and services, it did change the composition of demand by reducing private non-subsistence consumption of goods and services produced and distributed by local businesses. Squeezed by soaring unemployment and poverty and the political difficulties involved in raising new revenues, desperate local officials had nowhere else to turn but to the federal government in 1932.

Ideology now came to the forefront of America's politics, just as it did everywhere else in the industrialized world during the Great Depression. During the 1930s the Socialist and Communist parties each recruited tens of thousands of new members. So did the hundreds of new Fascist and anti-Semitic groups which emerged in all parts of the country. But most importantly, ever-worsening conditions and spreading protests tested mainstream political-economic policy assumptions. Often elected officials became prisoners of these assumptions even after their policies proved ineffective. This is what happened to Herbert Hoover in 1931–32. Although historians in recent decades have emphasized Hoover's lifelong progressive and humanitarian impulses and the steps he took to counter the Great Depression, what Hoover's contemporaries saw was a President who used conservative economic criteria to define his administration's response to the Great Depression.

To win the election of 1932 Herbert Hoover had to convince a majority of voters that America was truly on the road to economic recovery. By the end of 1931 the President's initial policy of securing voluntary pledges from industry leaders to maintain prices, employment, and wages had amounted to nothing more than a collection of broken promises. Promises made in 1930 to increase construction activity had proved equally ineffective against the depression. Even though a President's Emergency Committee on Employment had been established in October 1930 specifically to encourage new construction projects, private construction spending actually declined $4,000,000,000 in 1930–31. Overall, public works spending also declined. Falling tax revenues and soaring demands for poor relief forced drastic cuts upon local and state governments. In December 1931 Senator Robert Wagner proposed adding $2,000,000,000 in additional federal public works spending to the President Hoover's State of the Union recovery plan. Hoover resisted, but a coalition of Democrats and progressive Republicans in Congress were able to raise federal public works spending to $670,000,000 in 1932. This unprecedented peacetime appropriation still failed to stimulate economic recovery because concurrent reductions in private construction, as well as state and local public works, were so much larger.

Herbert Hoover had urged counter-cyclical public works spending in 1922 and again in 1930, but in 1932 he successfully blocked the public works program proposed by Senator Wagner on the grounds that it would enlarge the federal deficit. In May 1932, in an open letter to one of many groups then lobbying for greater federal spending on construction, President Hoover declared,

> the balancing of the Federal budget and unimpaired national credit is indispensable to the restoration of confidence and to the very start of economic recover. . . . A public works program such as is suggested

by your committee and by others through the issuance of Federal
bonds creates at once an enormous further deficit.

Hoover's reversal on public works was just one sign of his
growing conservatism. In 1932 he displayed dogged determination to defend the three pillars of an orthodox conservative
political economy: the gold standard dollar, balanced government budgets, and local responsibility for poor relief.

Like the bankers who advised him – Eugene Meyer, the governor of the Federal Reserve Board; Treasury Secretary Mellon;
and Mellon's successor in 1932, Ogden Mills – Hoover believed strongly that a fixed gold standard was essential for
international economic stability and growth. His 1931 moratorium on war debts and reparation payments had clearly expressed this belief. After the moratorium failed to prevent the
collapse of the universal gold standard, Hoover never considered following Britain's example. In fact he denounced all suggestions that the United States use an inflationary devaluation
to fight the depression's relentless deflation.

Herbert Hoover also strongly believed, as did most contemporary politicians and editorial writers, that the federal
government should balance its annual budgets except in wartime. In 1931, declining tax revenues had created an unexpected $1,000,000,000 federal deficit. Herbert Hoover was
mortified that he had presided over this largest peacetime deficit
in American history, and he was determined not to let it happen again. Beginning in December 1931, Hoover repeatedly
lectured Congress in public speeches and in personal appearances at committee hearings on what he called "the absolute
necessity of a balanced budget." The President also vetoed
congressional measures he deemed fiscally irresponsible. Hoover's vetoes of bills that increased public works spending, extended federal assistance to states for poor relief, and speeded
up payment of federal bonuses to war veterans became occasions to remind Congress that a balanced budget was in his
words, "the foundation of all public and private financial stability."

Hoover blocked billions of dollars of new spending proposed by congressional Democrats and progressive Republi-

cans. In June 1932, Congress finally approved a 1932–33 budget that included $1,000,000,000 in new federal taxes as well as $300,000,000 of the $700,000,000 in spending cuts requested by the President. This budget deal reduced federal expenditures to less than 1929 levels, but investor confidence was not restored. The downward economic spiral persisted, further reducing tax revenues, and creating an even larger budget deficit during Hoover's last year in office.

An unusual number of special elections due to deaths and retirements transformed the 72nd Congress. By 1932 Herbert Hoover had to deal with a divided legislature instead of a co-operative Republican Congress. His party held only a single seat majority in the Senate, while the opposition Democrats narrowly controlled the House of Representatives. Hoover's difficulties were compounded by the fact that a significant number of progressive Republicans including Nebraska Senator George W. Norris and New York Congressman Fiorello LaGuardia usually voted with liberal Democrats on economic issues.[3] Many of the President's opponents in Congress had by now concluded that the depression was a national emergency comparable to war which required new government initiatives, new borrowing, and unavoidable deficits. They were joined by Governor Franklin Roosevelt of New York who had launched the nation's first state-funded relief program on this basis.

Always a fine public speaker and a charismatic public personality, Governor Roosevelt had been re-elected in 1930 by a landslide margin that brought him to the attention of Democrats around the country. Aided by his longtime political advisor, former newspaperman Louis Howe, and by his politically active wife, Eleanor Roosevelt, FDR courted party officials and influential Democratic office holders outside of New York throughout his second term as governor. His frequently broadcasted and widely reported speeches earned Roosevelt the reputation as a leader who spoke to working people and farmers with warmth and empathy about their problems, and about the ways he proposed to have government help them to solve those problems. By early 1932, Franklin Roosevelt had made himself the leading spokesman for a liberal Democratic response to the Great Depression.

The differences between Hoover's conservatism and Roosevelt's liberalism were always most evident when the issue of poor relief arose. Herbert Hoover consistently resisted the idea that the federal government had a responsibility to provide for direct aid to unemployed workers and their families. In August 1931 Hoover responded to the growing relief crisis by replacing his Emergency Committee on Unemployment with a new organization, the President's Organization on Unemployment Relief (POUR), made up mostly of leading businessmen. Hoover named Walter Gifford, president of American Telephone and Telegraph, POUR's chairman. Launched as if it were a major federal program, POUR was only intended to advise local relief agencies; it had no funds to distribute to the unemployed. POUR never tried to raise any money for relief or make any direct contact with the needy. Called to Capitol Hill to testify on January 8, 1932, Walter Gifford could not even tell members of Senator LaFollette's Subcommittee on Manufacturing how many people in the United States were receiving relief payments. Gifford explained "the responsibility [for relief] was to be left squarely with the States, counties, and communities."

Franklin Roosevelt demonstrated a very different approach to the mounting unemployment crisis. Fourteen days after President Hoover announced POUR, Governor Roosevelt called New York state legislators into a special session asking them to approve direct state funding for relief "not as a matter of charity, but as a matter of social duty." The resulting New York Temporary Emergency Relief Administration (TERA) became a model alternative to the Hoover response to the relief crisis. TERA's method of using bonds to fund matching state grants to local authorities and its preference for work relief over the dole were copied by other industrial states in 1932, and then implemented nationally in the New Deal's first relief program. Harry Hopkins, the social worker who directed New York's TERA in 1932 became the head of the new Federal Emergency Relief Administration (FERA) in May 1933.

From the outset of the presidential election year, Franklin Roosevelt distinguished his response to the Great Depression from that of the Hoover administration. In his annual message to the state legislature on January 6, 1932, Governor Roosevelt stated that the depression had already inflicted upon New York and the nation the greatest suffering since the Civil War. "We face the necessity of employing new measures of value for the good reason that many of the old values have disappeared," Roosevelt declared. He continued, "We know now from bitter experience that the theory that a nation could lift itself up by its own bootstraps was not sound." On January 29th, Governor Roosevelt followed up his call for a new way of thinking in a special proclamation promising government-funded relief to all needy New Yorkers. "No one who is out of work today can rightfully feel that he or she is personally responsible for having lost his or her job," Roosevelt proclaimed. Tracing what he called "the most serious depression in economic history" to "complex and impersonal forces," Roosevelt insisted that "if responsibility is to be lodged at any door it cannot be and will not be lodged at the door of those who need help today."

FDR, like Hoover's opponents in Congress, had decided the depression was an extraordinary national calamity that required government to act in extraordinary ways. By fusing inspiring words and effective actions, Franklin Roosevelt was trying to lift the psychological burden that American individualism imposed on the poor. At the same time he was paving the way for reforms in the capitalist system that would prevent a future depression. The promises Governor Roosevelt made to the people of New York in 1932 about providing government-guaranteed economic security were the foundation of what every American was soon calling the "New Deal."

Franklin Roosevelt had long believed that government had a duty to intervene when economic difficulties created serious social problems. He also believed that government had a responsibility to provide necessary infrastructure and services for future economic development and social welfare, especially when profit-oriented businesses seemed incapable or unwilling to do so. Thus, as Governor of New York he had called for state-funded unemployment benefits and old age pensions, continued the extensive road and park building projects of the previous administration, and established a state power authority to develop cheap hydroelectricity for all New Yorkers.

In March 1932, Roosevelt's chief speechwriter Samuel Rosenman suggested that the Governor needed a group of experts to help him plan his campaign for the Presidency. FDR agreed, and Rosenman recruited three Columbia University faculty members. Raymond Moley, a professor of government and public law who had worked previously with FDR, was the first recruit and probably the most influential. He was soon joined by agricultural economist Rexford Tugwell, and Adolph Berle, an expert on corporations and the law. A reporter for the *New York Times* dubbed the trio, "the Brains Trust." Together, and with the assistance of Rosenman, the Brains Trust provided Roosevelt with a series of memoranda and speeches which proposed to fight the Great Depression by reforming American capitalism.

As a group, the Brains Trust were economic nationalists. They believed the federal government had to borrow to pay for emergency relief, intervene in domestic markets to raise prices and wages, reform banking and finance, and provide permanent unemployment insurance and old age pensions. But there were significant differences, especially in their long-term objectives. At the time Moley seemed most interested in bringing about an ideological realignment of the parties: all conservatives in the Republican Party and all liberals enrolled as Democrats. Tugwell believed strongly in comprehensive national economic planning, an idea Moley thought unnecessary and impractical. Berle shared some of Tugwell's interest in economic planning, but he emphasized redistribution of income as the best way to insure recovery and long-term growth.

To get his campaign for the Democratic presidential nomination into high gear, Roosevelt outlined his response to the Great Depression in a much-discussed national radio address that was originally drafted by Raymond Moley. On April 7, 1932 FDR told listeners, "In my calm judgment, the nation faces a more grave emergency than in 1917." It was time, Roosevelt declared, "for plans like those of 1917 that build from the bottom up not from the top down, that put their faith once more in the forgotten man at the bottom of the economic pyramid." A month after this now famous "forgotten man" address, Roosevelt made an unmistakable call for fundamental changes in America's free enterprise system that especially reflected the ideas of Tugwell and Berle. At Oglethorpe University in Georgia he described the basic cause of the depression as "an insufficient distribution of buying power coupled with an over sufficient speculation in production." In the future FDR proclaimed, "we are going to have to think less about the producer and more about the consumer." He continued,

> Do what we may to inject life into our ailing economic order, we cannot make it endure for long unless we bring about a wiser, more equitable distribution of national income . . . the reward for a day's work will have to be greater, on average, than it has been, and the reward to capital, especially capital that is speculative, will have to be less.

Roosevelt's call for a new political economy in which the federal government insured a more equitable distribution of income could not have been clearer.

Unlike FDR, Herbert Hoover never wavered in his belief in the fundamental soundness of the New Era political economy. "The great problem before the world today is a restoration and maintenance of confidence," Herbert Hoover still insisted in 1932. He saw Franklin Roosevelt's ideas about government guaranteed economic security and income redistribution as dangerously radical. Where Roosevelt called for "a fundamental change in our popular economic thought" and "bold, persistent experimentation" to relieve poverty, redistribute income, and spur economic recovery; President Hoover insisted, "The sole function of government is to bring about a condition of affairs favorable to the beneficial development of private enterprise." Above all else, in 1932 Hoover insisted that private enterprise would be best served by a balanced federal budget, proclaiming "it is the basis of recovered unemployment and agriculture."

During the presidential campaign in the fall of 1932 Roosevelt appeared to retreat from some of the ideas he had expounded during his springtime drive for the Democratic nomination. On the campaign trail, Herbert Hoover won the approval of most political pundits and newspaper editorial writers because he could rightfully claim that "We fought the battle to balance the budget." Speaking to voters, the President condemned recent Democratic attempts to increase spending on public works and relief nothing more than "raids upon the Federal Treasury" which proved his Democratic opponent would also be fiscally irresponsible if elected. Afraid that Hoover's appeal to America's traditional wisdom that balanced budgets were a *moral necessity* might win over conservative Democrats, Roosevelt felt compelled to try to one-up the Republican President on this issue. In September, Roosevelt began blaming Hoover for waiting too long to take up the fight for a balanced budget. Speaking in Pittsburgh in October, FDR promised voters he would balance the federal budget by cutting deeply into "the ordinary costs of conducting Government" while raising "by taxes whatever sums may be necessary to keep them [American citizens] from starvation." As President, Franklin Roosevelt never actually produced a balanced federal budget, but initially he did try to make good on this campaign pledge. During his very first week as President in March 1933 he proposed, and Congress approved, an Economy Act which trimmed the Hoover administration's last budget by reducing government salaries and payrolls, and by cutting veterans' benefits.

Franklin Roosevelt's support for a balanced federal budget in the campaign of 1932 and the Economy Act of 1933 are often presented as evidence that, like Herbert Hoover, he was really an economic conservative at heart. Such reasoning fails to appreciate the dynamic context of FDR's evolving policy ideas. In 1932–33, like almost all American politicians, Franklin Roosevelt was trying to understand a twentieth-century economic depression by using political-economic concepts acquired in the late nineteenth century. As young men Roosevelt and Hoover had absorbed similar political-economic ideas. So it is not surprising that during the early years of the Great Depression each man publicly subscribed to the balanced budget orthodoxy they had learned in school and college. What really distinguished Roosevelt from Hoover during the depression decade was how their thinking and policies changed in response to economic catastrophe. Hoover reached back and defended inherited conservative maxims, proceeding on the belief that a basically sound free enterprise economy needed only renewed investor confidence to prosper. Roosevelt slowly abandoned this old way of thinking, displaying the will to create a new political-economy in which government regulated markets, redistributed income, and guaranteed economic security to all Americans.

By 1932–33 Franklin Roosevelt believed that government had a duty to provide adequate relief to the poor even if relief programs had to be funded through borrowing. Already as Governor of New York, FDR had distinguished between what he called "normal budget" expenditures and "emergency" spending. He argued that the "normal budget" had to be balanced to insure government's ability to borrow for emergencies such as war and depression. Governor Roosevelt submitted a bond issue to New York's voters in 1932 to fund his Temporary Emergency Relief Administration even as he requested cuts in spending by regular state agencies. As President of the United States, FDR continued this approach to funding relief. Four years later, writing in the introduction to the first published volume of his presidential papers, FDR explained,

> To balance our budget in 1933 or 1934 or 1935 would have been a crime against the American people. To do so we should have had to make a capital levy [tax on wealth] that would have been confiscatory, or we would have had to set our face against human suffering with callous indifference. When Americans suffered, we refused to pass by on the other side. Humanity came first.

Roosevelt's use of the word "crime" here is important because it signals a critical ideological distinction between the conservative and liberal responses to mass unemployment and poverty that first emerged in the campaign of 1932.

Herbert Hoover emphasized ideology throughout his re-election campaign. Speaking at New York's Madison Square Garden on October 31, 1932 he explained,

> This campaign is more than a contest between two men. It is more than a contest between parties. It is a contest between two philosophies of government.

About this Hoover was absolutely right. In 1932 American voters also sensed that they were being offered a truly significant choice. Herbert Hoover clearly stood for a federal government which used conservative financial criteria to guide its anti-Depression policies, while Franklin Roosevelt promised to treat the Great Depression as an emergency and put social justice ahead of fiscal orthodoxy. But voters alone could not decide whether Hoover's conservative or Roosevelt's emerging liberal politics would lead to a restoration of prosperity. The Great Depression itself was the ultimate test of both the Old and New Deals.

FURTHER READING

Primary Sources

Freedman, Max. *Roosevelt & Frankfurter: Their Correspondence, 1928–1945*. Boston: Little, Brown and Company, 1967.

Hoover, Herbert. *American Individualism*. Garden City: Doubleday, 1928.

Hoover, Herbert. *Memoirs, Volume Two: The Cabinet and the Presidency*. New York: Macmillan, 1952.

Hoover, Herbert. *Memoirs, Volume Three: The Great Depression, 1929–1941*. New York: Macmillan, 1952.

Myers, William Starr and Newton, Walter eds. *The Hoover Administration: A Documented Narrative*. New York: Charles Scribner's Sons, 1936.

Roosevelt, Eleanor. *This I Remember*. New York: Harper & Brothers, 1949.

Roosevelt, Franklin Delano. *The Public Papers and Addresses of Franklin D. Roosevelt, Volume One: The Genesis of the New Deal, 1928–1932*. New York: Random House, 1938.

Roosevelt, Franklin Delano. *The Public Papers and Addresses of Franklin D. Roosevelt, Volume Two: The Year of Crisis, 1933*. New York: Random House, 1938.

Secondary Sources

Allen, Frederick Lewis. *Since Yesterday*. New York: Harper & Brothers, 1939.

Burner, David. *Herbert Hoover: A Public Life*. New York: Alfred A. Knopf, 1979.

Cooney, Terry A. *Balancing Acts: American Thought and Culture in the 1930s*. New York: Twayne, 1995.

Davis, Kenneth S. *FDR: The New York Years*. New York: Random House, 1985.

Friedel, Frank. *Franklin D. Roosevelt: The Triumph*. Boston: Little, Brown and Company, 1956.

McElvaine, Robert S. *The Great Depression: America 1929–1941*. New York: Random House, 1984.

Romasco, Albert U. *The Poverty of Abundance: Hoover, the Nation, the Depression*. New York: Oxford University Press, 1965.

Rosen, Elliot. *Hoover, Roosevelt, and the Brains Trust: From Depression to New Deal*. New York: Columbia University Press, 1977.

Schlesinger, Arthur M. Jr. *The Age of Roosevelt: The Crisis of the Old Order, 1919–1933*. Boston: Houghton Mifflin, 1957.

3

Why the Old Deal Failed

"We have done all we can do; there is nothing more to be done."
President Herbert Hoover, March 4, 1933

The Failure to Ignite Recovery

In 1932 Herbert Hoover confronted a Congressional coalition of Democrats and progressive Republicans who wanted the federal government to provide unprecedented federal funding for job programs and poor relief. Hoover had outlined a more limited economic program in his State of the Union address in December 1931. He remained convinced that provision of new financial credits would be enough to jump-start an investment-led economic recovery that would silence the swelling demand for federally funded relief. The centerpiece of Hoover's recovery plan was the Reconstruction Finance Corporation (RFC). Eager to do something to halt the downward economic spiral, Congress quickly approved establishment of this new federal lending institution.

"Its purpose is to stop deflation in agriculture and industry and thus to increase employment by the restoration of men to their normal jobs," the President explained when signing the RFC into law on January 22nd. Congress capitalized the RFC at $500,000,000 and gave it the authority to raise an additional $1,500,000,000 by selling bonds. The RFC was authorized to make loans to needy railroads, banks, insurance corporations, mortgage loan companies, credit unions, and other financial institutions. Calvin Coolidge immediately criticized the RFC as "socialistic;" other conservatives called it "state capitalism" and wondered whether the United States was now on the slippery slope to socialism. RFC supporters countered that the agency would be temporary, and that it would put itself out of business as soon as the emergency had passed. The RFC did not actually close its doors until 1953.

The RFC was a new departure in economic tactics for the Hoover administration. However, its lending policy remained grounded in the conservative assumption that America's economic problem was financial panic, a mind-changing collapse of confidence which had snapped the financial circuits that normally transformed the savings of individuals and institutions into investments made by corporations, entrepreneurs, and farmers. By making more credit available to banks and other private institutions that were not creditworthy by current market standards, RFC was intended to be a domestic lender of last resort and thus a new source of capital and renewed confidence for lenders and investors.

Restoring confidence by increasing bank liquidity and available credit was also the intent of the other important parts of the Hoover administration's election year recovery program. The day after the RFC was established, President Hoover approved $125,000,000 in additional capital for the Federal Land Banks. The Federal Land Bank system had been set up in 1929 to provide assured credit to banks in agricultural regions. As the depression developed, small independent country banks found agricultural mortgages were frozen assets (that could not be sold) and that increasing numbers of them were in default. Adding capital to the Federal Land Banks, as well as the establishment in July 1932 of a parallel system of Federal Home Loan Banks to provide rediscounting of residential mortgages, was intended to stabilize two important sectors of the banking industry and stimulate new investment in agriculture and residential construction.

The Bank Credit Act of 1932 also played a large role in the Hoover administration's recovery program. Congress passed it without debate on February 27th. The Bank Credit Act changed Federal Reserve rules to permit more of the system's money to become available to member banks. It allowed member banks to rediscount a broader range of their assets, and it permitted each of the 12 regional Federal Reserve banks to hold a portion of their reserves in government securities. As soon as it was signed, the Federal Reserve banks started buying government securities in open markets.

By the end of 1932, the Federal Reserve had acquired $1,850,000,000 in securities; during the same period RFC had extended nearly $2,000,000,000 in loans. *Business Week* magazine called this program, "perhaps the most powerful monetary medicine that has ever been applied to the strengthening of the banking system in a similar period of time." For a few months, this monetary medicine seemed to have a positive effect. Stock prices bottomed out in the summer of 1932, and commodity prices also rose a bit. Bank openings actually exceeded failures for several months. At the same time industrial production and employment increased slightly.

Herbert Hoover tried to make the most of this handful of positive economic signs during the fall presidential campaign. In his address at Madison Square Garden in New York, the President claimed that his administration had developed "measures and programs which are now demonstrating their ability to bring about restoration and progress." After he was defeated by Franklin Roosevelt in November, the economy completely collapsed and social disorder spread throughout the country. Herbert Hoover went to his grave believing that the economy was recovering right up to election day. He blamed the final turn of the downward spiral on fears generated by the prospect of Roosevelt's New Deal. In a long memorandum that he prepared at the request of Republican Senator Simeon Fess on February 21, 1933, Hoover explained that since the election,

> every development has stirred the fear and apprehension of the people. They have begun to realize what the abandonment of a successful program of this administration, which was bringing rapid recovery last summer and fall, now means and they are alarmed at possible new deal policies indicated by current events.

For a long time conservatives argued that the Hoover recovery program was working in mid-1932 and that had Hoover been re-elected in November a "natural" recovery led by confident private investors would have ensued. This counterfactual hypothesis was wishful thinking. In 1932 most voters were skeptical about Herbert Hoover's claim that the economy was recovering; and their skepticism was justified. Even at the height of the brief economic upturn in early September, stock prices remained 80 percent below their 1929 peak, while the *New York Times* index of economic indicators (including freight car loadings, steel production, electrical power output, automobile production, and cotton cloth production) was just 2 percent above its all-time low a month earlier. By the time voters went to the polls on November 8th, commodity prices were again tumbling, bank and business failures were increasing, and unemployment was again on the rise.

The Hoover recovery program was conceived and administered by conservative bankers, and it most directly served the banking industry. The RFC, Bank Credit Act, and the capitalization of Federal Land Banks and Federal Home Loan Banks were designed to save the banking system and to stimulate private lending for investment in job-creating economic activity. This conservative, banker-dominated approach to recovery was a total failure. In the 14 months following Herbert Hoover's signing of the Reconstruction Finance Corporation into law, thousands of banks failed and private investment virtually ceased. These developments confounded Herbert Hoover, his advisors, and most bankers. The outgoing Republican administration blamed a combination of financial crises overseas and the incoming New Deal for the ever-worsening depression. As late as February 13, 1933, in his farewell address to the American people, President Hoover claimed "During the past two years the crash of one foreign nation after another . . . has dominated our whole economic life." By sticking to the diagnosis that the Great Depression was a crisis of confidence brought on by what economists call "exogenous" events, Herbert Hoover never had to question his own orthodox economic assumptions or his confidence that America's free enterprise economy was structurally sound.

The Hoover recovery program failed because it rewarded conservative financial decision-making. Credit availability was not a problem in 1932. As journalist Gilbert Seldes observed, "the Government had created a deep pool of credit, with clearly marked paths to the water line; but the horse would not drink." In 1932, steeply declining demand for output and falling prices destroyed the expectation of profits from investments while the erosion of the value of assets undermined the financial condition of most banks. For good reasons, fear of failure – not risk-taking for profit – dominated individual and institutional decisions. When the Federal Reserve purchased government securities in open markets, banks selling securities used the proceeds to reduce their indebtedness to the central bank, instead of making risky new loans. Similarly when the RFC decided which loans to approve, it applied conservative criteria which meant large banks and corporations with substantial assets received the largest share of federal money. Many small institutions were aided in 1932, but institutions seriously at risk did not receive RFC loans. The mid-summer news that RFC's biggest loan of $90,000,000 had gone to former Republican Vice President Charles Dawes' family bank in Chicago just three weeks after he had resigned from the RFC board seemed to confirm Democratic charges that President Hoover's recovery program favored elites over "the forgotten man."

The Federal Land Bank and Federal Home Loan Bank programs also failed to protect the most vulnerable property holders in their sectors of the economy. Although these programs offered mortgage lenders new financing, neither program offered refinancing directly to people struggling make mortgage payments. Defaults and foreclosures continued to rise in 1932 because the incomes of farmers and workers fell while their mortgage payments remained constant. By the winter of 1932–33, the nation faced a coast to coast foreclosure crisis, record numbers of bank failures, and widespread organized resistance to local enforcement of property laws.

The Failure to Provide Jobs or Relief

The Hoover recovery program failed to reverse America's downward economic spiral. By mid-1932, nearly one in four workers had no income. The Hoover administration never found a way to provide the vast majority of these unemployed workers a paycheck. Reductions in normal federal operations ordered in the attempt to balance the budget, and cutbacks in state and local payrolls negated the employment effects of the limited public works program that Congress was able to get past the President. Hoover's April 1931 order to expand the activities of the Department of Labor's Employment Service did help many workers find (especially temporary agricultural) private sector jobs in 1931–32, but the Employment Service itself created no new jobs. The Administration's only other employment program, an attempt to reduce the numbers of alien workers in the labor market, also failed to directly address the problem of mass unemployment.

In the mid-1920s, Congress had sharply curtailed immigration from eastern and southern Europe and all but eliminated immigration from Asia, Africa, and the Pacific islands. In 1929 only 280,000 people entered the United States as legal immigrants, still about four times as many as emigrated to other countries. By early September 1930, as it became clear that unemployment was a growing problem, President Hoover looked to eliminate job seekers from those applying to live in the United States. On September 8th, he ordered American consulates and immigration officials to strictly enforce a provision of the immigration code that excluded people likely to become public charges. In practical terms, this meant people hoping to work in the United States and their dependents were blocked from entering the country. At the same time, the President ordered the Immigration and Naturalization Service to step up efforts to deport illegal aliens and political radicals.

The Hoover administration's policy of using immigration law to reduce unemployment reflects the way that the Great Depression encouraged xenophobia even in the United States.

Taking their lead from the federal government, local authorities began to repatriate foreigners to reduce the financial burdens of poor relief. Mexicans, who had not been subject to immigration quotas, were especially vulnerable in these circumstances. Like black workers they were often the first employees laid off when companies cut payrolls. In cities with large Mexican populations relief offices used the names of people who applied for public assistance to compile lists for deportation. Altogether, more than 57,000 people were deported during President Hoover's last three years in office including 9,000 Mexicans from Chicago and 13,000 *repatriados* from Los Angeles.

Depression America was no longer a land of opportunity. There were three times as many registered emigrants as immigrants in 1932, an extraordinary reversal of one of the most consistent patterns of American history. Official figures show that 151,000 people voluntarily left the United States during President Hoover's last three years in office. It also seems likely that tens of thousands of Mexicans who never showed up in official statistics also returned to their native land after realizing neither jobs nor relief were available in the United States. In 1932 over 100,000 American citizens applied to work in Russia after the Soviet industrial agency Amtorg advertised for just 6,000 skilled machinists. Thousands of Americans actually did take jobs in the Soviet Union during the depths of the Great Depression. But the absolute number of people leaving the country remained small. In a global depression, there was really nowhere that unwanted Americans could go where labor was in short supply.

Herbert Hoover boasted that his tough immigration and deportation policies were effective responses to rising unemployment. In his December 1931 State of the Union message, the President proclaimed that his efforts had reduced immigration by "about 300,000 individuals who otherwise would have been added to our unemployment." Campaigning in August 1932, Hoover proudly announced that he had "by Executive direction, in order to relieve us of added unemployment, already reduced the inward movement [to the United

States] to less than the outward movement." President Hoover claimed his immigration and deportation policies had reduced unemployment by at least half a million persons. Of course, most Americans were not really impressed by this argument. They knew the President had not created 500,000 new jobs, and they probably realized that half a million was just 4 percent of the total number of unemployed workers in the summer of 1932.

By that summer, many millions of the unemployed had been out of work for months, and some had not received a paycheck for over a year. Declining wages and shrinking tax collections left charities, local governments, and the states without funds to provide even minimal subsistence to all those who needed it. Reports of people starving and of children going hungry multiplied. As we shall see in greater detail in the next chapter, the real possibility of total destitution now struck fear into the hearts of most Americans.

The failure of his recovery program and the breakdown of local poor relief put candidate Herbert Hoover in an impossible political position in November 1932. Hoover's difficulties were compounded by what was easy to interpret as the elitism of his administration's policies – there seemed to be millions of federal dollars for well-connected bankers such as Charles Dawes, but not a federal penny for unemployed workers and their families. Accepting the Democratic Party's nomination for President in July, Franklin Roosevelt struck one of the keynotes of New Deal politics when he mocked his opponent as belonging to "the party of Toryism" that "first sees to it that a favored few are helped and hopes that some of their prosperity will leak through, sift through, to labor, to the farmer, to the small businessman." It was a theme that FDR would return to again and again during the next eight years.

In the late spring of 1932, Congress was bombarded with requests to provide direct assistance to the victims of the Great Depression. It also received reports of hungry mobs breaking into Red Cross food warehouses and daily demonstrations at big city relief offices. Charitable organizations, the American Federation of Labor, the National Association for the Advancement of Colored People, and urban mayors all warned Congress and the President that greater disorders would follow if funds for poor relief ran out in the states. Illinois was already in crisis. After providing $20,000,000 early in the year the state legislature simply refused to appropriate any more money for poor relief in Chicago even though 750,000 workers were unemployed in that city. When Mayor Anton Cermak came to Washington in June to testify on behalf of a Democratic bill that would allow the RFC to lend money directly to states for relief and public works, he told Congress to provide either federal relief or troops to maintain order.

At this critical moment, Herbert Hoover still refused to treat the relief problem as an emergency. In June 1932, he worked tirelessly to block various relief proposals put forward by Democrats and progressive Republicans in Congress. His veto of a bill authored by Senator Wagner on July 11th stated that "my major objection to the measure, as now formulated, lies in the inclusion of an extraordinary extension of authority to the Reconstruction Finance Corporation to make loans," and "upon the extreme undesirability of increasing non-productive public works beyond the $500,000,000 already in the budget." Only after Congress changed the proposal to limit and tightly regulate RFC lending for relief to states and greatly scale down the measure's public works provisions did President Hoover approve the Emergency Relief and Construction Act. This law authorized RFC to lend up to $300,000,000 to the states for poor relief and up to $322,000,000 for public works projects. It also restricted the amount each state could request, and required governors to justify in great detail every single dollar requested; federal loans to the states did briefly stabilize the relief crisis. But this expansion of RFC's lending authority proved to be too little and too late to prevent a breakdown of social order in the winter of 1932–33.

Mayor Cermak had said the choice was between federal funds for relief or troops. Fighting to preserve the tradition of local responsibility for the poor to the bitter end, Herbert Hoover finally had opened the door to federal assistance to the poor when he signed the Emergency Relief and Construction Act on July 21st. But just one week later his administration demonstrated a willingness to use troops against victims of the depression. The result was the biggest single political fiasco of Hoover's presidency.

At issue was the payment of a bonus to veterans of World War I that was scheduled to be made in 1945. As early as the spring of 1931, unemployed veterans had begun lobbying Congress to pay the bonus early to relieve economic distress and pump several billion dollars into economic circulation. In May 1931 Congress passed a bill over President Hoover's veto that put $1.3 billion of the promised bonus into the hands of veterans. Exactly one year later, a dramatic movement for immediate payment of the remainder of the bonus developed when Texas Democrat Wright Patman introduced such a bill in Congress.

In early May 1932 a group of unemployed veterans in Portland, Oregon decided to ride the rails to Washington to demonstrate their support for the Patman bill. Kept under strict discipline by a former army sergeant named Walter Waters, the Bonus Army (as it soon became known) clashed with Illinois National Guard troops in the Baltimore and Ohio railroad yards in East Saint Louis on May 21st. The confrontation made front-page news, and soon thousands of other unemployed veterans including many with families were streaming into Washington to lobby on behalf of the Patman bill. As they arrived, the unemployed veterans took up residence in a few deserted buildings on the Mall in downtown Washington and in a sprawling shantytown on the Anacostia flats within sight of the Capitol. On June 15th, the House of Representatives passed the Bonus bill. President Hoover threatened a veto. He urged the Senate to block the bonus, arguing it would dangerously destabilize the 1932–33 budget. A majority of the Senate apparently agreed with Hoover; they defeated the Bonus bill on June 17th. Despite this setback, thousands of veterans spurred on by retired Marine Corps General Smedley Butler decided to stay in Washington and continue their lobbying efforts.

In mid-July there were still approximately 15,000 Bonus

Army veterans camped out in Washington. Pennsylvania's State Secretary of Welfare reported to Governor Gifford Pinchot that "They represented a cross section of America, as had the army in 1919 ... Their real demand was for security ... American flags were everywhere." President Hoover had steadfastly refused to meet any Bonus Army leaders. Instead he convinced Congress to approve $100,000 in travel loans to veterans willing to go home (the amount borrowed to be deducted from their bonus payments in 1945). This token gesture established a deadline of July 24th for the start of the Bonus Army's withdrawal. In the meantime District of Columbia commissioners in consultation with the President and members of his cabinet secretly worked out a plan to force the Bonus Army to leave the city.

The climax of the Bonus Army march on Washington came just after Congress adjourned without reconsidering the Patman bill. On July 28th, clashes with local police erupted when marchers were evicted from the empty buildings on the Mall. Over their own police chief's objections, the District Commissioners asked the President to have the U.S. Army to clear the city of demonstrators. Four troops of calvary, four infantry companies, a motorized machine gun squadron, and six tanks were ordered into the city. General Douglas MacArthur commanded their movements from horseback with his adjutant, Major Dwight Eisenhower, at his side. Major George Patton directed the tank squadron. This small army moved against the unarmed veterans, many in uniforms and displaying American flags. MacArthur's force cleared the Mall in the afternoon according to a prearranged plan. Then in the evening MacArthur ordered the Anacostia shantytown cleared and burned. The Bonus Army was driven into the Maryland countryside. Casualties included two veterans and one child killed, and other people including bystanders wounded by gunfire, swords, and bayonets. About 1,000 people suffered injuries from tear gas.

This whole military operation was reported and photographed by the Washington press corps. Most of the nation's newspapers ran selected pictures the next day along with edi-

torials that condemned the Hoover administration for employing excessive force. But President Hoover remained publicly
unrepentant. He refused to see a delegation of writers led by
Sherwood Anderson who wanted to protest the Army's actions, and he never apologized to veterans. In fact, months
later, in one of his last campaign speeches in St. Paul, a visibly
exhausted Hoover angered many in the audience when he let
slip, "Thank God we still have a government that knows how
to deal with a mob." It is impossible to know if voters subsequently punished Herbert Hoover for the Bonus Army affair.
But to this day, the forcible eviction of the Bonus Army from
the nation's capital on July 28, 1932 remains the preeminent
symbol of the failure of the Old Deal.

The Voters' Verdict

When voters went the polls on November 8, 1932, less than
40 percent of them cast ballots for Herbert Hoover. Franklin
Roosevelt defeated the incumbent President by a greater margin than Hoover's landslide over Al Smith four years earlier.
Roosevelt won 57.4 percent of the popular vote, slightly less
than Hoover's 1928 percentage, but his 472 electoral votes
were more than Hoover had collected four years earlier.[1] FDR
rolled up majorities in every region, while Hoover won just
five Northeast states: Maine, New Hampshire, Vermont, Connecticut, and Pennsylvania. Roosevelt re-established his party's dominance in the upper South, and he swept every state
West of the Mississippi, something no Democrat had ever done
before. He was also supported by very large majorities in most
industrial cities.

The election of 1932 decisively changed the partisan balance of power in the United States. FDR was the first Democrat to receive an absolute majority of the popular vote for
President since Franklin Pierce in 1852. His victory helped the
Democratic Party all around the country. Democrats made
significant gains in state legislatures and in races for governor. And they established a majority presence in both houses

of Congress that would endure with only two brief interruptions until 1980. The new 73rd Congress which convened in March 1933 was dominated by Franklin Roosevelt's Democratic Party. Democrats outnumbered Republicans 310 to 117 in the House and 60 to 35 in the Senate. New reform parties, which established an important electoral presence in few Upper Midwest and Western states in the 1930s, held five seats in the House and one seat in the Senate in the 73rd Congress.

The Democratic Party's enormous new congressional majorities appeared to give Franklin Roosevelt a free hand to propose and get enacted the most sweeping reform program in American history. But ideological divisions within the Democratic Party greatly complicated FDR's political task. The most ardent New Dealers were drawn from the disparate ranks of urban reformers, Midwestern and Far Western progressives, and Southern populists. These liberal factions agreed government should take positive steps to promote economic recovery, provide public works jobs for the unemployed, and speed relief to the poor. Yet they also were often at odds with one another over monetary policy, regional priorities, and civil rights issues. Conservative Democrats included Al Smith supporters with close ties to Northern businessmen and corporate lawyers, but they were especially entrenched in the South's congressional delegation during the 1930s. Conservative Democrats wanted to balance the budget and spur economic recovery by subsidizing agriculture, industries, and banks. They especially did not want the federal government to extend legal protection to labor unions and racial minorities. During his first term Franklin Roosevelt would have to hold this ideologically divided Democratic Party together to make his New Deal, while each of its historic factions tried to use the opportunity to get FDR to conform to their own priorities.

The Republican Party would struggle for years to overcome the effects of its staggering defeat in 1932. Voters had handed Herbert Hoover the greatest rebuke ever received by a sitting President. Hoover received 5,600,000 fewer votes in 1932 than he had in 1928. This fact led contemporary observers to conclude that millions of voters had switched from the Republican to the Democratic column in these four years. But very careful study of the 1932 election has called this contemporary conclusion into question. It is certainly true that many previous Republican voters, including a surprising number of high-income voters disillusioned with the Hoover administration's failures, did switch parties in 1932. But many more Republicans seemed to have simply sat out the election. In 1932, new voters, especially young people and recently naturalized ethnic working people, contributed greatly to the Democratic victory margin. Between 1932 and 1936, millions more working class citizens registered to vote for the first time in their lives, and most of them registered as Democrats. As a result, the coalition of voters that eventually gave Franklin Roosevelt his greatest electoral victory in 1936 was something new in American history. It was dominated by working people and farmers, and it included most white workers as well as overwhelming majorities of Mexican-American, and African-American voters. For conservatives, this class-based coalition of groups who previously had never acted together was a most ominous aspect of the "Roosevelt Revolution."

Had Herbert Hoover's recovery program reversed the downward economic spiral, he might well have been given the chance to serve a second term as President. And the Roosevelt coalition probably would not have formed during the 1930s. Most American voters could have forgiven Hoover's resistance to federal funding of poor relief if unemployment had been significantly reduced in 1932. But Hoover and his conservative Republican allies in Congress did not develop a successful recovery program, and America's voters held them responsible for this failure.

The Hoover administration never recognized the enormous suffering created by the Great Depression. Even progressive Republicans, who once had once been friendly with Herbert Hoover, were repulsed by the elitism of his administration's response to the relief crisis. Petitioned by 70 of his state's newspaper editors to endorse Hoover just three weeks before election day, California's Republican Senator Hiram Johnson replied, "I cannot and will not support Mr. Hoover . . . Government belongs to all the people, not just a privileged few." In the years that followed his crushing defeat, Herbert Hoover would repeatedly accuse FDR and the New Deal of having injected class conflict into politics, but as Hiram Johnson's words illustrates, by 1932 Hoover's "Old Deal" had already raised political class consciousness. On November 8, 1932 most Americans made it clear that they were ready for a new approach to solving the problems of the Great Depression. But the nation would have to wait, and survive, the worst winter in modern American history before it discovered the details of what Franklin Roosevelt intended to include in his promised New Deal.

FURTHER READING

Primary Sources

Farley, James A. *Behind the Ballots: The Personal History of a Politician.* New York: Harcourt, Brace and Company, 1938.

Hoover, Herbert. *Memoirs, Volume Three: The Great Depression, 1929–1941.* New York: Macmillan, 1952.

Jones, Jesse. *Fifty Billion Dollars: My Thirteen Years with the RFC.* New York: Macmillan, 1951.

Myers, William Starr and Newton, Walter eds. *The Hoover Administration: A Documented Narrative.* New York: Charles Scribner's Sons, 1936.

Roosevelt, Franklin Delano. *The Public Papers and Addresses of Franklin D. Roosevelt, Volume One: The Genesis of the New Deal, 1928–1932.* New York: Random House, 1938.

Secondary Sources

Allswang, John M. *The New Deal and American Politics: A Study in Political Change.* New York: John Wiley, 1978.

Brock, William R. *Welfare, Democracy, and the New Deal.* New York: Cambridge University Press, 1988.

Burner, David. *The Politics of Provincialism: The Democratic Party in Transition, 1918–1932.* New York: Alfred A. Knopf, 1968.

Craig, Douglas B. *After Wilson: The Struggle For the Democratic Party, 1920–1934.* Chapel Hill: University of North Carolina Press, 1992.

Daniels, Roger. *The Bonus Army March: An Episode of the Great Depression.* Westport: Greenwood Press, 1971.

Dawley, Alan. *Struggles for Justice: Social Responsibility and the Liberal State.* Cambridge, Massachusetts: Harvard University Press, 1991.

Gamm, Gerald, *The Making of New Deal Democrats: Voting Behavior and Realignment in Boston, 1920–1940.* Chicago: University of Chicago Press, 1989.

Huthmacher, J. Joseph. *Senator Robert F. Wagner and the Rise of Urban Liberalism.* New York: Atheneum, 1968.

Lisio, Donald. *The President and Protest: Hoover, Conspiracy, and the Bonus Riot.* Columbia, Missouri: University of Missouri Press, 1974.

Romasco, Albert U. *The Poverty of Abundance: Hoover, the Nation, the Depression.* New York: Oxford University Press, 1965.

Sundquist, James L. *Dynamics of the Party System: Alignment and Realignment of the Political Parties of the United States.* Washington: Brookings Institution, 1973.

4

America Impoverished

"SHALL AMERICANS STARVE? This is, after all, the greatest issue
which confronts the United States this winter.
                                        The Nation, November 30, 1932

The Worst of Winters

The winter of 1932–33 was a desperate season. The drought
that had begun two years earlier in Arkansas spread west to
Kansas, Colorado, Oklahoma, and Texas carving out the soon
infamous Dust Bowl. Unusual frosts ruined California fruit
and vegetable crops in December. Two months later Arctic
winds sent blizzards as far south as Atlanta, killing at least 65
people. Yet the weather alone did not make the winter of 1932–
33 uniquely cruel and frightening. Extraordinary poverty
turned the four months following Franklin D. Roosevelt's election victory into the worst winter in American history.

Then as now poverty and protests by poor people seldom
made headlines. Newspapers maintained their predictable for-
mat, focusing more attention on crime and political scandal
than policymaking, more on sports and entertainment than
on business, and more on high society and celebrities than on
breadlines and hunger marches. In the winter of 1932–33 congressional and state actions initiating the repeal of prohibition were reported on front pages across the nation while news
of spreading social disorder was buried in the back pages, or
ignored altogether.[1]

Newspaper advertising also conveyed the illusion of nor-
malcy. Today people who survey daily newspapers from the
depths of the Great Depression are surprised to see page after
page of ads for the entire array of modern consumer goods.

The sheer volume of this advertising obscures the extent of the economic collapse from our view. By the winter of 1932–33 millions of unemployed and underemployed workers had been squeezed out of America's mass-consumer economy. Between 1929 and 1933 wholesale and retail sales declined 55 percent in cities with populations over 500,000. By early 1933, cash business transactions had nearly ceased in many rural areas and in small towns where mines, mills, and banks were shut down. Corporate America responded to depressed sales with more advertising and more innovative advertising copy. Spurred on by agencies and newspapers which cut their rates, many businesses expanded their advertising efforts during the Great Depression. William Benton, who was assistant manager of the biggest advertising agency in Chicago, later recalled, "We didn't know that the Depression was going on. Except that our clients products were plummeting, and they were willing to talk to us about new ideas." Benton became a millionaire designing new advertising campaigns during the Great Depression, but very few Americans duplicated his success.

Masses of poor people – many resigned and frightened, others angry and ready to demonstrate – could be found everywhere during the winter of 1932–33. In port cities and metropolitan areas; in industrial cities and mill towns; in the cotton, corn, and wheat belts; in dairy country and cattle country; among the truck farms of the East and West coasts; in the mining villages of Appalachia and the Rocky Mountain states; and in the timber country of New England, the Upper Great Lakes, and the Pacific Northwest unprecedented numbers of Americans were hungry and cold that winter. Historians have used contemporary reports made by state and local governments, labor unions, and social work professionals to estimate the extent of this unprecedented poverty. Fifty million people living in poverty is a conservative estimate. More likely as many as 60,000,000 people out of a total population of 126,000,000 were living hand-to-mouth by March 1933.

Prices, investment, output, employment, and wages had been spiraling downward since the stock market crash in October

1929. By the winter of 1932–33 no one doubted that America had plunged into a "Great Depression." The prices farmers received for wheat, cotton, milk, and other commodities collapsed below the costs of even the most efficient producers. Midwestern farmers organized "holidays" and strikes, blockading roads and refusing to deliver their products to markets unless prices improved. New England fishermen dumped the largest mackerel catch ever rather than accept a price of one-half cent per pound. All across the country, construction of new homes and commercial buildings was halted. Big industrial corporations imposed additional wage cuts, drastic reductions in the hours of work, and unprecedented layoffs upon their workforces.

By the end of 1932 the business failure rate reached its highest point in American history as businessmen everywhere struggled to save their firms in the face of the continuing deflation. In early 1933 the price mechanism of free enterprise was not clearing markets of unsold inventories. Increased sales effort and continued price-cutting failed to revive demand for goods and services because employment and incomes were collapsing. Some capital-intensive firms continued to produce and sell well below the costs of production in order to cover at least a portion of their fixed obligations. U.S. Steel did this with a labor force made up entirely of part-time workers. But many other companies just gave up, leaving millions of workers without incomes. In Minneapolis, a city hit hard by the depression but not as hard as New York, Chicago, and Detroit, a quarter of the factories and wholesale businesses had permanently closed their doors by early 1933. Many companies stayed open with skeleton staffs who worked limited hours. In circumstances like these, businessmen had no incentive to invest in new inventories, buildings, and equipment; thus people lost hope for recovery through private initiative.

We have no accurate census of all those who went without work in the winter of 1932–33. Since the United States had no national unemployment insurance program and no national system of poor relief, no one was required to count the all of America's unemployed workers before Franklin Roosevelt became President. Widely cited Department of Labor average annual estimates of unemployment show about one-quarter of the labor force were out of work and looking for jobs in both 1932 and 1933. But these annual averages really tell us little about the winter months that connect these two worst years of the Great Depression. *Unemployment did not hover around 25 percent that winter; it soared.* Writing a few months later, Adolph Berle estimated that "roughly 40 percent of all wage earners were out of job" when "we hit the bottom of that mad spiral." Berle's estimate still seems close to the mark. In February and March 1933 nearly two of every five non-farm workers were unemployed. Blue-collar workers were three times as likely to be without jobs as white-collar workers. African-Americans, Mexicans, and other first generation immigrants usually suffered much higher rates of unemployment than native born white workers. About two-thirds of the labor force in Harlem and South Chicago, the nation's largest African-American communities, were out of work. People lucky enough to hold onto their jobs that winter struggled to make ends meet as wages were cut and work schedules reduced. It seems likely that close to half of all those still receiving pay checks in early 1933 had been forced into part-time work; work that was often irregular, the kind of work that made individuals wait, sometimes for days, to be called in for just a few hours of paid activity.

Falling prices helped cushion the effects of wage cuts and reduced hours, but only a minority of all workers managed to keep full-time jobs. These lucky few were spared drastic reductions in material living standards. The average annual real earnings of full-time workers were just 3 percent lower in 1933 than they had been in 1929, but the majority of workers were either unemployed or part-timers. Average annual family income had fallen almost 40 percent since 1929 while per capita disposable income declined even more steeply. Almost everyone felt some economic pain as incomes shrunk. Yet the deprivations experienced by America's upper-income families only slightly diminished the quality of their lives. Edward Ryerson, a steel company executive who also directed Chicago's Welfare Council, fired his chauffeur and drove his own car. "We had to cut ourselves down so that it would not look too far out of line. After all, I was in the midst of a very close relationship with a lot of people who had nothing," he later explained. Ryerson's concern about flaunting his affluence was rather unusual. Most wealthy Americans continued to live in conspicuous luxury, turning out for fashion shows and opening nights, gathering at debutante balls and banquets, and vacationing at posh resorts.

These well-publicized displays of wealth at a time of massive poverty angered many citizens who would later join political movements and unions dedicated to a redistribution of income. But in the winter of 1932–33, most newly poor Americans were simply struggling to come to terms with unforeseen poverty. That winter social workers all across the country reported millions of new applications for public assistance, and for the first time since 1929 the new applicants included large numbers of middle class men. By early 1933, three of every ten new applicants for public assistance in New York were unemployed white-collar workers.

Working class men and women who had previously lived through spells of unemployment and part-time work often coped better than craftsmen and middle class managers who were more likely to feel ashamed and guilty about their poverty. Ben Issacs, a clothing salesman, had made as much as $500 a week before he lost his job in the Great Depression. Years later he recalled,

> I didn't want to go on relief. Believe me, when I was forced to go to the office of the relief, tears were running out of my eyes. I couldn't bear myself to take money from anybody for nothing. If it wasn't for those kids – I tell you the truth – many a time it came to mind to go commit suicide. Than go ask for relief.

Just a few years earlier men such as Ben Issacs had been confident in their status as "breadwinners." Many of these middle class breadwinners now found themselves idle and demoralized, their families eating fewer and poorer meals, patching and repatching worn clothes, and evading bill collectors.

Contemporary descriptions of the unemployed emphasized the demoralization of those men who had never before suffered long bouts of joblessness. Social work professionals, such as New York City's Lillian Wald, testified that "the loss of the dignity of man is the first and most tragic" effect of unemployment. Another social worker Harry Lurie explained,

> The previous experience of wage-earners had demonstrated to them that only by participating in the work of the world can they achieve real economic security or feel the sense of importance that comes from belonging to ranks of persons who really matter because they are productive.

Uncounted millions of people were psychologically depressed by their inability to stem the loss of everything they had worked for in their lives. Lillian Wald listed "the loss of home, of ties, of position, the humiliation of bread lines, the appeal to relief agencies" as each contributing to "the overwhelming sense of failure" felt by the unemployed in the depths of the Great Depression.

Reformers such as Wald and Lurie had long argued that forces beyond the individual's control caused many of society's problems. But most middle class and wealthy Americans still clung to the traditional belief that poverty was usually the result of some individual failing, such as laziness, drunkenness, profligacy, or hedonism. During the Great Depression, many hard-working believers in American individualism were deeply confused by their own slide into poverty, and unable to see how it could be reversed. A man from Waterloo, Iowa, a town devastated by layoffs at the John Deere tractor factory, recalled, "The dominant thing was this helpless despair and submission. There was anger and rebellion among a few, but by and large, that quiet desperation and submission."

Many Americans who had believed that hard work and thrift would enable them to own a home saw their dream shattered by the Great Depression. Urban and rural homeowners faced evictions and public auction of their properties when they were unable to pay property taxes. Owners of mortgaged property were doubly vulnerable in the winter of 1932–33. Foreclosures and evictions for failure to make mortgage payments had been increasing since the mid-1920s when declining farm prices began squeezing heavily indebted farmers off their land in the wheat and cotton belts. In the early 1930s, urban homeowners also found it harder and harder to meet their mortgage obligations. Neither of the Hoover administration's attempts to address this crisis – the Federal Land Banks and Federal Home Loan Banks – had stemmed the rising tide of foreclosures. In 1930, 150,000 Americans lost their homes in foreclosure actions. There were 200,000 more foreclosures in 1931, more than a quarter of a million in 1932. By February 1933 over half of all home mortgages in the United States were in default, and more than a thousand families a day were being evicted in foreclosure actions. For millions of Americans, the Great Depression had turned the dream of home ownership into a nightmare of worry and loss.

Unemployed workers who failed to pay rents on time were also subject to evictions. When tenants refused to move, landlords sought assistance in the courts. Court-ordered actions multiplied especially where massive unemployment undercut the ability of local relief offices to provide meaningful assistance to renters. In New York City, the nation's largest manufacturing center, court-ordered evictions climbed from just over 12,000 per month in early 1930 to nearly 37,000 per month by late 1932. Similar increases occurred in other hard hit industrial cities.

Newly destitute Americans had to make extremely difficult adjustments in the way they lived. Foreclosures and evictions were especially traumatic. Children of the Great Depression carried vivid memories of these experiences for the rest of their lives. Years later a woman from Cleveland related her story:

> I remember all of a sudden we had to move. My father had lost his job [and house] and we moved into a double-garage. The landlord didn't charge us rent for seven years. We had a coal stove and we each had to take turns, the three of us kids, warming our legs. It was awfully cold when you opened those garage doors.

In the long run this type of personal experience built voter support for the federal economic security programs ushered in by the New Deal. But during the early years of the Great

Depression, most newly impoverished people had to impro-
vise their own responses to the downward economic spiral.

Young adults moved back in with parents and grandpar-
ents and families doubled up. Others took in boarders, but
still homelessness spread like an epidemic across America. In
1932, hundreds of thousands of mostly male transients were
thrown off railroad property by company police, and scores
were killed trying to leap on and off moving trains. By the end
of the year, at least two million homeless people were roam-
ing the country looking for work or adequate relief. Over
200,000 of these transients were children, mostly boys, 14
years and younger. For society's leaders, this development
appeared especially ominous. In December, former Secretary
of War Newton D. Baker sounded the alarm, writing in the
New York Times that "all too impressionable young people"
thrown into the transient life would "pick up the vices and
crimes of the underworld – gambling, stealing, drug addic-
tion, prostitution, and sexual perversion."

The hobo "jungles" that could be found near the railroads
all across rural America, and the shantytowns that by early
1933 had appeared alongside garbage dumps, railroad yards,
and abandoned waterfronts in most cities were the focus of
these fears about moral decay. Sometimes more than 1,000
people clustered together in hovels thrown together out of scrap
wood and metal and discarded boxes. One such settlement in
New York City stretched for a mile and a half along the Hudson River on Manhattan's Upper West Side. In Oakland, California several hundred unemployed men who had hoped to
find work on the Golden Gate Bridge project lived in abandoned sewer pipes during the winter of 1932–33. These ramshackle urban places where the homeless gathered were
sarcastically called "Hoovervilles" by residents and non-resi-
dents alike. Hoovervilles were constant reminders of what lay
in store for those who had become too poor to pay their bills.

The additional funds Congress and some states had made
available for relief proved to be woefully inadequate to meet
the needs of the America's poverty-stricken population. New
York, one of the nation's most progressive states, provides a

good example. Voters there approved a $30,000,000 bond act in November 1932 that Governor Roosevelt promised would keep the state's Temporary Emergency Relief Administration afloat for two years. But the new funds were rapidly exhausted when the relief caseload jumped over 50 percent in just three months. Moreover, TERA benefits, among the most generous in the nation, enabled only one in every five families receiving relief to pay their rent, heating and other bills. In early 1933 TERA investigators discovered that most recipients spent almost every penny of their relief checks on food.

The Specter of Starvation

The specter of starvation, humanity's most basic fear, cast a wide shadow across the United States in the winter of 1932–33. In September 1932 *Fortune* magazine had optimistically declared, "No one has starved yet." But people forced into destitution, their relatives and neighbors, and the social workers who tried to help them knew better. Just as there was no accurate national census of the unemployed during the early Great Depression, there was no national accounting of death from starvation and exposure. In fact there are no reliable local figures either. All across the United States elected officials, hospitals, and medical examiners seemed determined to hide the facts about hunger and starvation from the public. In 1931, the case of a man who died on a park bench in Grand Circus Park in Detroit murmuring "I am hungry, I am hungry" reached the newspapers only after 16 witnesses gave sworn testimony refuting the city's denial of the incident. In the spring of 1932 New York's Welfare Council hired Eleanor Flexnor to test the truth of that city's insistence that only two people had starved to death in the previous year. Miss Flexnor looked at the records of just four of New York's largest hospitals and found 95 such deaths. Moreover, she concluded many other people who died of starvation were listed as casualties of something else. Flexnor explained, "A starvation case is more than likely to be suffering from an infection. If the starving person dies, death may be credited to pneumonia or some other disease, but none the less starvation is the primary cause."

In November 1932, *The Nation* magazine estimated 20 million people, about one-sixth the population were at risk of starvation during the upcoming winter, but no one really knew for sure. Today, all that remains are scattered accounts of people starving to death during the Great Depression. Most of these stories came from urban areas that had highly developed relief agencies. Nonetheless, this fragmentary evidence suggests that millions of Americans who had no regular incomes had good reasons to fear starvation during the early Great Depression. For instance, a Brooklyn baby died in her mother's arms as they were evicted for non-payment of rent in April 1931; a doctor reported "malnutrition" as the cause of the death. A year later a newspaper reporter discovered 13 unidentified bodies in the Boston city morgue; all showed signs of starvation. In June 1932, the *San Francisco Chronicle* described the death of four-year-old Narcisso Sandoval from starvation; the child's family had been denied subsistence level public relief because they were Mexicans. Narcisso's bitter mother told reporters of stealing food and following vegetable trucks to pick up anything edible that fell to the ground. In Albany, New York a ten-year-old child collapsed and died of starvation at her elementary school desk in September 1932. The girl's starving brother survived only because his teacher insisted that he be hospitalized. In November in nearby Schenectady a man reported missing by his family was found after three weeks, "his stomach and digestive tract absolutely empty and . . . shriveled by disuse." A front-page story in the *San Francisco Chronicle* on December 15th headlined "Starvation Hits 14,000" described Chicago, where nearly half the labor force was unemployed, as having the largest population in danger from lack of food. In January 1933, investigators from New York City's Children's Welfare Bureau found "no food at all" in the homes of many black children. They estimated 160,000 of the city's children were suffering from malnutrition. Two months later, Brooklyn police answering a call placed by a concerned neighbor found a family of six collapsed from hunger in their Hull Street apartment.

Conditions were, if anything, even worse in the South. Barefoot, ragged, and hungry, more and more of the region's hardworking farm, mill town, and mining families were falling victim to pellagra, hookworm, tuberculosis, and malaria in the early 1930s. Most Southern state governments were dominated by small groups of landowners and businessmen whose principal concern was holding down taxes; they did little to relieve the suffering of poor blacks and whites who were effectively disenfranchised by poll taxes and other devices. Some Southern cities created committees to coordinate relief efforts in 1930–31, but others continue to delegate all responsibility for the poor to private charities. Birmingham, Alabama, a big city devastated by the collapse of its steel industry, relied solely on the Red Cross to administer relief throughout the Hoover years. By early 1933 Birmingham's Red Cross was trying to provide food, fuel, and medicines to nearly 21,000 families while getting just $1,000 per month from the municipal government and nothing at all from the state. Conservative Southern Democrats in Congress finally supported federal funding for relief because it alleviated pressure on state governments to tax local elites, but also because private charities simply could no longer cope with the poverty-stricken population.

Already poor before the Great Depression, the South's mill workers, coal miners, and cotton farmers were especially hard hit by wage cutting, unemployment, and low cotton prices. In the Southeast, cotton textile workers earned an average of just ten cents an hour on the eve of the New Deal. As early as 1931 a third of the upper South's coal miners were completely out of work, while another third relied on uncertain part-time shifts to survive. By 1932 hunger was so widespread in Kentucky and West Virginia that the American Friends Service Committee was forced to restrict its food relief to people who weighed at least ten percent less than normal for their height. Further south conditions were just as bad. Congressman George Huddleston of Alabama told a Senate committee in

January 1932 that "men are actually starving by the thousands today" in the Cotton Belt, especially where failed crops had reduced many farm incomes to zero. The first reports of mobs looting food emerged from drought-stricken Arkansas and Oklahoma as early as the spring of 1931. In response to these incidents the Red Cross started its emergency food relief programs in the region. But even after Congress directed farm surpluses being stored by Federal Stabilization Corporations to be turned over to the Red Cross in March 1932, poor people in the expanding Dust Bowl continued to go hungry.

By early 1933 when cotton prices hit their lowest levels of the twentieth century, a million Southern tenant farmers and their families teetered on the brink of starvation. Forced by landlords to plant almost all their land with the cash crop (not food), these farm families had been squeezed between declining cotton prices and the annual costs of borrowing for seed, foodstuffs, and other supplies. Cotton which had sold for as much as 35 cents a pound after World War I and 18 cents a pound in 1929, brought in as little as 5 cents a pound by the winter of 1932–33. Low cotton prices forced thousands of landowners to put their farms on the auction block. But 5 and 6 cent cotton hit tenants even harder. Many were evicted, and most of those who stayed on the land could not repay what they owed landlords and storeowners. Even tenants who realized a little cash after settling their debts struggled to feed their families through the winter. Where it reached destitute farmers, Red Cross relief prevented starvation. But in the drought-stricken western Cotton Belt desperate mobs again looted stores for food during the winter of 1932–33.

The Relief Crisis

The International Labor Office reported in January 1933 that private charities in the United States were providing only 1 percent of the total wages lost to unemployment. State and local governments had also failed to keep up with the soaring demands for relief. Even after President Hoover signed the amended version of Senator Wagner's Emergency Relief and Construction bill into law in July 1932, federal assistance to the states for poor relief still fell woefully short of meeting the actual needs of the poor. By the beginning of 1933, not a single public works project authorized by that emergency legislation had been started, nor had newly available federal relief monies flowed freely to the poor.

The Reconstruction Finance Corporation was authorized to loan up to $300,000,000 to the states for relief purposes, but each state had to prove it could effectively distribute relief before federal loans were granted. Many agricultural states were forced to create new relief agencies to qualify. Moreover, RFC doled out its loans in amounts too small to provide adequate assistance to millions of needy people in the hardest industrial hit states such as Pennsylvania, Michigan, and Illinois. RFC compounded this problem by using promised loans to induce the states to do more to pay for their own relief efforts. This policy infuriated elected officials in the states, including Pennsylvania's Republican Governor Gifford Pinchot. In July 1932 Pinchot requested $45,000,000 "for an irreducible minimum of food alone until next April and no longer." He was rebuffed and told the state could do more on its own. In August, Governor Pinchot managed to persuade the legislature to raise taxes to pay for an additional $12,000,000 in emergency relief. He then reapplied to RFC for assistance. After scrutinizing the new application for several weeks, RFC granted Pennsylvania just $2,500,000 (to be repaid via deductions in future federal highway assistance). Such was the way the Hoover administration handled the relief crisis. RFC rationed its authorized funds by extending small loans, probably saving many absolutely destitute people from death by starvation. Yet the lack of sufficient funds for relief also left millions of Americans weakened and scared from want of adequate food, shelter, and warmth.

Compelled by law to balance their budgets and restrained by powerful taxpayer lobbies that refused to endorse new taxes or borrowing, most politicians in charge of local and state governments found themselves trapped in an ever-worsening relief crisis. Urged on by conservative business organizations and press, they looked for ways to further reduce spending. Among big city mayors and state governors, only a few liberal Democrats such as Frank Murphy of Detroit and Franklin Roosevelt of New York insisted that issuing new bonds to fund relief was preferable to burying people who starved to death. In his dramatic acceptance speech at the Democratic national convention in Chicago in July 1932, FDR unambiguously rejected the conservative idea that "sacred, inviolable, unchangeable" economic laws compelled government to stand aside while people lacked food, clothing, and shelter. Instead Roosevelt expressed confidence that the federal government could develop effective measures to alleviate poverty. "When we get the chance," he told gathered Democrats, "the Federal government will assume bold leadership in distress relief."

FDR's campaign promises raised the hopes of millions of poverty-stricken Americans, but did nothing to immediately resolve the ever-worsening relief crisis. For three years local revenues from property and sales taxes had plunged while demands for public assistance soared. By early 1933 more than one in four urban property owners were delinquent in their tax payments, and at least one-fifth of the nation's farmers had not paid their property taxes. In Iowa the farm tax delinquency rate approached 50 percent. A growing tax revolt compounded the fiscal crises faced by most local and state governments. Since the start of the Great Depression over 3,000 local taxpayers' leagues had been formed to rollback taxes, and in some cases to urge property owners to refuse to pay their tax bills. In Chicago tens of thousands of people joined a tax strike organized by some of the city's leading citizens. More than half the city's property tax bills were unpaid in early 1933.

Many states and local governments adopted the tax and spending limitations urged by the taxpayer leagues, but political pressures to provide adequate relief could not be ignored. Most municipal governments slashed regular services including police, fire, and public health, and they cut the wages of remaining employees. But frequent public demonstrations that often resulted in clashes with police, and nearly constant lobbying by social workers, clergymen, and officials from charitable organizations forced them to maintain work and in-kind relief programs for the unemployed. As the numbers of desperate people seeking work or relief soared, municipal relief authorities had no choice but to ration their scarce resources.

Established residents who were married with children and had neither income nor savings were given highest priority by local relief agencies. Social workers felt a duty to stretch in-kind relief to insure that mothers and children would not starve or freeze to death, but as we have already seen they were not always successful. Relief authorities also tried to maintain the integrity of the patriarchal family, so they gave unemployed male breadwinners preference when assigning temporary work relief jobs such as cleaning streets and shoveling snow. Throughout the country needy single men and women often were ruled ineligible for public assistance, or they were harassed by local police who used vagrancy laws to keep them from becoming eligible for relief. Many states and localities also enacted strict residency requirements for those receiving publicly funded relief. California's legislature imposed a three-year minimum residency requirement that allowed officials in Los Angeles to refuse relief to over 70,000 applicants in 1932 alone.

Local control over relief also meant local racial preferences governed the distribution of public assistance. African-American, Hispanic, Asian-American, and Native American families seldom received assistance equal to that given to white families of European extraction. As early as 1931, over 1,000 black women formed a Harlem Housewives' League to protest against racial discrimination in New York City's family relief program. By 1932, in cities all over the United States thousands of African-Americans had joined the Communist Party's Unemployed Councils because the Councils openly protested the racial inequities imbedded in America's locally controlled relief organizations. Despite a rising tide of demonstrations, racial preferences in the distribution of relief continued into the New Deal years. Many letters written to President Roosevelt in the mid-1930s, after the New Deal had

of 1932.[2] The use of scrip was especially widespread in the urban South. Scrip circulated like cash but no one was legally bound to accept it as payment for goods purchased or debts due. Usually merchants accepted scrip but many did so only after sharply discounting it. In retrospect, the widespread use of scrip in the winter of 1932–33 looks like a sure sign the economy needed an immediate and drastic increase in the money supply as a matter of public policy. But at the time, most bankers, economists, editorialists, and politicians still vehemently opposed deliberate inflation.

When the Senate Finance committee held hearings on President Hoover's proposed austerity budget in February 1933, it presented a chorus of voices urging further deflationary actions. "I have no remedy in mind beyond retrenchment and budget balancing," U.S. Steel chairman Myron Taylor explained. The prominent Democratic financier Bernard Baruch was even more blunt. He advised the committee, "Cut government spending – cut it as rations are cut in a siege. Tax – tax everybody for everything." A few dissenters appeared among the host of conservative business leaders and bankers calling for further retrenchment. John L. Lewis, president of the then moribund United Mine Workers' union, declared, "The balancing of the Budget will not in itself place a teaspoon of milk in a hungry baby's stomach or remove the rags from its mother's back." But even at this late date, most people in positions of real economic power were unable to either comprehend or care about Lewis' message.

The Limits of Self-help and Cooperation

So how did hungry people feed themselves that winter? Impoverished Americans all across the continent ate fewer meals and a smaller variety of foods than they had in the 1920s. Hungry people wanted to feel their stomachs full. They ate lots of cheap bulky foods such as breakfast cereals and mass-produced white bread every day. Spaghetti, long identified as an ethnic Italian dish, became a regular part of the American diet for the same reason. Many families replaced expensive red meat proteins with peanut butter and cheap cold cuts such as baloney. Women's magazines were filled with tips on how to stretch the family's precious food dollars. Recipes for spaghetti sauces, stews, and soups that made the most out of dearly purchased meat were especially popular in these years.

Still, millions of Americans did not have enough money to purchase even simple foodstuffs that winter. Transients and people who lived in Hoovervilles swept floors, washed windows, and cleaned out basements in return for meals. Sometimes local governments could help out. Over 18,000 unemployed men were paid to shovel snow in New York on February 11, 1933. But these opportunities were unpredictable and they were disappearing. Boston paid five dollars a day to snow shovellers, but the city ran out of money to hire them in the last months of the winter. Most of the truly destitute tried to subsist on what little the public authorities and private charities could afford to dispense; by picking through garbage for eatable scraps, clothing, and something to burn to keep warm; and by begging and stealing food.

Warfare between the criminal gangs that controlled the illegal liquor trade, the exploits of bank robbers such as Pretty Boy Floyd, and the kidnapping of Charles Lindbergh's baby son (dubbed "the crime of the century" by newspapers) grabbed the headlines. Yet in most places violent crime decreased significantly while petty crimes, the kind that desperate people commit just to stay alive, increased sharply. In 541 cities, theft of goods worth less than $100 reported to police soared each winter of the early Great Depression, peaking in the winter of 1932–33. These statistics did not usually include theft of small amounts of food, the last resort of the hungry. Sometimes, if the incident had unusual characteristics, police were called in and food theft did make news. For instance, in June 1932 25 hungry children were caught raiding a Spanish–American War veteran's buffet in Boston. Two months later in Cleveland 52 rioters were arrested when a new grocery store offering free food to its first 1,500 customers could not satisfy the demands of a crowd of more than 6,000 people. By the winter of 1932–33 food theft was such a commonplace event that it seldom warranted the attention of either the police or the newspapers. Writing in *The Nation* magazine in December 1932, Mauritz Hallgren reported that in Detroit "frequently, grown men, usually in twos and threes" entered chain stores, scooped up all the food they could hold, and then walked out without paying. Hallgren observed, "Every newspaper in town knows of this practice and knows it is spreading, but none mentions it in print . . . And the chain store managers refuse to report such incidents to the police lest the resultant publicity encourage the practice."

Barter also increased as people without incomes improvised alternatives to the failing capitalist economy. Millions of men and women traded personal possessions and services (including sexual favors) for food, fuel, and shelter. By January 1933, down and out suburbanites in New York and several other metropolitan areas were exchanging clothes, furniture, and even works of art for food in barter markets organized by economist Ralph Borsodi and his wife. Only the publicity surrounding this development was unusual. No one will ever know how many Americans survived through private barter and by doing odd jobs for food during the winter of 1932–33. But we do know that various combinations of unemployed workers and middle-class reformers organized impressive barter economies in many urban areas.

The Unemployed Citizens' League (UCL) of Seattle developed a model barter network in the winter of 1931–32. Faculty and students from the Seattle Labor College had formed the first UCL chapters a few months earlier to pressure local authorities to increase work relief, provide food for needy children, and stop evictions of the unemployed. Local government's inadequate response to these demands led the League to establish a relief program in cooperation with the public authorities in September 1931. During the next six months several thousand unemployed workers were able to gather 60 tons of fish, 10,000 cords of woods, and eight freight carloads of potatoes, pears, and apples. These necessities were distributed to needy citizens through UCL-run centers in 21

Seattle neighborhoods. Seattle's UCL expanded its activities in 1932 to include gardening, canning of produce, house repairs, hauling services, and shoe repair. By mid-year, the UCL's gardens covered 450 Seattle acres, and its cobblers had repaired 42,000 pairs of shoes. The Seattle method was copied in many other cities including Tacoma, Portland, Cheyenne, Denver, and Houston in the West; Omaha, Milwaukee, and Columbus in the Midwest; and Pittsburgh and Paterson, New Jersey in the East. At its peak in the spring of 1933 the Unemployed Citizens' Leagues had at least 200,000 active members.

Other self-proclaimed barter groups came close to acting like cheap labor exchanges. One of the largest of these was Southern California's Unemployed Cooperative Relief Association. It used the slogan "Self Help Beats Charity" to encourage families to trade labor in the region's fruit and vegetable fields for food. During the winter of 1932–33 about 75,000 people including many Japanese-Americans were being fed by family members who put in two days' work each week for a seven-day supply of food consisting of second and third grade produce that growers would have had a hard time selling to the public. Salt Lake City's Natural Development Association was created during the harvest of 1931 by a real estate salesman who recognized unemployed workers would be willing to harvest fruits and vegetables for farmers who could only pay in kind. By the winter of 1932–33, the Natural Development Association had 19 units in six Western states; its 30,000 active members were feeding about a quarter of a million people. Other self-help organizations such as Minneapolis' Organized Unemployed Incorporated issued scrip redeemable only at its own distribution centers where prices on all items except those actually made by the unemployed tended to be higher than in standard retail outlets.

Altogether the number of working members in self-help and barter associations doubled to about 1,000,000 persons during the winter of 1932–33. Barter systems worked best in medium-sized cities located in agricultural regions, and were more difficult to establish in large metropolitan areas. New

York City's Emergency Exchange Association was set up by a group of social workers and philanthropists in August 1932, but it had just four units with only 1,500 active members in March 1933. New York's highly developed working class culture may have actually slowed the Exchange Association's growth. Working class radicals and union members were suspicious of self-help groups, especially those started by businessmen. California's Unemployed Cooperative Relief Association and Utah's Natural Development Association were frequently condemned in radical and union publications as schemes to exploit poor workers.

Of course workers were not opposed to all cooperative action. The most enduring alternative economy in the country was entirely the creation of working people in eastern Pennsylvania's anthracite coal-mining towns. Unemployed miners began surreptitiously working closed mine shafts and trading coal for food as early as 1930. By the winter of 1932–33, several thousand of these "bootlegging" miners continued to barter coal for food, but they also sold coal to hundreds of underemployed truck owners who hauled it to cities for resale to consumers. This elaborate bootleg coal economy persisted for years because miners elected sympathetic local government officials who refused to cooperate with coal company police. In the late 1930s, the companies were still trying to dynamite closed shafts rather than reopening them or allowing the bootlegging to continue.

Pennsylvania's bootleg coal miners took advantage of the unique characteristics of the anthracite industry and traditions of working class solidarity common in small mining towns to forge an especially successful alternative economy. They also clearly broke the law and flaunted established property rights. In this behavior the bootleg miners were not alone. By the winter of 1932–33, the legal means by which the poor could obtain food – from relatives and friends, through barter, on credit from sympathetic shopkeepers, from community, churches, and charitable organizations, and via public assistance – were all strained to the breaking point. As respect for contracts, law, and legal authority broke down all across the country established political leaders had good reasons to worry about the survival of America's social order.

FURTHER READING

Primary Sources

Banks, Ann ed. *First Person America*. New York: Alfred A. Knopf, 1980.

Burg, David F. *The Great Depression: An Eyewitness History*. New York: Facts on File Inc., 1996.

Hopkins, Harry L. *Spending to Save: The Complete Story of Relief*. New York: W. W. Norton, 1936.

Leuchtenberg, William ed. *The New Deal: A Documentary History*. New York: Harper & Row, 1968.

McElvaine, Robert S. *Down and Out in the Great Depression: Letters from the Forgotten Man*. Chapel Hill: University of North Carolina Press, 1983.

Sternsher, Bernard and Sealander, Judith. *Women of Valor: The Struggle Against the Great Depression As Told in Their Own Life Stories*. Chicago: Ivan Dee, 1990.

Terkel, Studs. *Hard Times: An Oral History of the Great Depression*. New York: Random House, 1970.

Wilson, Edmund. *The American Earthquake: A Documentary of the Twenties and the Thirties*. Garden City: Doubleday & Co., 1958.

Secondary Sources

Bird, Caroline. *The Invisible Scar*. New York: David McKay, 1966.

Beito, David. *Taxpayers in Revolt: Tax Resistance During the Great Depression*. Chapel Hill: University of North Carolina Press, 1989.

Bremer, William W. *Depression Winters: New York Social Workers and the New Deal*. Philadelphia: Temple University Press, 1984.

Cohen, Lizabeth. *Making a New Deal: Industrial Workers in Chicago, 1919–1939*. New York: Cambridge University Press, 1990.

Lynd, Staughton ed. *"We Are All Leaders": The Alternative Unionism of the Early 1930s*. Urbana: University of Illinois Press, 1996.

Mullins, William H. *The Depression and the Urban West Coast, 1929–1933*. Bloomington: Indiana University Press, 1991.

Patterson, James T. *America's Struggle Against Poverty 1900–1994*. Cambridge, Massachusetts: Harvard University Press, 1994.

Schwarz, Jordan A. *The Interregnum of Despair: Hoover, Congress, and the Great Depression*. Urbana: University of Illinois Press, 1970.

Smith, Douglas L. *The New Deal in the Urban South*. Baton Rouge: Louisiana State University Press, 1988.

Sternsher, Bernard ed. *Hitting Home: The Great Depression in Town and Country*. Chicago: Ivan Dee, 1989.

Trout, Charles H. *Boston, The Great Depression, and the New Deal*. New York: Oxford University Press, 1977.

Ware, Susan. *Holding Their Own: American Women in the 1930s*. Boston: Twayne, 1982.

5

Out of Disorder, a New Deal

"The situation is critical, Franklin. You may have no alternative but to
assume dictatorial power."
Walter Lippmann speaking to President-elect Roosevelt,
January 29, 1933

Whither Disorder?

When America's leading political columnist Walter Lippmann
sat down to a private lunch with Franklin Roosevelt at Warm
Springs, Georgia in late January 1933 their talk soon turned to
Adolph Hitler's rapid rise to political power in Germany. Events
in Germany were very much on the minds of Lippmann,
Roosevelt, and many other Americans during the winter of
1932–33. American newspapers were reporting German political developments almost daily, setting up on their front pages
an implicit comparison between the establishment of Hitler's
National Socialist government abroad and the emergence of
Roosevelt's New Deal at home. The parallels seemed clear
enough. Both the United States and Germany were big industrial nations with many millions of unemployed workers and
large rural populations suffering terribly from the collapse of
commodity prices. Since the onset of the Great Depression conservative governments in the United States and Germany failed
to maintain financial stability and develop effective recovery
policies. In both countries conservatives had forfeited the confidence of most voters when unemployment soared, people
starved, and protests grew more frequent and more violent.

By the winter of 1932–33, many Americans and many Ger-
mans wanted a strong leader to do whatever was necessary
to restore economic stability and law and order. Franklin

Roosevelt and Adolph Hitler each saw in this historical moment – the nadir of the Great Depression – a once in a lifetime
opportunity to transform the political-economic systems of
their respective countries, and both men seized the opportunity. Thus long before they were mortal enemies during World
War II, Roosevelt and Hitler had become ideological rivals
who presented to the world competing visions of the reformed
capitalist order that might emerge from the wreckage of the
Great Depression.

Looking back on Hitler's rise to power in Germany we see
clearly the corrosive effects of the Great Depression on democratic beliefs and institutions. Similar corrosive effects were at
work at the same time in the United States as well. The huge
crowd that gathered in a cold rain at the Capitol on March 4,
1933 to witness the inauguration of Franklin Roosevelt wanted
to be led out of the Great Depression. People listened atten-
tively to FDR's inaugural address, but for the most part they
displayed no emotions. In fact the crowd cheered loudly and
long only once, when near the end of the speech the new President proclaimed,

> In the event that the national emergency is still critical . . . I shall ask
> Congress for the one remaining instrument to meet the crisis – broad
> executive power to wage a war against the emergency, as great as the
> power that would be given to me if we were in fact invaded by a
> foreign foe.

That day, more than anything else he said, FDR's promise to
act like a dictator brought the multitude to life.

A few hours after her husband made this promise, Eleanor
Roosevelt used the words "solemn" and "terrifying" when
describing the inauguration in her first interview as First Lady.
"The crowds were so tremendous," she said, "and you felt
that they would do *anything* – if only someone would tell them
what to do." As Eleanor Roosevelt well understood, the line
separating public support for strong leadership and dictatorship was lot thinner in 1933 than it looks in retrospect.

America's democratic capitalism was severely tested by the
Great Depression. But was America, like Germany, on the brink
of dictatorship, or perhaps revolution, in the winter of 1932–

33? The question seems at first to answer itself. Since we know that democratic capitalism survived in the United States, it is easy to assume it was never in any danger. Moreover, and very importantly, since the United States had neither a multi-party parliamentary system nor mass fascist and mass communist parties like those that battled in the streets of Germany in 1932–33, it seems highly unlikely that either a fascist or communist dictatorship could have emerged in the United States.

Nonetheless many different types of government that concentrated political power in the hands of a single man and his minions were established in the world during the 1930s, including one in the state of Louisiana where Huey Long reigned supreme. In fact before he was slain by an assassin in September 1935, a significant number of Americans believed Louisiana's "Kingfish" would become the people's choice if the New Deal failed to end the Depression. However, during the winter of 1932–33, Americans who wanted a strong leader focused their attention on President-elect Franklin Roosevelt.

Important public figures began urging FDR to assume emergency powers in mid-January 1933, about the same time that Walter Lippmann proposed a limited dictatorship in a series of nationally syndicated newspaper columns. During the next few weeks, former Democratic presidential candidate Al Smith and future Republican presidential candidate Alfred Landon were just two of the prominent politicians who publicly endorsed Lippmann's proposal. During those same weeks, the Congress also seemed ready to turn over the whole crisis to a single man. On February 8th, the lame duck Senate actually approved a resolution urging Franklin Roosevelt to assume "unlimited power;" two days later Democratic leaders in the House proposed giving the new President what headline writers all over the country described as "Dictatorial Power" over the federal budget. Thus weeks before the disastrous financial panic that ultimately shut down all the nation's banks, the country was primed for a dramatic change in government.

"Justice above the Law"

In a democracy, politicians call for a leader with dictatorial powers only when truly extraordinary circumstances threaten the nation's social order. Such a situation developed in the United States during the early years of the Great Depression. In 1931–32 four types of disorder – agrarian protests against low prices and foreclosures, disorderly urban demonstrations to prevent evictions and demand adequate relief, brutal racial violence, and financial panics – emerged in scattered places all over the country. During the winter of 1932–33, these disordering developments intensified and converged, turning America's economic collapse into an extraordinary political crisis, a crisis so great that many Americans clamored for a strong leader to restore respect for authority and the rule of law. A complete history of the civil unrest of this period has yet to be written; the scope and scale of these events can only be suggested below.

Farmers faced crushing debts as prices for the harvest of 1932 plummeted far below the costs of production. When farm owners failed to make payments on their mortgages and crop loans, and tenant farmers failed to make rent payments, they were forced off the land by foreclosures and evictions. Many tens of thousands of farm families accepted this fate without protest, but equally large numbers did not go quietly. Instead, during the worst months of the Great Depression, militant farmers resisted both market forces and the forces of the law that tried to uproot them.

An agrarian revolt started in August 1932 in Iowa when the recently formed Farm Holiday Association proclaimed a 30-day ban on the marketing of oats, eggs, and dairy products as a way to limit supply and push up the prices farmers received for their produce. Using the slogan, "Stay At Home – Buy Nothing – Sell Nothing," Farm Holiday organizers spread their "farm strike" to neighboring Nebraska, Minnesota, and the Dakotas. Nine midwestern governors met in Sioux City on September 9th to discuss the crisis, but they agreed only on

the need for federal intervention. President Hoover turned a
deaf ear to the governors' plea. Subsequently, Hoover was
jeered by thousands of angry farmers during the opening of
his re-election campaign in Des Moines.

When prices continued to fall, striking farmers moved from
boycott to direct action. Groups of angry demonstrators sometimes numbering in the thousands blocked roads to prevent
trucks from reaching markets. There simply were not enough
state police and sheriff's deputies to keep all the roads in the
region open. Many trucks were taken over, their cargoes of
milk and produce dumped into ditches. On February 3, 1993
striking farmers shot four other farmers who tried to run a
roadblock in Riverside, Iowa. The next day another farmer
was killed under similar circumstances near Jefferson, South
Dakota. By the end of February new "farm strikes" against
low dairy prices had erupted in New York, Wisconsin, and
the Pacific Northwest. It was a desperate strategy. Journalist
Mary Heaton Vorse observed, "In ordinary strikes there is a
concrete organization to combat . . . The picketing farmers
have no such definite enemy. It is almost as if they were picketing the depression itself."

Resistance to farm foreclosures and evictions was even more
widespread than the Farm Holiday movement. "Justice above
the law," shouted a group in Iowa as they disrupted a foreclosure action. It was neither an isolated incident, nor an unusual sentiment. By March 1933 tens of thousands of farmers
in every farm state from Pennsylvania to Idaho in the North,
and from South Carolina to Texas in the South had taken the
law in their own hands to prevent the forced, but perfectly
legal removal of fellow farm families from their homes. "The
farmers broke the law, as a last resort," one man recalled,
"There was nothing else for them to do." Most often, crowds
of angry farmers silenced outside bidders, forcing auctioneers
to accept a few cents or few dollars for foreclosed property
which was then promptly handed back to its original owners.
But frequently physical force including fists, clubs, and whips
were used to disrupt auctions. On other occasions, crowds of
farmers took over county courthouses to stop foreclosure pro-

ceedings. Angry mobs threatened to kill bankers, sheriff's deputies, and even judges if they persisted in foreclosure actions. A bank agent was actually murdered in Nebraska. No one could be sure where it would all lead. A Farm Holiday leader in Nebraska threatened "200,000 of us are coming to Lincoln and we'll tear that new State Capitol to pieces." An official of the conservative American Farm Bureau Federation warned the lame duck Congress in Washington, "Unless something is done for the American farmer we will have a revolution in the countryside."

Since no such revolution occurred, it is tempting to dismiss that winter's radical rhetoric as exaggerated. But the militant farmers' words were fused to actions that confirmed their seriousness. Farmers who took the law into their own hands believed they were the backbone of the nation, and that the old American Dream of their ancestors had been destroyed by heartless capitalists and their government allies in the cities. "They think of themselves as fighting the banking interests of the East or the 'international bankers' about whom they are perpetually talking," Mary Heaton Vorse reported. Giving their organizations names such as "Minute Men" and "the Modern Seventy-Sixers," the agrarian rebels of 1932–33 forced national political leaders to recognize that only immediate government intervention in the market economy could prevent a complete breakdown of law and order in rural America.

"We have reached the end when a militant group resists the law at the very steps of the courthouse," Fiorello LaGuardia explained in the House of Representatives on February 3, 1933. In a less flexible political system the situation that LaGuardia described might have turned revolutionary. But even as LaGuardia spoke, Henry Wallace and Rexford Tugwell were preparing an emergency agriculture bill for the new Congress. Moreover, by the end of February at least six state governments had initiated farm foreclosure moratoria which gave Franklin Roosevelt's promised New Deal a chance to resolve the farm crisis.

In the same months that the farm revolt spread across rural America, even greater numbers of urban working people joined in demonstrations organized by Communists and other radicals. Both agrarian and urban demonstrators demanded extraordinary government intervention in the economy to remedy their distress, but the two movements were quite distinct. To meet the demands of urban protestors, New Dealers would have to develop very different programs than they were devising to meet the crisis in agriculture.

Most urban protests were led by men and women who saw in the Great Depression an opportunity for a radical restructuring of American society, but the vast majority of demonstrators had more limited aims. They wanted adequate relief, protection from evictions, opportunities to work, and a living wage if they were employed. We have already seen that hundreds of thousands of Americans responded to the Communist Party's protest against rising unemployment and insufficient relief on March 6, 1930. During the next three years, there was no comparable single day of nationwide demonstrations, but in cities across the country Communists enlisted at least a quarter of a million people into neighborhood-based Unemployed Councils. In Chicago alone over 22,000 people had enrolled in the Unemployed Councils' 45 neighborhood branches by the fall of 1932. Whenever unemployment soared or cutbacks in relief were announced, and frequently when neighbors were evicted, the Unemployed Councils called out hundreds and sometimes thousands of people to protest. Often when police tried to stop hunger marchers, bar protestors from entering public buildings, or prevent demonstrators from moving evicted people back into their apartments violence resulted. When police killed or seriously wounded demonstrators, even bigger demonstrations followed.

Confrontations between police and protestors organized by the Unemployed Councils first erupted during the late summer of 1931. A combination of the direct action tactics of the Communist-led demonstrators and police overkill was responsible for the increased violence. One of the most serious incidents occurred on August 3, 1931 as Chicago police prevented several thousand black residents from returning an old woman to the Southside apartment from which she had been evicted.

When angry demonstrators resisted arrest, white policemen opened fire immediately killing three unemployed workers and mortally wounding another. Fearing a riot, the mayor ordered 1,500 extra police into the district the next day. However, instead of mob violence, an estimated 40,000 blacks and 20,000 whites turned out for a peaceful funeral procession for the slain workers. The next day in San Jose, California over 1,500 demonstrators stormed the San Jose, California city jail in a failed attempt to free 11 striking workers who had been arrested during a police assault on picket lines outside a local cannery. Later that month hundreds of unemployed workers demanding jobs or food seized the Fruit Growers Express Company plant in Indiana Harbor, Indiana; they were routed by club-wielding police.

Street fighting continued in the fall of 1931. On October 5th, police and 2,000 Communist-led demonstrators battled on the steps of Cleveland's City Hall while 600 other people demanding increased relief broke into a City Council meeting inside the building. A couple of days later in the same city, nervous white police fired into a crowd of black residents trying to return an evicted family to their apartment. Two of the demonstrators were killed before the crowd overwhelmed and disarmed the police. In November Detroit police and thousands of protestors called out by the Unemployed Councils fought for over a week in the middle of the downtown business district after the city tried to enforce a ban on demonstrations in Grand Circus Park.

The Communist Party had only 20,000 members in 1932, but these activists led hundreds of thousands of people in demonstrations that were increasingly designed to disrupt the routine work of public officials. In the biggest cities demonstrations involving fewer than 1,000 people were rarely reported by the press unless arrests or injuries occurred. Larger demonstrations were covered on the back pages of local newspapers, but only spectacularly violent clashes made national news. The most famous of these incidents occurred on March 7, 1932 when Detroit's Unemployed Councils led about 3,000 working people on a hunger march to the employment gate of Henry

Ford's giant River Rouge plant. Dearborn police and Ford's own security men greeted the marchers with a hail of bullets that left four workers dead and another 50 wounded. Several days later at least 30,000 people attended a funeral for the fallen demonstrators in downtown Detroit that featured eulogies by Communist leaders who stood beneath a red banner proclaiming "Ford Gave Bullets For Bread."

The Ford Hunger March marked the beginning of the most disorderly year since the Civil War. With unemployment hovering around 25 percent of the workforce, the Unemployed Councils stepped up their campaign for greater public assistance by picketing relief stations and demanding audiences with municipal authorities. Radicals also organized increasingly effective tenant unions to prevent evictions and demand lower rents. Demonstrators frequently blocked entrances to public buildings, occupied relief offices, and battled police at evictions. In the biggest cities these kinds of daily disorders influenced public policy. Chicago's Mayor Cermak was forced to rescind announced cutbacks in relief after mass marches in June 1932 during which thousands of protestors carrying banners that read "Fight, Don't Starve!" and "We Want Bread" refused to obey police orders to disperse. Cermak's reaction was not unusual. Contemporary observers generally agreed that the constant pressure brought by the Unemployed Councils resulted in efforts to improve relief services for the swelling numbers of urban poor. After touring the country for the *Forum* magazine in the September 1932, C. R. Walker wrote "In the cities I visited the economic status of the unemployed workers, the amount of relief, etc. was directly proportional to the strength of the Unemployed Councils." A few months later *The Nation*'s Mauritz Hallgren reported, "Social Workers everywhere told me that without the street demonstrations and the hunger marches of the unemployment councils no relief whatever would have been provided in some communities."

Urban demonstrations did not taper off after voters had cast their ballots for a New Deal in November 1932. Indeed as the chronology presented in this book's Appendix makes clear, urban protest actually intensified during the winter of 1932–33, the very same months that the agrarian revolt spread across rural America. In late November 1932, the Unemployed Councils showed their strength by staging meetings and demonstrations in 46 states. At these events 3,000 delegates were selected to present petitions for immediate federal relief to Congress when it convened its lame duck session in Washington. For a week the delegates traveled in eight caravans of trucks and cars that slowed down to parade through the downtown streets of cities and towns across the United States. Usually they were watched by nervous police and greeted by large crowds who offered donations. In Trenton, New Jersey sympathetic workers staged a one-hour general strike to support the hunger march. But the same column of marchers was broken up by club-wielding police in Wilmington, Delaware. Another racially integrated column of hunger marchers that approached Washington from the South was stopped in Virginia by 500 hooded Klansman. Somehow approximately 3,000 delegates from the Unemployed Councils arrived on the outskirts of the District of Columbia on December 4th. Over 1,200 policemen promptly confined them to a remote city street without food, water, or toilets for three days. A parade down Pennsylvania Avenue was finally permitted only after several Congressmen protested the denial of the marchers' right to present petitions to their representatives.

One can only wonder how this National Hunger March and the scores of other major confrontations between police and urban demonstrators that followed might have appeared if America had been wired for 24-hour cable television news during the nadir of the Great Depression. As it was the dramatic events of January–February 1933 – such as the running battle against evictions conducted by the 5,000-member Bronx Tenants' Union; four days of racially charged fighting between mostly black demonstrators and white police in Chicago; the mass picketing of state capitols in New Jersey, Pennsylvania, South Carolina, Indiana, Illinois, Nebraska, Washington state, and California; and the dramatic seizures of city–county government office buildings in Salt Lake City and Seattle – each remained local news stories. Rumors of a "red revolution" abounded and are remembered to this day, but no national media covered the many daily disorders "live," framing them as part of a larger single national story.

Nevertheless the relief crisis was made an urgent national problem by this unprecedented wave of urban protest and by the local officials and governors who pleaded for immediate federal assistance. In mid-February Senator Wagner responded to the mounting pressure by trying to force a last-minute emergency appropriation for relief through the lame duck Congress. "We are in a life and death struggle with forces of social and economic dissolution," Wagner told his colleagues. Wagner's bill was approved in the Senate on February 20th by a lopsided 54–16 margin, but the House failed to act on it before it adjourned. As a result Franklin Roosevelt would have to rush emergency relief legislation to Congress shortly after he became President on March 4th.

Race Wars

Both the rural and urban crises of the early 1930s were compounded by a frightening rise in racial scapegoating and racial violence. From the very beginning of the Great Depression, African-Americans and other minority workers had been pushed out of the labor market to make room for whites. In many places, especially in the South, the pressure to dismiss non-white workers was overt and sinister. After the Communist Party demonstrated its ability to bring blacks and whites together in demonstrations against unemployment in Atlanta on World Hunger Day 1930, a fascist-style organization calling itself the Black Shirts recruited an estimated 40,000 members using the slogan "No Jobs for Niggers Until Every White Man Has a Job!" The Black Shirts disintegrated in October 1930 when federal, state, and local authorities cracked down on it, but its racist response to the Great Depression flourished in the South.

During the next three years a widespread "Negro Removal"

campaign sparked a regional revival of the Ku Klux Klan. Thousands of blacks were forced out of jobs once thought reserved for "Negroes only" – jobs as street cleaners, garbagemen, hotel employees, ushers, elevator operators, janitors, and domestic servants – only to see whites take their places. "Negro Removal" was particularly vicious in those parts of Tennessee, Mississippi, and Louisiana where white vigilante groups wanted African-American firemen taken off the Illinois Central Railroad's payroll. Racist thugs were paid $25 to maim and $100 to murder black workers. By 1934, white terrorists had killed ten black firemen and wounded at least seven others in the nation's most brutal "Negro Removal" campaign.

The Communist Party's reputation as a tireless fighter for racial justice helped it recruit several thousand African-Americans in both the North and the South. Communists were admired by many blacks because they insisted that their Unemployed Councils and labor unions be integrated. Other widely publicized activities also contributed to the Communist party's stature in black America. For several years beginning in 1931, the party provided a legal defense team that refused to let stand guilty verdicts and death sentences repeatedly handed out by Alabama courts to the Scottsboro boys, nine black teenagers falsely accused of rape in Scottsboro, Alabama. Moreover in 1932 Communists nominated an African-American, John Davis, as their candidate for Vice-President of the United States.

Black Communists were for many white Americans a worst nightmare come to life. White fears of Communist-organized black workers split the working class in many cities, making it easier for white police to use excessive force against black demonstrators. In Alabama especially, white fears of black Communists resulted in repeated incidents of officially sanctioned vigilante violence. As early as July 1931, at least 500 armed white men terrorized the black sharecroppers of Tallapoosa County, Alabama for nearly a week after a sheriff and several other policemen trying to break up a meeting of a Communist-organized sharecropper's union were fired upon by a lone black man. Groups of white gunmen began to gather immediately after this incident around the small town of Camp Hill. "Negro Reds Reported Advancing" screamed a headline in the Birmingham *Age-Herald*, knowing this particular hysterical framing of the news would provoke swift white vigilante retaliation. At Camp Hill, a white posse hunted down the original assailant and riddled his body with hundreds of bullets. Dozens of black sharecroppers were beaten, African-American homes were fired upon, and cars driven by blacks were filled with buckshot. Although no whites were arrested for perpetrating these atrocities, about 60 black men were thrown in jail.

Despite this terror, or perhaps because it inspired fierce resentments, the Communist Party increased its strength in Alabama. By May 1932 its Sharecroppers Union included 600 African-American members in 28 locals. In Birmingham dozens of younger black workers were recruited by Communist activists. At the same time, a resurgent Ku Klux Klan signed up racist zealots. On November 7th, just two days after FDR's election victory, more than 7,000 blacks and a handful of whites gathered on the steps of Birmingham's Jefferson County Courthouse community to show support for the Scottsboro boys. When a speaker called for racial equality under the law, Klansmen attacked and beat the demonstrators while city police stood aside. White vigilantes struck again in mid-December 1932 after 15 members of the Sharecroppers' Union in Reeltown, Alabama prevented a sheriff from seizing a farmer's livestock. Scores of blacks were beaten and at least 12 others were shot in this white racist rampage. To protest these killings, more than 3,000 blacks marched in a Birmingham funeral parade behind coffins draped with hammer and sickle flags.

The organization of minority farm workers provoked white terror in California too. There a Communist-organized Cannery and Agricultural Workers Industrial Union had been bringing together white Anglos, Mexican, and Asian-American fruit pickers since 1931 to resist wage cuts imposed by white landowners. Open warfare erupted in the winter of

1932–33. On December 7th the *San Francisco Examiner* called for "MINUTE MEN TO FIGHT REDS AT VACAVILLE." As Christmas approached all-white groups of vigilantes given a free hand by local authorities used whips and clubs to break this latest mixed race strike by California farm workers.

The nation's most brutal racial ritual, lynching, was also revived in the early Great Depression. Between January 1930 and February 1933, on at least 140 different occasions, white mobs tried to abduct, torture, and kill black men accused of crimes. Most of the intended victims were saved by timely removal to a more distant jail. On a few occasions local authorities and state police successfully dispersed lynch mobs. But murderous whites had their way 38 times during these years. In 1932, 29 of 35 attempted lynchings of blacks were frustrated by preventive actions. In 1933, preventive actions almost ceased; and 20 of 21 attempted lynchings were successful.

The lynchings of this era were, like their early twentieth-century predecessors, demonstrations of well-organized white supremacist communal violence. For instance a vigilante firing squad executed a black man accused of killing a white girl before a large crowd in Vicksburg, Mississippi in March 1931. This incident was unusual only for its restraint. More typical were the events of February 1, 1930 in Ocilla, Georgia, where a black man accused of killing a white girl was tortured, mutilated, and then burned alive at the stake. White mobs commonly inflicted a combination of torture, mutilation, dismemberment, and disfiguring upon their victims' bodies. For example, on February 19, 1933, a black man who had confessed to burglary, murder, and attempted rape was taken by a mob from jail in Ringgold, Louisiana. The victim was beaten, dragged to the scene of the crime, and hung; then his lifeless body was riddled with bullets by gun-toting members of the white community.

Most lynchings occurred in the South where mob violence had long played a role in maintaining white supremacy, but there were several lynchings outside the region. White mobs tortured and murdered black men in Pueblo, Colorado; West

Chester, Pennsylvania; Anoka, Minnesota; and Massilon, Ohio during the early Great Depression. The ritualized character of lynching and the underlying reason for its revival in this period of economic disintegration are especially apparent in an episode that occurred on September 15, 1932 in Linden, Virginia. That day searchers found the hanging body of a black man who had been accused of rape two months earlier. A crowd of whites gathered. Sheriff's deputies surrendered the body to the crowd who proceeded to burn and then dismember it. The victim's teeth were distributed as souvenirs, and his charred skull was placed on public exhibition in nearby Warrenton. The behavior of these white Virginians cannot be explained by revenge; their black victim was long dead. But the community went through the motions of a lynching anyway, celebrating the maintenance of white supremacy, using the ritual as a frightening demonstration of their collective defiance of the social disintegration that occurred during the Great Depression.

The dramatic increase in lynching incidents in the early 1930s reveals the horrible irrational potential of human beings caught up in destructive events larger than themselves. In December 1932 *Harper's* staff writer George Leighton observed, "The citizen can only ask himself: What will this army [of the unemployed] do if the barriers give way? Will they not demand retribution?" In retrospect, such contemporary fears of a bloody uprising seem to us greatly exaggerated. But we must remember that in the midst of that terrible winter of 1932–33 crowds of demonstrators led by anti-capitalist radicals were a very visible and troubling presence for local authorities and the many still comfortable members of the business class whose wealth and income had been diminished but not destroyed by the depression. Moreover, if we add to George Leighton's query the question, "retribution on whom?" the outcome of what happens "if the barriers give" becomes even more problematic and disturbing. White supremacist politics and race war were not inconceivable outcomes of the collapse of American capitalism. America's black newspapers were very much attuned to the possibility. Unlike their white counterparts, they covered racial attacks and lynchings with extensive front-page stories, not occasional back-page paragraphs. As readers of the African-American press realized all too well, by the winter of 1932–33 the Great Depression had fostered a terrifying rise in brutal racial scapegoating in both the United States and Germany. For Franklin Roosevelt to achieve a genuine New Deal, he would somehow have to reverse this development without forcing the millions of voters who believed in white supremacy out of his Democratic Party.

The Last Straw

The agrarian revolt, relief crisis, and racial violence of the winter of 1932–33 were compounded by the most destructive financial panic in American history. A great fear about the security of the nation's banks surged through the nation during February and early March 1933. With financial institutions failing in record numbers, more and more people decided to turn their accounts into cash and gold. Treasury Secretary Andrew Mellon had advised America's capitalists to seek liquidity shortly after the stock market crash of 1929. For three years investors had generally followed this orthodox prescription, but not as a herd. The urge to simply hoard money remained restrained. But by February 1933, when most people saw the economy collapsing, a genuine stampede to liquidity developed. This final panic swept away one-fourth of all the nation's banks before it was tamed during the early days of the New Deal.

The depression undercut the value of bank assets and diminished reserves increasing the risk that many, and perhaps all, of America's privately owned banks would fail if nervous depositors' demanded cash. Runs on banks had been a common occurrence in American history, especially in rural areas during winters when unexpectedly low agricultural prices made it difficult for farmers to keep up mortgage and tax payments, repay old crop loans, and negotiate new crop loans. The dramatic collapse of already depressed farm prices after 1929 caused a large increase in rural bank failures. Bigger urban banks were also hit hard by the steadily declining value of their loan, equity, bond, and real estate portfolios. Over 5,000 banks had failed in the three-year period 1930–32, about as many as had failed in the entire decade 1919–29. Yet these failures were just a prelude to the catastrophic panic that followed.

As 1932 ended, for the first time in 63 years, America's national banks distributed no net profits to their stockholders. In January–February 1933 fears about the solvency of banks led increasing numbers of Americans to hoard what was left of their savings. At the same time growing worries that the United States would follow Britain off the gold standard led many foreigners to turn their dollar holdings into gold. Depositors all over the United States and the world withdrew record sums from America's banking system in early 1933. In the last full week of February, withdrawals reached a record $2,670,000,000. The following week, the last before Franklin Roosevelt's inauguration, withdrawals from the system exceeded $3,500,000,000. Gold losses at the New York Federal Reserve Bank were staggering. Nonetheless the Chicago Federal Reserve Bank, worried about a gold drain of its own, refused to loan gold to its troubled sister bank in New York. Fear was paralyzing the major units of the Federal Reserve itself.

The reluctance of the 12 Federal Reserve Banks to risk their own reserves only compounded problems created by the Federal Reserve Board's reluctance to intervene in the crisis. Previously, in 1928 and 1931, losses of gold had prompted the Board to require higher interest rates to protect the fixed value of the gold standard dollar. In both cases the higher rates had encouraged foreign investors to hold onto their dollar accounts. But higher interest rates also discouraged domestic borrowing and investment, slowing domestic economic activity. In late 1931 this policy had contributed to accelerated deflation and unemployment. The Federal Reserve Board feared repeating this mistake during the catastrophic panic of early 1933, so it did not act decisively. Instead Federal Reserve and Treasury

Department staff worked together on a case-by-case basis to shore up the weakest big city banks. As February ended, Federal Reserve Board chairman Eugene Meyer informed outgoing President Hoover that the central bank would be unable to support these rescue operations for much longer. On March 1st Meyer urged Hoover to close all of the nation's banks by decree, but the President refused to consider the suggestion. The next day, the Federal Reserve Board presented Herbert Hoover with drafts of two different executive orders closing the banks, but Hoover still refused to act unless President-elect Franklin Roosevelt cooperated with him.

Throughout his last lame duck months in office President Hoover continued to insist that the nation's financial system was fundamentally sound. Bitter about the country's preference for Franklin Roosevelt and about FDR's unwillingness to cooperate with him, Hoover offered no new last-minute initiatives to bolster confidence. Instead, Hoover wanted the President-elect to pledge to defend the gold standard and deny rumors his new administration would adopt inflationary policies, but Roosevelt refused. FDR had not ruled out inflation; nor would he publicly commit himself to policies developed by the Hoover administration. Roosevelt wanted responsibility for whatever happened before March 4th to rest solely on Herbert Hoover's shoulders.

Roosevelt's strategy of non-cooperation made good political sense, but it was not necessarily good for the country. Critics of the New Deal have long argued that the President-elect should have cooperated more closely with the President during the banking crisis. After all, Hoover and Roosevelt shared the same policy goal; they both wanted to save the private banking system. Unlike Western progressives such as Senators Norris, Cutting, Costigan, and LaFollette, neither Hoover nor Roosevelt saw the crisis as an opportunity to nationalize the banks. Nonetheless, the two men differed significantly about how to save the banks. Hoover repeatedly refused suggestions made by Federal Reserve officials and his own Secretary of the Treasury to declare a national emergency, something Roosevelt was determined to do as soon as he took over the presidency. Moreover, Roosevelt was considering taking the United States off the gold standard. Hoover adamantly opposed both these steps. Indeed Hoover believed that abandoning gold would be disastrous and even immoral.

Washington's inaction forced states to devise their own emergency policies when panic arose among their citizens. As early as December 1932, Nevada's governor had imposed a 12-day "holiday" – a mandatory closing of all banks – to break a run on the banks in his state.[1] In January, bank failures increased sharply in the Midwest and the South. Extremely low cotton prices put Southern banks in an especially vulnerable position. Serious runs on banks occurred in Chatanooga, Little Rock, Memphis, Mobile, and St. Louis. In each case, Treasury and Federal Reserve officials in Washington coordinated intercity transfers of reserves. By the end of January they were warning the President that nervous central city bankers were increasingly reluctant to draw down their own reserves in this type of high risk operation.

The next crisis occurred in Louisiana. The collapse of a big insurance company in New Orleans threatened to snowball into a run on one of the city's biggest banks. On February 4th, Louisiana's governor declared a two-day business holiday to allow his political boss, Senator Huey Long, time to arrange in secret an emergency RFC loan to the endangered institution. Long had the militia seize a newspaper that tried to publish the real reason for the holiday. Huey Long's actions prevented panic in Louisiana, but they also indicated how the collapsing economy could threaten democracy itself. On the day Louisiana's banks reopened, 12 other state legislatures were considering proposals to allow their governors to regulate or close banks by decree.

In these circumstances Congressional actions taken to make private banks more accountable to the public were actually counterproductive. As we have already seen the Reconstruction Finance Corporation did not act as a true lender of last resort. Instead of risking large sums to save weak units, the RFC board generally followed conservative banking guidelines. Still many small banks got some RFC money, and usu-

ally the loans were kept secret. This secrecy rankled Democrats, especially Speaker of the House and Vice-President elect
John Nance Garner of Texas who suspected a partisan bias in
RFC policy. On January 6, 1933 Garner got the Democratic
majority in the House of Representatives to pass a resolution
requiring the RFC to make its activities public. But publicity
only made matters worse. Many anxious depositors learning
that their bank had received or had just applied for RFC assistance headed to the withdrawal windows, so bankers increasingly shied away from requesting RFC help. President
Hoover tried to stop the practice of leaking news about RFC
loans, but it continued until the new Roosevelt administration took office.

Front-page newspaper stories about the Senate Banking
Committee's ongoing investigation into the links between the
stock market crash of 1929 and the investment policies of big
commercial banks further undermined public confidence in
the nation's financial system. In January and February 1933,
committee counsel Ferdinand Pecora interrogated leading
bankers who admitted risking depositors' money in speculative investments, and even worse, using unsecured interest-
free loans for their own speculations. Pecora's hearings
eventually led to the enactment of reforms that included the
legal separation of commercial and investment banking in the
United States. The reputations of several of the nation's financial leaders were ruined. But at the time, the unethical practices Ferdinand Pecora uncovered seemed to many Americans
confirmation of the anti-capitalist politics of agrarian and urban radicals.

On February 14th, Michigan's Republican Governor
William Comstock proclaimed an eight-day bank holiday that
sent shock waves across the country. Imposed as a last-ditch
effort to buy time for big banks in an important industrial
state, Michigan's bank holiday signaled the beginning of three
panicky weeks during which all confidence in America's banking system dissolved. The same sequence of events repeated
itself in state after state. At the request of bankers looking at
devalued assets and rapidly increasing withdrawals, the gov-

ernor first proclaimed those banks within his jurisdiction to be sound, only to retreat a few days later when growing panic forced him to impose either an embargo on withdrawals or the total suspension of banking activities. By the end of business on March 3rd, 32 states had imposed bank holidays or severe restrictions on withdrawals. Outgoing Treasury Secretary Ogden Mills advised a banker friend planning a trip to the Bahamas, "If you go, don't get a round trip ticket – when you're ready to return, there'll be nothing worth returning to."

New York's governor Herbert Lehman, himself a banker, spent March 3rd in conferences with Wall Street financiers and Federal Reserve Bank officials. These men urged Lehman to close all New York banks or risk the complete collapse of the nation's biggest financial institutions. At 2:30 a.m. on March 4th, after demanding and getting a formal petition from Wall Street bankers, Governor Lehman closed New York's banks. An hour later, Illinois' governor proclaimed a bank holiday upon receiving a similar petition from Chicago's major banks. Before dawn broke in the East that Inauguration Day, the Federal Reserve Board warned the governors of Reserve Banks in the few cities where banking was still permitted to expect panicky runs on local institutions. Over 6,500 banks had failed in just two months. Unless unprecedented federal action was initiated immediately, a financial catastrophe sure to plunge the nation into chaos would result. The stage, agenda, and priorities were finally set for the New Deal.

FURTHER READING

Primary Sources

Burg, David F. *The Great Depression: An Eyewitness History*. New York: Facts on File Inc., 1996.

Hallgren, Mauritz. *Seeds of Revolt: A Study of American Life and the Temper of the Times*. New York: Alfred A. Knopf, 1933.

Lynd, Staughton and Lynd, Alice eds. *Rank and File: Personal Histories by Working-Class Organizers*. New York: Monthly Review Press, 1988.

Moley, Raymond. *After Seven Years.* New York: Harper & Brothers, 1939.

Painter, Nell Irvin. *Narrative of Hosea Hudson: His Life as a Negro Communist in the South.* Cambridge, Massachusetts: Harvard University Press, 1979.

Roosevelt, Eleanor. *This I Remember.* New York: Harper & Brothers, 1949.

Simon, Rita James ed. *As We Saw the Thirties: Essays on Social and Political Movements of a Decade.* Urbana: University of Illinois Press, 1967.

Terkel, Studs. *Hard Times: An Oral History of the Great Depression.* New York, Random House, 1970.

Yoneda, Karl G. *Ganbatte: The Sixty Year Struggle of a Kibei Worker.* Los Angeles: UCLA Asian American Studies Center, 1983.

Secondary Sources

Allen, Frederick Lewis. *Since Yesterday: The Nineteen-Thirties in America.* New York: Harper & Brothers, 1939.

Bernstein, Irving. *The Lean Years: A History of the American Worker 1920–1933.* Boston: Houghton Mifflin, 1966.

Folsom, Franklin. *Impatient Armies of the Poor: The Story of Collective Action of the Unemployed, 1808–1942.* Niwot, Colorado: University of Colorado Press, 1991.

Friedman, Milton and Schwartz, Anna Jacobson. *A Monetary History of the United States 1867–1960.* Princeton: Princeton University Press, 1963.

Garraty, John. *The Great Depression.* New York: Doubleday, 1987.

Goodman, James. *Stories of Scottsboro.* New York: Random House, 1994.

Kelley, Robin. *Hammer and Hoe: Alabama Communists During the Great Depression.* Chapel Hill: University of North Carolina Press, 1990.

Kennedy, Susan Estabrook. *The Banking Crisis of 1933.* Lexington: University of Kentucky Press, 1973.

Lynd, Staughton ed. *"We Are All Leaders": The Alternative Unionism of the Early 1930s.* Urbana: University of Illinois Press, 1996.

Newton, Michael and Newton, Judy Ann. *Racial & Religious Violence in America: A Chronology.* New York: Garland, 1991.

Piven, Frances Fox and Cloward, Richard A. *Regulating the Poor: The Functions of Public Welfare.* New York: Random House, 1971.

Prago, Albert. *The Organization of the Unemployed and the Role of the Radicals, 1929–1935.* Ann Arbor: Xerox University Microfilms, 1976.

Saloutos, Theodore and Hicks, John D. *Agricultural Discontent in the Middle West 1900–1939.* Madison: University of Wisconsin Press, 1951.

Starr, Kevin. *Endangered Dreams: The Great Depression in California.* New York: Oxford, 1996.

Sternsher, Bernard ed. *Hitting Home: The Great Depression in Town and Country.* Chicago: Ivan Dee, 1989.

6

A New Deal in One Hundred Days

> "We knew that a leaderless system of economy had produced and would
> again produce economic and social disaster ... Government leader-
> ship was the only method left."
> *Franklin Roosevelt recalling the origins of the New Deal, 1937*

FDR

As Franklin Roosevelt readied a new federal administration
to combat the Great Depression, his image appeared everywhere in newspapers, magazines, and newsreels. The FDR seen
by the public was a big man who displayed broad shoulders
and an even broader smile. In contrast to the dour Hoover,
Roosevelt appeared intensely alive, often joking and laughing
freely with reporters and bystanders. Although some intellec-
tuals worried over what Edmund Wilson described as FDR's
"slightly unnatural sunniness," most reporters welcomed the
public Roosevelt's good humor, boundless energy, and infec-
tious optimism. And more importantly, tens of millions of
frightened Americans found a much-needed tonic in the self-
assurance and strength that FDR projected through the mass
media.

Among American presidents, Franklin Roosevelt had an
unmatched ability to radiate confidence and to hide fears and
self-doubts. FDR rarely shared his inner life with anyone. He
almost always tried to please the people around him, even
when this meant concealing his own thoughts and desires.
Roosevelt's critics seized upon this characteristic behavior as
evidence of a devious and manipulative nature. But this way

of living – learned while he grew up the only child on a Hudson River estate otherwise populated by adults, and perfected during his desperate struggle to survive polio – was one of Franklin Roosevelt's greatest political assets.

He had been struck down by polio in August 1921 while vacationing on Campobello Island with his family. After nearly killing him, the disease left the 39-year-old Roosevelt with totally paralyzed legs. FDR never recovered from this paralysis; he learned to live with it. Every day for the last 24 years of his life, he needed help getting out of bed, getting dressed and undressed, as well as getting in and out of chairs. Heavy steel braces on his legs enabled FDR to balance himself in an upright position, but he always required a handhold to prevent himself from falling. Franklin Roosevelt had to exert enormous physical effort whenever he moved in public and great mental effort to appear to move without exertion. He invariably used extravagant head movements, a flashing smile, playful banter, and hearty laughter to draw attention away from his dead limbs and put the people around him at ease.

Polio could have easily ended Franklin Roosevelt's political career, but instead his disability endowed him with greater strength and wisdom than he had previously possessed. At first he seemed deeply depressed; then he became obsessed with rehabilitating his paralyzed legs. Surviving polio reinforced FDR's quiet faith in a God who worked through human beings, as well as a personal conviction that he was destined to achieve greatness. Spurning his mother's entreaties to retire to the family home in Hyde Park, in the mid-1920s Roosevelt tried desperately to regenerate his legs while Eleanor and his faithful political aide Louis Howe kept his name alive among Democrats around the nation.

Before polio Franklin Roosevelt had been a rising Democratic star, but as the pampered son of a very wealthy family he really did not understand the everyday problems of most Americans. Ironically, paralysis created opportunities for him to fill that void in his understanding. During his long convalescence, Franklin spent many happy days at Hyde Park with Rose Schneiderman and Maud Schwarz, two union activists whom

Eleanor knew from her membership in the Women's Trade Union League. Schneiderman and Schwarz were the first working class Americans that FDR ever got to know as friends. From them Roosevelt gained insights into the lives of working people and the labor movement. FDR also learned about the diversity of American life from his fellow polio sufferers. In 1926, he established what soon became the nation's leading rehabilitation center for polio victims at a run-down resort in Warm Springs, Georgia. The Warm Springs project brought Roosevelt into extended contact with Americans from less privileged backgrounds than his own. At Warm Springs, FDR shared the pool, exercise rooms, and leisure time with other polio victims. Frances Perkins, FDR's Secretary of Labor and someone who had observed him since 1911, later explained that after polio, "He was serious, not playing now. . . . He had become conscious of other people, of weak people, of human frailty."

By 1928, Franklin Roosevelt was ready to re-enter politics. In public he appeared vigorous and strong. Years of strenuous exercise had not restored his withered legs, but it had given him a massive upper body. During the early New Deal, cartoonists seized upon this feature, frequently portraying FDR as a muscular athlete who smashed home runs, scored touchdowns, and knocked out his opponents. With the cooperation of his family and his closest associates FDR had also devised a way to "walk" in public by using a cane and leaning heavily on the arm of a person (often one of his sons) next to him. New York Republicans tried to turn FDR's polio against him when he first ran for Governor in 1928, but the tactic failed and was never revived. Convinced he could not be elected President if the full extent of his paralysis were widely known, Franklin Roosevelt asked reporters to refrain from publicizing his disability. At the same time he also offered them unprecedented access, holding daily press briefings as Governor, and bi-weekly press conferences when he was President. During the 16 years that Franklin Roosevelt was Governor of New York and President of the United States, a cooperative press corps never once showed the public the full extent of his paralysis.

During the winter of 1932–33, Franklin Roosevelt radiated confidence in public. Yet we know from the recollections of family members that FDR doubted whether he had the strength and wisdom to lead the country out of the worsening Depression. On the evening of his election victory over Herbert Hoover, Roosevelt had confided this apprehension to his oldest son James. These inner doubts may have persisted all through the long interregnum. As late as the morning of March 6th, the day on which he shut down the nation's banks by presidential proclamation, FDR experienced a terrifying panic attack when left alone in the President's office for the first time. Yet never for a minute, on that day or any other, did Franklin Roosevelt reveal his fears to the public.

FDR's best qualities – a quiet courage that calmed all around him, and a genuine compassion for suffering people – were showcased on one of the most tumultuous days of the interregnum, February 15, 1933 (see Appendix for details). That evening, a 33-year-old anarchist named Guiseppe Zangara tried to kill the President-elect as his open car slowly moved through a crowd of 20,000 well-wishers in a Miami park. Zangara's bullets missed Roosevelt, but hit five bystanders including Chicago's Mayor Anton Cermak who was standing next to FDR's car. After Cermak was shot, Roosevelt ignored Secret Service orders to leave the scene immediately. Instead he directed his driver to put the bleeding Cermak on the back seat of the car. While FDR wrapped an arm around the wounded man and spoke encouraging words into his ear, the driver took them to the nearest hospital. FDR did not leave Anton Cermak's side until he had been assured that the Mayor would survive the night. By then everyone around him, including his closest advisors and reporters, recognized there was much more to Franklin Roosevelt than he had previously showed them.

When FDR returned to New York City on February 17th, his motorcade was guarded by over 1,000 policeman who stood with guns drawn. This show of force heightened tensions surrounding Roosevelt's last New York homecoming before he moved onto the White House, but the continued concern for his life seemed prudent. During an incredibly speedy trial for attempted murder, Guiseppe Zangara had declared, "I do not hate Mr. Roosevelt personally. I hate all presidents . . . and I hate all officials and anyone who is rich." Who could assure Roosevelt and the country that there were no more men or women like Zangara out there, their grievances becoming murderous as the economic foundations of everyday life crumbled around them? On February 20th, just five days after he was arrested at the scene of his crimes, Guiseppe Zangara was pronounced guilty on two counts of attempted murder and sentenced to 80 years of hard labor in a Florida prison. The next day a bomb was discovered in mailbag sent to FDR.

Reports of the events in Miami and their aftermath dominated the headlines for days.[1] Franklin Roosevelt's magnificent behavior on February 15th soon became part the mythology of the New Deal. According to this popular history, the courage and compassion FDR demonstrated in Miami so inspired the American people with hope that they simply hunkered down for the next three weeks waiting for their heroic leader to take charge of the federal government. In reality, the events in Miami did not arrest the nationwide disintegration of law and order. During the two weeks following the attempt on Roosevelt's life, farms strikes, anti-eviction and foreclosure riots, seizures of public buildings, and incidents of racial violence grew more frequent and numerous.

Throughout the winter of 1932–33, FDR carefully avoided the appearance of alarm or excessive worry, but he was well aware of the deteriorating economy and social instability. Since he was not sure how to reverse the Great Depression, Roosevelt made himself available to scores of people who hoped their ideas would be included in the New Deal. During these months, Roosevelt never publicly committed himself to a single course of action. Instead, like most of his principal advisors, FDR treated the Great Depression as a collection of separate crises each of which could be handled by emergency actions of the national government.

The New Deal was planned in piecemeal fashion by the President-elect himself, his Brains Trust, and other experts.

Just two days after the election, Adolph Berle sent Raymond Moley a long memorandum outlining an agenda for a special session of Congress based on the correct assumption that "the economic situation may change very much for the worse." Berle thought farm relief, stabilization of industrial prices and employment, and poor relief would be the most critical problems; and that new fiscal and monetary problems would have to be solved quickly. Shortly after Berle drew up this outline, FDR and the Brains Trust decided on an initial division of responsibilities at a series of meetings in Warm Springs. Moley worked most closely with Roosevelt recruiting experts and filling positions in the new administration. In February he played a major role in developing its response to the banking crisis. William Woodin, a New York businessman, lifelong Republican, former director of the New York Federal Reserve Bank, trustee of the Warm Springs Foundation, and personal friend of FDR was also given major responsibility for developing financial policy. Rexford Tugwell coordinated the effort to create a coherent agricultural policy, and soon he was working closely with Henry Wallace and Henry Morgenthau, a neighbor and close friend of Franklin Roosevelt who had served the Governor as chairman of the New York's Agricultural Commission. Adolph Berle directed efforts to deal with the farm foreclosure crisis, business bankruptcies, and the imminent threat of financial collapse in the railroad industry.

Soon dozens of men drawn mostly from university faculties, business and finance, and agriculture organizations had been divided into small groups, each assigned the preparation of specific legislation for the expected special session of Congress.

Franklin Roosevelt himself provided the only real coordination for these working groups. The President-elect spent most of his days in meetings held variously at Hyde Park, his Manhattan townhouse, and Warm Springs. With Raymond Moley often at his side, FDR used these meetings to size up potential appointees and discuss particular policy problems. Sometimes these meetings accomplished both purposes. "I can see now exactly what they were doing," Henry Wallace later said of his first meeting with FDR at Warm Springs. "They wanted to see what ideas I had regarding the farm program and see how I would handle myself vis-à-vis Franklin Roosevelt; vis-à-vis Ray Moley . . . and later vis-à-vis members of the House agricultural committee."

Roosevelt was trying to build as broad a political coalition of support as possible for his New Deal. FDR was especially concerned because his Democratic Party's majority delegation in the new Congress remained divided along regional and ideological lines. Conservative Democrats, including Southerners who dominated the leadership of important committees, believed in limited federal power. More numerous liberal Democrats wanted the federal government to take charge of relief and recovery efforts, and they realized emergency programs would require unprecedented borrowing. Yet the liberals were divided among themselves on specific issues. Western and Southern liberals generally favored extensive federal aid to farmers and big water projects, while urban liberals from the Northeast and Midwest thought federal monies should be spent on massive job-creation programs and slum clearance. Many Democratic liberals (and progressive Republicans) endorsed the anti-trust ideas long championed by Supreme Court Justice Louis Brandeis and his protege, Professor Felix Frankfurter of Harvard University; but others like Senator Wagner believed that planning and regulated markets were inevitable and good.

FDR supported the nationalist ideas of the planners in 1933, but he also expressed the anti-trust liberals' belief that the unrestrained accumulation of wealth and economic power was anti-social and undemocratic. Roosevelt saw no contradiction in this combination, and was confident that all liberals would remain loyal to his new administration. He also knew the support of conservative Democrats hinged on making the New Deal palatable to business interests and Southern plantation owners. So he deliberately included people more conservative than himself in the planning and execution of the early New Deal. For example Lewis Douglas, a conservative Arizona Congressman, was assigned the task of finding $500,000,000 to cut from the already austere budget of the outgoing Hoover administration. Douglas' work emerged as the Economy Act which Congress passed on March 20, 1933, just a few weeks after FDR had named him Director of the Budget.

FDR also acted conservatively, using regional balance and political service as criteria, when making most of his cabinet appointments. Roosevelt selected three Southerners: Cordell Hull of Tennessee as Secretary of State, Claude Swanson of Virginia as Navy Secretary, and Daniel Roper of South Carolina for Secretary of Commerce; and two men from the West: Utah's George Dern to head the War Department, and Montana's Thomas Walsh as Attorney General. When the elderly Walsh died suddenly on March 2nd, Roosevelt called upon Homer Cummings, a long-time party activist from Connecticut, to replace him. FDR picked James Farley, his campaign manager since 1928, to be Postmaster General. He also reached out to progressive Republicans from the Midwest by naming Harold Ickes of Chicago, an advocate of public power development and racial equality, Secretary of the Interior; and Henry Wallace of Iowa his Secretary of Agriculture.

FDR rounded out his first cabinet by sending William Woodin to the Treasury Department; and Frances Perkins, New York State's Industrial Commissioner, to the Department of Labor. Frances Perkins was the first woman ever appointed to a Cabinet position, and the first Secretary of Labor not drawn from a labor union background. The Perkins' appointment angered union leaders, but pleased Democratic women's groups who had lobbied FDR on her behalf. As a former social worker, Perkins saw herself as representing all working people, not just organized labor. She wanted to immediately enact federal emergency relief, a public works employment program, and minimum wage and maximum hours legislation.

Roosevelt's desire to achieve political balance in his early New Deal created serious divisions among those charged with solving the problems created by the Great Depression. For example, conservatives determined to balance the federal budget were almost always at odds with proponents of new programs that required federal borrowing. Advocates of anti-trust action against big business found themselves at logger-heads with planners who wanted to suspend anti-trust laws to allow businesses to stabilize prices. Those working on agricultural price adjustment included proponents of export subsidies, monetary inflation, and domestic allotment. Using charm, humor, guile, and persuasion Franklin Roosevelt made these ideologically diverse people work together. In 1933 FDR's loosely coordinated policy-making method worked because the collapsing economy and rising social disorder created a desperate national emergency in which cooperation and compromise were imperative. As time passed, however, the ideological differences among New Dealers became harder to reconcile.

The New Deal that took shape under Franklin Roosevelt's supervision in early 1933 was a series of problem-specific actions developed by various groups of people who held often conflicting ideas about what should be done to reverse the effects of the Great Depression. Inevitably it created some overlapping programs and contradictory policies. Moreover this first New Deal dealt exclusively with those problems which were brought to FDR's attention by the experts he gathered together in the winter of 1932–33. Except for Frances Perkins, these experts were all white men drawn from major institutions of the contemporary establishment. Whole classes of people with little or no political power – including blacks and other racial minorities, and even organized labor – were simply not invited to participate in planning the early New Deal. However, after he assumed the duties of the President, Franklin Roosevelt would confront growing demands from all these groups of Americans to be included in the New Deal.

Restoring Confidence

The advent of the New Deal stands out as one of the most dramatic episodes in American history. As the President-elect's special train pulled into Washington's Union Station on the

evening of March 2nd, it was surrounded by a huge crowd of
well-wishers. At the same time in cities all over the country
several hundred thousand members of the Unemployed Councils and Unemployed Citizens' Leagues were readying themselves for Inauguration Day demonstrations. FDR and the press
paid them little attention. Roosevelt was genuinely saddened
by the news of the unexpected death of his Western champion, Attorney General designate Walsh, earlier in the day.
But the news of further state-mandated bank closures and secret reports of fast-dwindling reserves at the nation's largest
private banks and the Federal Reserve itself were even more
troubling. Late in the afternoon of Friday May 3rd, Herbert
Hoover turned the President-elect's traditional ceremonial visit
to the White House into a final desperate appeal for a joint
declaration on the banking crisis. Yet Hoover still refused to
declare a national bank holiday, and as Raymond Moley later
reported, FDR insisted "that, until noon on March 4th, the
baby was Hoover's anyhow." The drama would be played
out according to Roosevelt's script. There would be no visible
signs of cooperation between the outgoing and incoming administrations, nor any public indications of how the new President intended to prevent the now imminent collapse of
America's banking system.

A sanguine Franklin Roosevelt already had made several
crucial decisions. Most importantly, and much to the chagrin
of Western progressives who hoped for nationalization, FDR
had decided that the private banking system was fundamentally sound, and that it could be restored to health by federal
insistence on proper financial management. Unlike Hoover,
he was ready to follow the Federal Reserve's recommendation
to close all the nation's banks. All through the night of March
3rd, outgoing Treasury Secretary Ogden Mills and his staff
secretly met with Raymond Moley and Treasury Secretary-
designate William Woodin hammering out the details of what
FDR wanted done. By the time he was sworn in as President
of the United States by Chief Justice Charles Evans Hughes on
the afternoon of Saturday March 4th, Franklin Roosevelt was
prepared to (1) invoke an obscure and never repealed law (the

1917 Trading-with-the-Enemy Act) to temporarily close all of the nation's banks; (2) use the authority of the same law to stop all transactions in gold and silver; (3) immediately summon leading bankers to Washington for consultations on the content of emergency legislation; and (4) call Congress into special session to extend the bank holiday and pass legislation that would provide for an orderly reopening of most banks.

Franklin Roosevelt betrayed none of these decisions in his inaugural address. In a steady serious voice he told the tens of thousands gathered on the east side of the Capitol, and the tens of millions listening on their radios, that they had nothing to fear because "Nature still offers her bounty and human efforts have multiplied it." When Roosevelt blamed "unscrupulous money changers," "self-seekers," and the stubborn and incompetent "rulers of the exchange of mankind's goods" for the Great Depression the crowd applauded briefly. Then they listened quietly as FDR made vague promises to raise agricultural prices, increase purchasing power, save homeowners and farmers from foreclosure, provide federal monies for relief, reform banking and finance, and "put people to work." These promises would be remembered as each was made good in the coming weeks, but that day the commanding tone of Roosevelt's words, not their specific content, was most arresting. FDR told Americans he had a mandate "for direct, vigorous action," and their role should be to respond with "discipline and direction under leadership." He spoke as a commander-in-chief, instructing citizens "if we are to go forward, we must move as a trained and loyal army willing to sacrifice for the good of a common discipline." But he also promised his New Deal would "apply social values more noble than monetary profit," and place "the joy of achievement" and "the thrill of creative effort" over "the mere possession of money."

FDR's first inaugural address combined the fierce nationalism of Theodore Roosevelt and the moral idealism of Woodrow Wilson into what the *New York Herald Tribune* rightly described as "A Call to Arms." And it seems that this was just what most Americans wanted to hear. The next day editorial greatly expanded federal relief programs, confirm the widespread persistence of this form of economic discrimination. "The way they are treating Darkies here is A Shame," a Vicksburg, Mississippi man complained as late as September 1935. "They wont give them food nor Cloths nor Work to do [and] When they Ask for Any thing they drive them away as they were dogs." Eliminating racial discrimination in locally administered public assistance programs proved to be one of the most difficult problems confronting New Dealers.

The relief crisis greatly compounded urban America's fiscal problems. During the winter of 1932–33 over 1,000 city, town, and county governments defaulted on debts due to bondholders. These defaults helped create broad political support for more extensive federal relief in 1933. But before the New Deal rescued financially strapped cities and their creditors, local governments were forced to slash payrolls. Since almost every municipal government in the United States answered to an electorate dominated by white voters, minority workers increasingly found themselves denied both regular and temporary municipal employment. For example, in September 1932 the city of Los Angeles dismissed 74 experienced Japanese-American transit workers so as to continue employment for less-senior Anglo workers. New Orleans went even further. The Crescent City not only fired black workers; it also passed an ordinance prohibiting the employment of African-Americans on city-owned docks. Fortunately, a U.S. Court of Appeals prevented the city from enforcing this ordinance.

Despite efforts to cut spending, in the winter of 1932–33 many city governments had to adopt draconian policies to stay afloat. Atlanta, Memphis, and New Orleans forced municipal workers to "donate" several days of work each month. New York City and Boston deducted "contributions" for relief from workers' paychecks. In Alabama, most public schools shut down in January 1933 as state aid dried up and local school boards went bankrupt. Chicago's schoolteachers were simply not paid from November 1932 to March 1933.

Local governments also began issuing scrip in lieu of cash payments to employees, suppliers, and contractors in the fall opinion across the country was united in praise of the speech. Even more remarkably, 450,000 letters and telegrams flooded the White House mailroom during the week following the inauguration, almost all of them strongly supportive of the President's message.[2]

Yet FDR's words alone did not dispel the desperation and anger that gripped the nation. The new President took immediate steps to turn his promise of bold leadership into concrete and effective actions. On Saturday evening, while the inaugural reception was just getting underway downstairs in the White House, FDR moved to the Oval Room upstairs to watch while Justice Benjamin Cardozo swore in his entire cabinet. This action was unprecedented and only possible because FDR had obtained prior Senate confirmation of his appointments. The new President immediately conferred with Treasury Secretary Woodin and Attorney General Cummings about plans for proclaiming a national bank holiday. On Sunday afternoon Roosevelt briefed the whole cabinet on the banking crisis. He next met Congressional leaders, telling them that he wanted a special session to be convened on March 9th to enact the emergency banking bill then being prepared under the direction of Secretary Woodin. That night, he asked four reporters to witness his signing of a proclamation calling Congress into special session, and at one o'clock in the morning of Monday March 6th, a second proclamation closing all the banks in the United States for four days.

The big city bankers whom Roosevelt had summoned to Washington were too demoralized and divided among themselves to offer any coherent advice to the new administration. By Tuesday morning William Woodin and Raymond Moley had put together the essential elements of the emergency banking bill on their own. Roosevelt's men presumed this was no time for radical reform. Woodin wanted to restore depositors' confidence by combining what he termed "swift and staccato action" with conventional banking methods. Working from an outline originally produced by Hoover's Treasury, he and Moley decided the federal government had to act as both overseer and lender of last resort. Bank openings would be staggered according to financial condition. Weak banks could issue preferred stock to secure loans from the RFC. Federal Reserve loans would be available in the form of notes backed by government securities, not specie. Woodin also decided to have the Federal Reserve issue $200,000,000 in notes backed only by government securities to meet the expected demand for cash from bank customers. The President approved this plan on the evening of March 7th. For the next 36 hours a drafting committee labored over the precise language of the bill, limiting participation to members of the Federal Reserve at the insistence of two conservative Southern Democrats: Carter Glass, chairman of the Senate Banking Committee, and Jesse Jones, the new director of the Reconstruction Finance Corporation.

On Wednesday morning Franklin Roosevelt held the first of the 337 press conferences of his first term. It was an unqualified success. From the start FDR made it clear that he wanted press conferences to be a give-and-take in which he answered questions freely as long as reporters played by his rules. The President was not to be quoted directly unless the quotation was released by his press secretary Stephen Early; some of what he said was treated as "background information" that could be described without identifying the White House as a source; and other statements were completely "off the record" (not to be used at all in print). Surrounded by over 125 reporters who crowded into his office, Roosevelt was alternately humorous and serious, but always charming. He talked with reporters, not down at them, conveying a genuine respect for their work and intelligence. FDR made these particular reporters feel like insiders who were privy to inside information. That morning, and in the twice-weekly meetings with reporters that followed, FDR acquired one of the New Deal's greatest political assets, the respect of the White House press corps.

The 73rd Congress convened on the afternoon of March 9th to consider the President's request to pass the hastily drafted banking bill. The fate of the bill was never in doubt. Democrats outnumbered Republicans nearly two to one in the Senate and almost three to one in the House. And even more importantly, in that moment of great national crisis, partisan and ideological differences were put aside. "Our first task is to reopen all sound banks," FDR explained in the message that accompanied the bill. To achieve that end, he asked Congress to give "the Executive branch of the Government control over banks for the protection of depositors." FDR's bold request for expanded presidential power was approved almost without deliberation. The Senate Banking and Currency Committee heard two hours of testimony, including a prediction that only 10 percent of the nation's banks could reopen without the emergency legislation. The full Senate approved the banking bill 73–7 just three hours after receiving it from the committee. The lower house had worked even faster. In little more than an hour, before copies of the bill could be produced, the House of Representatives approved the President's proposal on a voice vote.

Franklin Roosevelt signed the law granting him extraordinary powers over the nation's banks that evening, and immediately proclaimed an indefinite extension of the bank holiday. Then he called Congressional leaders to his office to inform them that he wanted to balance the federal budget by slashing veterans' benefits, federal salaries (including Congressional pay), and other programs. The next day, Friday March 10th, FDR formally asked Congress to grant him special powers to obtain what he called "drastic retrenchment at this time." Advancing an argument prepared by Budget Director Lewis Douglas, FDR told the legislators they had no time to waste, that they had to give him the power to reduce the budget set to take effect on July 1st by 25 percent. The President insisted that "the unimpaired credit of the United States government" – upon which rested nothing less than "the safety of deposits, the security of insurance policies, the activity of industrial enterprise, the values of our agricultural products and the availability of employment" – was at stake. Roosevelt would later explain that this argument referred exclusively to "the normal budget," not the new programs he envisioned to extend emergency relief. This important distinction was not made clear at the time.

Conservatives in both parties hailed what appeared to be the President's embrace of conservative fiscal policy, while many liberal Democrats felt betrayed by FDR's economy message. Others in Congress feared proposed reductions in veterans' benefits (which were consuming one-fourth of total federal expenditures) would provoke a political fight with the powerful American Legion. FDR still got what he wanted in short order. Ninety Democrats deserted the President on Saturday when the House approved his economy measure by a comfortable 266 to 138 margin. The Senate took a few more days to approve the extraordinary request, but when it voted only four Democrats and nine Republicans opposed the Economy Act.

Franklin Roosevelt addressed a national radio audience in the first, and probably most important, of his "fireside chats" on the evening of Sunday March 12th. FDR knew that he had to establish public confidence in his emergency banking plan if it were to have any chance of success. With nearly half the American population listening, he began, "My friends, I want to talk for a few minutes with the people of the United States about banking." Then, in a voice that was quietly confident and reassuring, the President explained the basics of the banking crisis and how the federal government planned to reopen financial institutions. He informed listeners, "We shall be engaged not merely in reopening sound banks but in the creation of more sound banks through reorganization." Banks with assets equal to liabilities would be immediately reopened; most other banks would be allowed restricted business under the supervision of federal conservators as soon as financial assistance could be arranged. FDR ended with a plea for renewed national confidence. "Let us unite in banishing fear," he proclaimed. "We have provided the machinery to restore our financial system; and it is up to you to support and make it work."

Both the Comptroller of the Currency's office and the nation's 12 Federal Reserve banks were at that moment frantically inspecting bank records. Federally chartered banks were licensed by the Comptroller's office while the 12 Federal Reserve banks handled licenses for state-chartered member banks in their districts. State banks that were not members of the Federal Reserve were reopened by state authorities who generally followed Federal Reserve guidelines. Using very liberal criteria, these authorities started issuing licenses for reopening banks on Monday, March 13th. Since all banks had been closed for at least a week, there was good reason to fear withdrawals would outnumber deposits. But the reverse occurred. Individuals and businesses took money they had been hoarding and put it back into the nation's banking system. In New York City alone $15,500,000 in cash and coin, and $11,500,00 in gold certificates, were deposited on the first day banks were opened. By week's end, about the half the nation's banks were back in business, prices were rising on reopened stock exchanges, and cash customers were returning to stores. FDR's combination of decisive action and inspiring rhetoric had broken the financial panic. The New Deal was off to a most auspicious start.

What the New Deal Accomplished in 100 Days

On Sunday March 12th, President Roosevelt decided to ask Congress to permit the manufacture and sale of beverages with up to 3.2 percent alcohol content while the constitutional amendment totally repealing prohibition worked its way through the states. He knew this proposal would be popular, especially among urban liberals who had opposed prohibition and were now troubled by his budget-balancing economy bill. The President's recommendation was greeted with shouts of "Vote – vote – we want beer" when it was read in the House of Representatives the next day. Although prohibition's dwindling number of supporters opposed it, the beer bill sailed through Congress and was signed by the President on March 22nd.

President Roosevelt had by then already signaled his intention to keep Congress in Washington for the purpose of passing additional legislation. During his third press conference

FDR told reporters "even if we can get through the three measures – banking economics, the economy bill and the beer bill – we shall have done nothing on the constructive side, unless you consider the beer bill partially constructive." The President then outlined two measures he wanted enacted before Congress adjourned: a plan to raise agricultural prices, and a program that would put single unemployed men to work on public lands. This second proposal soon became the Civilian Conservation Corps (CCC). It was of FDR's own making and remained his favorite New Deal program. As Governor of New York, Roosevelt had set 10,000 unemployed young men to work in reforestation projects, and now he wanted to do something similar across the nation. "The idea is to put people to work in the national forests and on other Government and State properties," he told reporters.

On March 21st, the President formally asked Congress for authority to enroll 250,000 young men in reforestation, flood control, and soil conservation work on public lands. FDR's argument for the CCC reflected what he had learned long ago from his cousin Teddy. He told Congress that "It will conserve our precious natural resources . . . [and] make improvements in national and state domains." At this time Franklin Roosevelt clearly articulated his unwavering faith in the importance of work, a belief that informed all of his administration's subsequent relief programs. "We can take a vast army of these unemployed out into healthful surroundings," he explained. "We can eliminate the threat that enforced idleness brings to spiritual and moral stability."

Ten days later, after deciding to allow the President to settle contentious pay questions, Congress approved the Civilian Conservation Corps. By August, the CCC had stationed nearly 275,000 young men in 1,300 camps built by the Army. Military officers managed and maintained discipline in the camps. CCC workers were paid $30 a month plus room and board, and they were required to send at least $22 of their monthly pay back home to their families. At its peak in September 1935, more than half a million CCC workers between 17 and 25 years old were living in 2,500 camps all over the country. The average CCC "boy" was 18, and enrolled in the corps for nine months. More than half of the 2,900,000 young men who served in the CCC before it was shut down in 1942 came from rural and small town backgrounds. Most had been desperately poor. The combination of outdoor labor, regular sleep, and hardy meals improved the health of enrollees. CCC boys gained between 12 lb. and 30 lb. while in the program. "Oh, they really fed us, especially breakfast," one veteran recalled. The camps also provided their residents with night classes that stressed basic literacy and vocational skills. "I'd only gone to third grade." another former CCC worker remembered. "The C's gave me the confidence that I was as good as anybody."

The CCC was not without problems. About one of every ten enrollees dropped out, often due to disciplinary problems. And most CCC camps remained strictly segregated. At first some states even refused to establish segregated CCC camps. This was especially true in the South where planters feared the loss of cheap labor to government work relief programs. "There are few negro families who . . . need an income as great as $25 a month in cash," Georgia's state director explained. Protests by civil rights leaders had little effect on the color line during CCC's first years. But after 1936, when African-American voters played an important role in electing Democratic candidates in Northern cities, black participation in the CCC increased from less than 6 percent to 11 percent of the total enrollment. In the late 1930s, Labor Secretary Perkins and Interior Secretary Ickes pressured the CCC to integrate camps outside the South. By 1942, about one-tenth of the more than 200,000 blacks with CCC experience had worked in integrated camps.

The Civilian Conservation Corps was a tremendously popular program. When President Roosevelt announced cutbacks in the CCC in early 1936, a petition signed by 233 Congressmen convinced him to rescind the order. The benefits created by CCC could be seen in the lives of "the boys" and their families, in the local businesses from which the agency purchased millions of dollars in supplies each month, and in useful work it performed nearly everywhere in the country. "I know what we did was lasting, and that's what matters," a CCC veteran from Tennessee remembered. In addition to conservation work, the CCC constructed roads, bridges, and trails in national and state forests, and built and improved thousands of public parks and campgrounds. Most are still in use today.

President Roosevelt had sent his farm relief bill to Congress on March 16th. As soon as it became clear that Congress needed time to approve that complex measure, FDR decided to submit additional legislation. He hoped to enact all the measures his advisors had been preparing since the election before the broad coalition of New Deal supporters that had emerged during the banking crisis disintegrated. Along with farm relief, a bill extending federal assistance to the unemployed was at the top of FDR's priority list. The initiative for the emergency relief bill that FDR sent to Congress on March 28th came from two former social workers, Labor Secretary Frances Perkins and Harry Hopkins, director of New York's Temporary Emergency Relief Administration. Senators Wagner, LaFollette, and Costigan drafted the final measure after meetings with Secretary Perkins. It represented a sharp break with the policies of the Hoover administration. Their emergency relief bill called for $500,000,000 to be spent over two years in *direct* federal assistance (not loans) to the unemployed. Half of the appropriation was to go straight to state and local relief agencies, while the other half would consist of matching grants that required the states to put up three dollars for every federal dollar received. It was hoped that this provision would lead to increased state spending on relief. The bill also required relief recipients to be means tested by social work professionals; and it emphasized the creation of work relief projects, not the dole. In other words, like the CCC, the Federal Emergency Relief Act that Congress approved in early May was designed to do more than relieve poverty. It was, in Harry Hopkins words, a response to "a still further destructive force, that of worklessness."

Hopkins was named director of the new Federal Emergency Relief Administration (FERA). Never in good health, he nonetheless had an enormous capacity for sustained hard work. Harry Hopkins was a pragmatic doer who detested bureaucratic red tape, and he was passionate about getting assistance to the needy. Within hours of assuming his new duties on May 22nd Hopkins wired the requirements for federal relief funds to all the Governors; the next day he signed and sent out checks totaling $5,000,000 to seven states in the Midwest and the South. The brilliant, cynical but idealistic Hopkins soon became the most visible New Dealer, and one of Franklin Roosevelt's closest advisors.

The early New Deal's planning impulse was most strongly expressed in its creation of the Tennessee Valley Authority (TVA). The TVA originated in legislation authored by Senator George Norris, a progressive Republican from Nebraska who had tried for a decade to reopen the federally owned hydroelectric dam and nitrate manufacturing plant at Muscle Shoals, Alabama. Built to supply weapons grade nitrates during World War I, Muscle Shoals had the potential to provide cheap electricity and fertilizers to the hundreds of thousands of impoverished people who lived in the seven-state region defined by the Tennessee River and its major tributaries. Calvin Coolidge and Herbert Hoover had both vetoed Norris' attempts to reopen Muscle Shoals, but Franklin Roosevelt was a different story.

FDR saw in the Tennessee Valley an opportunity to test his own ideas about using public hydroelectric power to develop balanced agricultural/industrial communities in rural places. He also understood the importance of securing the support of Southern Democrats at the outset of his New Deal. Much to the delight of editorial writers throughout the South, the President-elect announced his intention to reinvigorate Muscle Shoals while touring the Tennessee Valley with Senator Norris in January 1933. Once in office, Roosevelt acted quickly to fulfill this promise. In early April he recommended to Congress a bill authorizing creation of the TVA, a government-owned corporation which would actually do far more than run Muscle Shoals. FDR proposed to have TVA build and operate additional dams, distributing low-cost electric power to the region's people on its own transmission lines. And there was more. As he explained at the time, "envisioned in its entirety, [TVA] transcends power development." Roosevelt said TVA would promote "flood control, [control of] soil erosion, afforestation, elimination from agricultural use of marginal lands, and distribution and diversification of industry." This was indeed the New Deal's boldest experiment, a truly visionary project intended to counter what Roosevelt called "the human waste . . . [that] results from lack of planning."

In normal times, such a proposal would have been doomed to failure in Congress. But the spring of 1933 was not a normal time. Although power company executives led by Commonwealth and Southern's Wendell Wilkie condemned the bill for taking away their market, and Republicans denounced the measure as a "Russian idea" and "one of the soviet dreams," Congress approved the TVA bill just six weeks after it was introduced. Arthur Morgan, a civil engineer and president of Antioch College who shared FDR's vision of balanced growth through comprehensive regional planning, was named first chairman of TVA's three-person board of directors. He took charge of dam building and immediately started a model town at the site of the proposed Norris Dam on the Clinch River in Tennessee. Harcourt Morgan (no relation to Arthur), an agricultural expert and president of the University of Tennessee, ran the TVA's fertilizer and farm programs; while David Lilienthal, a young Harvard-trained lawyer who had been serving on Wisconsin's Public Service Commission, directed the power program.

TVA was under constant legal assault from private power companies, attacked by landowners who claimed it usurped their rights, and criticized by reformers who claimed it ignored poor farmers. Differences in philosophy and temperament eventually split TVA's board, giving Arthur Morgan's opponents a chance to scale back his most ambitious plans. But TVA still scored a great many successes. Its dams controlled flooding, improved navigation, and most importantly, generated cheap hydroelectric power. TVA-sponsored power-cooperatives speeded rural electrification while setting prices that became what FDR liked to call a "yardstick" for private producers. In the long run, plentiful cheap power encouraged industrial development throughout the Southeast. TVA also encouraged agricultural modernization. Working with the Department of Agriculture's Extension Service, the agency sponsored farms that demonstrated how to greatly improve productivity. TVA's agricultural programs mostly benefited larger landowners, while tenants and sharecroppers bore the heaviest burden of forced evictions when dams were built. Even so, after World War II TVA was studied around the world as a model for developing poor agricultural regions.

By the time the special session of Congress adjourned in June exactly 100 days after being called to order, it had passed 14 pieces of major legislation (see Figure 6.1). The Hundred Days still defies strictly narrative historical exposition. Each of the legislated innovations can be chronicled, but the whole story of the Hundred Days is much more than the sum of its parts. In retrospect, this opening stage of the New Deal appears to us as a sequence of laws each designed to address distinct problems, and will be treated as such in subsequent chapters. But first we should recognize that the Hundred Days was experienced, as one Washington reporter put it, as a "whirlwind of changes in the old order." This bundle of legislation transformed the role of the federal government in American life, and the balance of power within the federal government itself. During the Hundred Days all the various pieces of the emerging New Deal were still simultaneously in process: either undergoing preliminary discussion, bill writing, amendment and approval in Congress, or initial implementation. Rexford Tugwell remembered, "There was confusion, conflict, and some mistaken policies, but everything was fluid and nothing could be considered settled finally." President Roosevelt – acting as a coordinator and prod to action behind the scenes, and rallying the public and Congress in special messages, public addresses, press conferences, and fireside chats – played the crucial role in pushing his New Deal forward.

Contemporary observers accustomed to Presidential restraint and Congressional deadlocks were amazed at both the pace

Program	Bill introduced	Enacted
Emergency Banking Act	March 9th	March 9th
Economy Act	March 10th	March 15th
3.2 Beer and Light Wine	March 13th	March 22nd
Farm Relief Act	March 16th	May 12th
Civilian Conservation Corps	March 21st	March 31st
Emergency Relief Administration	March 21st	May 12th
Public Works Administration	March 21st	June 16th
Securities Regulation	March 29th	May 27th
Farm Mortgage Assistance	April 3rd	May 12th
Tennessee Valley Authority	April 10th	May 18th
Home Owners Loan Corporation	April 13th	June 13th
Railroad Coordination Act	May 4th	June 16th
National Recovery Administration	May 17th	June 16th
Glass-Steagall Banking Act	March 9th	June 16th

Figure 6.1 Legislative Record, Special Session of 73rd Congress, 1933

and scope of the transition from Old Deal to New Deal. "Never was there such a change of government," Supreme Court Justice Harlan Stone wrote Herbert Hoover. "More history has been made during these fifteen weeks than in any other comparable peacetime period," the *Baltimore Sun*'s J. Frederick Essary exclaimed. "The New Deal was so abruptly different it was startling," recalled United Press' Washington Bureau chief Kenneth Crawford. But different how? So much happened so quickly that it was hard to judge the character and significance of the Hundred Days.

One thing was certain. Washington hummed with an energy not felt in many years. "The capital is experiencing more government in less time than it has ever known before . . . it is now as tense, excited, and sleepless and driven as a little while ago it was heavy and inactive," Anne O'Hare McCormick reported in the *New York Times*. Franklin Roosevelt was partly responsible for this change, but the transformation was more than the product of one man's inspiring words and actions.

The New Deal was initiated by a new generation of public servants. Washington was suddenly filled with new faces including hundreds of young, energetic lawyers, economists, and other professionals who filled lesser positions in cabinet departments, new agencies, and congressional staffs. These people brought new ideas and a passionate dedication to public service to their work. They did not think or act like stereotypical "bureaucrats." Thomas Eliot, who at age 26 became the number two lawyer in the Department of Labor in July 1933, later wrote, "one thing many young New Dealers shared, whether they were starry-eyed or merely hungry for personal advancement, was joy in the work they were doing. It was absorbing, mentally. It was exciting." During the next few years, some of the brightest of these young New Dealers rose quickly to positions of real power (Eliot was principal draftsman of the Social Security Act at age 28). Not all stayed in Washington, but a significant minority did win Congressional seats or high appointments that gave them influence over federal policies for many years after the Great Depression.

The youthful, college-educated character of so many New Dealers would soon grate on many older members of the business and political establishments. But in the early summer of 1933, praise of the President and his program filled the country's newspapers and magazines. To many observers who had previously underestimated FDR, he now seemed a giant. *The Nation*'s editor confessed, "Many of us who have know him long and well ask ourselves if this is the same man." Once skeptical Walter Lippmann wrote that Roosevelt had transformed "a congeries of panic-stricken disordered mobs and factions" into "an organized nation confident of our power to provide our own security." Likewise, the New Deal itself seemed of momentous importance. The downward momentum of the Great Depression had been broken; prices and employment were rising steadily. Most of the nation's newspapers, including the conservative Chicago *Tribune* and Hearst chain, strongly supported of the administration's recovery efforts. *Collier*'s magazine went further than most, proclaiming, "We have had our revolution, and we like it."

Of course, praise for Roosevelt and the New Deal was not universal; criticism of the Hundred Days emerged from both the political Left and Right. Radical journalist Suzanne LaFollette complained that Roosevelt had revealed himself to be "a liberal meliorist in a revolutionary situation." Socialist writers agreed, pointing out that the administration's reliance on emergency legislation failed to provide what one described as a "basis for permanent protection against the evils of capitalism." Other socialists and communists suggested the New Deal's industrial recovery program was really the basis for establishing a fascist state. These radicals could cite no less an authority than Italy's "Il Duce," Benito Mussolini, who in July told the *New York Times*' Anne McCormick, "Your plan for coordination of industry follows precisely our lines of cooperation."

Although radicals would persist in comparisons between the New Deal and fascism, an even more important line of criticism emerged among conservatives who were skeptical of the Hundred Days. One of their spokesmen, the *Baltimore Sun*'s J. Frederick Essary, described the Hundred Days as "practically unchallenged Executive domination." These critics, the forefathers of today's anti-big government politicians, feared the Hundred Days had destroyed the balance of power within America's system of divided government. They claimed Congressional grants of authority and FDR's assertive use of executive powers had transformed the Presidency into what Essary described as "a virtual Dictatorship."

There were real reasons for this kind of conservative dissent. FDR had boldly expanded the President's power as promised in his inaugural address. He got around statutory limits on the size of the President's staff by appointing key aides (such as Moley and Tugwell) to positions in cabinet departments and then using them for other tasks. He issued hundreds of proclamations and executive orders, using some of them to make important government policy. The executive orders which enabled FDR to seize control of monetary policy and take the United States off the gold standard especially worried these critics (see Figure 6.2). They were also alarmed by Congress' rapid delegation of extraordinary powers to the Executive branch. Most of the legislation FDR proposed during the Hundred Days gave existing Cabinet departments and new agencies very broad authority to intervene in virtually all economic markets. Congress gave the President power to close and then reopen the banks, provide relief to the poor, adjust agricultural prices, and revive industry. They left it up to FDR and his appointees to define the specific policies that would achieve these goals. This enabling legislation allowed Roosevelt's administration to respond quickly to the desperate crises created by the Great Depression. But it also exposed the New Deal to serious constitutional challenges.

In 1933 conservative criticism of FDR as a dictator was as far out of step with views of the majority of the public as the socialist charge that New Deal was fascism. Throughout the

Date	Presidential action
March 5th	Proclamation 2038: calls Congress into special session.
March 6th	Proclamation 2039: imposes four-day bank holiday and embargo on gold and silver.
March 9th	Proclamation 2040: bank holiday and embargo on gold and silver extended.
March 10th	Executive Order 6073: established procedure for reopening banks, and demonetarized gold.
March 27th	Executive Order 6084: consolidated farm credit agencies.
April 5th	Executive Order 6102: prohibits hoarding of gold and gold certificates.
April 20th	Executive Order 6111: permitted foreign exchange transactions under supervision of the Treasury.
June 10th	Executive Order 6166: consolidation and abolition of federal agencies.[1]

[1] This was the first of many such actions authorized by the Economy Act; it abolished eight federal commissions and services, and consolidated ten other programs.

Figure 6.2   Selected presidential proclamations and executive orders, 1933

country, most Americans shared the sentiments of a group of citizens from Brooklyn who wrote Senator Wagner express- ing "sincere appreciation for the unified action of Senate and House . . . pulling in harmony with our courageous President." Fear of total economic collapse and social disorder, as well as his own great political skills, had enabled Franklin Roosevelt to bring together an extraordinary coalition of supporters that included most of the press, business community, plantation owners, farm families, and working people. For the next two years FDR would try to hold this first New Deal coalition together. But in the words of the letter writers from Brooklyn, "Fear was gone." As a result, Roosevelt was never again able to convince so many different groups of Americans that the New Deal was for them.

FURTHER READING

Primary Sources

Burg, David F. *The Great Depression: An Eyewitness History*. New York: Facts on File Inc., 1996.

Dudley, William. *The Great Depression: Opposing Viewpoints*. San Diego: Greenhaven Press, 1994.

Eliot, Thomas. *Recollections of the New Deal: When the People Mattered*. Boston: Northeastern University Press, 1992.

Freedman, Max ed. *Roosevelt and Frankfurter: Their Correspondence, 1928–1945*. Boston: Little, Brown and Company, 1967.

Hopkins, Harry L. *Spending to Save: The Complete Story of Relief*. New York: W. W. Norton, 1936.

Ickes, Harold. *The Secret Diary of Harold L. Ickes: The First Thousand Days 1933–1936*. New York: Simon and Schuster, 1954.

Lilienthal, David. *The Journals of David E. Lilienthal, Volume I: The TVA Years*. New York, Harper & Row, 1964.

Loucheim, Kate ed. *The Making of the New Deal: The Insiders Speak*. Cambridge, Massachusetts: Harvard University Press, 1983.

Moley, Raymond. *After Seven Years*. New York: Harper & Brothers, 1939.

Morgan, Arthur. *The Making of the TVA*. Buffalo: Prometheus Press, 1974.

Nixon, Edgar B. *Franklin D. Roosevelt & Conservation 1911–1945*. Washington: Government Printing Office, 1957.

Perkins, Frances. *The Roosevelt I Knew*. New York: Viking Press, 1946.

Roosevelt, Eleanor. *This I Remember*. New York: Harper & Brothers, 1949.

Roosevelt, Elliot ed. *F. D. R.: His Personal Letters 1928–1945*. New York: Duell, Sloan, and Pearce, 1950.

Roosevelt, Franklin D. *On Our Way*. New York: John Day, 1934.

Roosevelt, Franklin Delano. *The Public Papers and Addresses of Franklin D. Roosevelt, Volume Two: The Year of Crisis 1933*. New York: Random House, 1938.

Schneiderman, Rose. *All For One*. New York: Paul S. Eriksson, 1967.

Zinn, Howard ed. *New Deal Thought*. Indianapolis: Bobbs-Merrill, 1966.

Secondary Sources

Blum, John Morton. *From the Morgenthau Diaries: Years of Crisis, 1928–1938*. Boston: Houghton Mifflin, 1959.

Burns, James Macgregor. *Roosevelt: The Lion and the Fox*. New York: Harcourt, Brace & World, 1956.

Davis, Kenneth S. *FDR: The New Deal Years 1933–1937: A History*. New York: Random House, 1979.

Friedel, Frank. *Franklin D. Roosevelt: Launching the New Deal*. Boston: Little, Brown and Company, 1973.

Gallagher, Hugh. *FDR's Splendid Deception*. New York: Dodd, Mead, 1985.

Goldberg, Richard Thayer. *The Making of Franklin D. Roosevelt: Triumph Over Disability*. Cambridge, Massachusetts: Abt Books, 1981.

McGraw, Thomas. *TVA and the Power Fight, 1933–1939*. Philadelphia: Lippincott, 1971.

Rosen, Elliot. *Hoover, Roosevelt, and the Brains Trust: From Depression to New Deal*. New York: Columbia University Press, 1977.

Salmond, John. *The Civilian Conservation Corps, 1933–1942: A New Deal Case Study*. Durham: Duke University Press, 1967.

Schlesinger, Arthur Jr. *The Coming of the New Deal*. Boston: Houghton Mifflin, 1959.

Tugwell, Rexford G. *The Democratic Roosevelt: A Biography of Franklin D. Roosevelt*. New York: Doubleday, 1957.

Ward, Geoffrey. *A First Class Temperament: The Emergence of Franklin Roosevelt*. New York: Harper & Row, 1989.

White, Graham J. *FDR and the Press*. Chicago: University of Chicago Press, 1979.

Winfield, Betty Houchin. *FDR and the News Media*. Urbana: University of Illinois Press, 1990.

7

The Problem of Recovery

"I see one-third of a nation ill-housed, ill-clad, ill-nourished."
Franklin D. Roosevelt, January 20, 1937

Growth but not Recovery

President Roosevelt offered the above description of poverty in America during his Second Inaugural Address. By then the New Deal was nearly four years old, and as FDR acknowledged, the problems of mass unemployment and widespread poverty had not been solved. As most Americans now know, full employment and dramatic reductions in poverty were not achieved until 1942–43 when 13,000,000 men and women were serving in the armed forces and the United States was supplying huge quantities of war materials and food to its wartime allies. These facts alone force us to conclude that the New Deal failed to promote real economic recovery; and that it took massive government borrowing, investment, and spending during World War II to end the Great Depression.

Americans who listened to FDR's second inaugural Address had a different perspective than ours. Although hindsight allows us to see that the New Deal failed to promote sustained investment-driven growth, the economic record of the New Deal did not appear so dismal to contemporaries. The recent past, not an unknown future, was the public's reference point. Thus the great majority of voters who had returned FDR to the White House probably agreed with him when he proclaimed on January 20, 1937, "we have come far from the days of stagnation and despair."

The nation's economy grew significantly after bottoming

out in March 1933. By the beginning of FDR's second term total output of goods and services (gross national product or GNP) actually exceeded the levels reached in 1929. In fact the four-year average annual growth rate achieved from 1934 to 1937 has never been bettered in peacetime (see Figure 7.1). Economic growth during these years was also impressive by international standards. During the mid-1930s industrial production expanded faster in the United States than in any other industrial democracy. Only rapidly arming Nazi Germany and Japan outpaced American industry.

During the first four years of the New Deal, employed workers felt economic conditions improve even though mass unemployment persisted. As early as the summer of 1934 sports writer Rud Rennie reported much larger crowds turning out for baseball games all over the country. "They may not be rolling in wealth, but evidently they have a few bucks to spend on amusements. That's something they did not have last year," Rennie noted. Tens of thousands of Americans wrote directly

Year	Gross national product (billions of 1929 dollars)	Real weekly earnings (1929 = 100)
1929	104	100
1930	94	95
1931	87	94
1932	75	86
1933	73	89
1934	80	94
1935	88	100
1936	100	108
1937	105	115
1938	101	108
1939	109	118

Sources: Historical Statistics of the United States: Colonial Times to 1957, 1961; and Peter Temin, Lessons from the Great Depression, 1989.

Figure 7.1   The Depression Decade: measures of improvement

to the White House to express their appreciation for the improvements. A typical letter from a woman in Orangeburg, South Carolina to Eleanor Roosevelt explained, "We feel that he [FDR] has brought us out of a great depression and will continue to keep us going for Peace and Prosperity." By 1937 over 8,000,000 workers had been added to the nation's payrolls. That year average real weekly earnings were 30 percent higher than they had been when FDR took office, and a full 15 percent higher than in 1929 (see Figure 7.1). At the same time in many industries the standard work week had been reduced to 40 hours. New Deal labor policies including wage and hours standards of its recovery program and support for rapidly expanding unions were responsible for these changes.

The economic revival was fitful at first. In the late spring of 1933 farm prices, industrial production, employment, and the value of the dollar were all rising. But as inventories of unsold goods mounted, a contraction set in that sent unemployment soaring in the winter of 1933–34. Recovery began again in the spring and steady advances in many sectors continued for two years. By 1936, a growing volume of commercial loans seemed to indicate a genuine restoration was underway. The much disputed one-time lump sum payment of $1,700,000,000 to veterans that Congress passed over FDR's veto, and greater spending on work relief also contributed to rising incomes which in turn insured a Democratic landslide in the November elections. By the summer of 1937, employment in the automobile, chemical, non-ferrous metals, food products, and textile industries all exceeded pre-Depression levels. Highways, railroads, and resort towns were jammed with travelers. *Business Week* proclaimed, "Business is good. This fall it will be better."

Such optimism was misplaced. Much investment in 1936–37 was part of a worldwide inventory stocking boom. Private investment in new production remained weak. Even at its peak, the economic revival never lifted the massive construction and associated lumber products industries out of depression. Capital tied up in huge investments in older industries such as the nation's largest employer, iron and steel products, remained underutilized. Only a handful of older industries producing basic consumer goods and a few new ones such as synthetic fibers and frozen foods actually exceeded pre-Depression output records. In short, growth of aggregate demand was insufficient to employ all of America's productive capacity and workers.

The economic revival abruptly halted in the fall of 1937. During the winter of 1937–38 demand for many goods and services collapsed, prices and investment plummeted, unsold farm surpluses mounted, and employment again fell to Depression levels. Franklin Roosevelt popularized the term "recession" to distinguish this latest downward spiral from what had happened during Herbert Hoover's presidency, but he could not prevent a serious erosion of confidence among his supporters. Representative Maury Maverick of Texas, an ardent New Dealer, confessed to his colleagues, "we Democrats have to admit we are floundering . . . We are a confused, bewildered group of people." Other liberals thought stagnation might be a permanent condition. New York's Mayor Fiorello LaGuardia told South Carolina's Senator Byrnes, "that instead of considering the situation as an emergency, we accept the inevitable, that we are now in a new normal." However, economic growth resumed again during the second half of 1938. By 1940 FDR's determination to push military preparedness at home while sending aid to future allies abroad had sparked a broad-based industrial expansion, raising hopes that this recovery could be sustained.

In retrospect we can see clearly that the New Deal failed to resolve two critical problems: mass unemployment and low prices. Despite impressive GNP growth and improvements in the wages and hours of employed workers, widespread joblessness persisted until Franklin Roosevelt's third term as President. For eight long years many workers never found regular work while most others lived in fear of unemployment. The occasional layoffs suffered by most workers prevented increased real *weekly* earnings from producing significantly higher *annual* incomes and higher levels of consumption. Wage increases mandated by new legislation and new union contracts may have actually contributed to unemployment by limiting rehiring by cost-conscious employers. Nonetheless the nation's basic unemployment problem stemmed, not from high wages, but from the underutilization of capital in major industries.

Persistent unemployment was especially concentrated in old industries burdened by what appeared to be overcapacity including cotton textiles, leather products, iron and steel, lumber and wood products, and construction. Older workers and very young inexperienced workers nearly everywhere also found it difficult to stay employed. The administration's relief programs helped unemployed workers and their families survive both temporary and long-term losses of private sector

Year	Bureau of Labor Statistics average annual estimates ("the official rate")	BLS rate less those employed in work relief programs[1]
1931	16%	15%
1932	24%	23%
1933	25%	21%
1934	22%	16%
1935	20%	14%
1936	17%	10%
1937	14%	9%
1938	19%	13%
1939	17%	11%
1940	15%	10%

Sources: *Historical Statistics of the United States: Colonial Times to 1957*; and Michael Darby, "Three and Half Million U.S. Employees Have Been Mislaid," *Journal of Political Economy*, 1976.

[1] The BLS counted people in work relief programs as unemployed because work relief was considered an "emergency" measure that would be terminated once recovery was achieved.

Figure 7.2   The Depression Decade: unemployment

jobs. Work relief projects also contributed enormously to improvements in economic infrastructure. But even if the often
more than 3,000,000 relief workers are counted as employed,
it is clear that New Deal failed to generate enough employment and income to stimulate real recovery (see Figure 7.2).

An often overlooked, very large increase in the size of America's labor force contributed to the New Deal's failure to create jobs for all who wanted them. While total population
increased just 7 percent during the depression decade (the lowest 10-year growth rate in American history), the labor force
expanded by more than 16 percent between 1929 and 1940.
The Depression itself generated this unusual combination of
slow population growth and rapid expansion of the labor force.
Lower annual incomes forced many members of households
who had not previously sought work, especially wives and
older children, to look for jobs. Violation of the widely accepted single breadwinner custom provoked protests by male
and female workers all over the country. "I think the government should pass a law so that married women cannot be
employed in factories or stores, that would give the single girl
a chance to get a job," a young woman from Dayton, Ohio
wrote to Labor Secretary Perkins.

Sentiments like this prompted three-quarters of the nation's
local school districts to prohibit the employment of married
women, and some private businesses followed suit. But financial pressures still forced many married women to seek work.
At the same time, life expectancy was increasing, but most
older workers could not afford to retire.[1]

The rapid growth of the labor force compounded the New
Deal's unemployment problem. Full employment required
more than creating 12,000,000 jobs for workers made redundant during the Hoover years. Full employment also required
8,000,000 additional jobs for all the new workers who entered the labor force between 1930 and 1940. Until the
Roosevelt administration embraced the task of becoming the
"Arsenal of Democracy," and until the armed forces workers
pulled millions of workers out of the private labor force, mass
unemployment seemed intractable. As the editors of the *New*

Republic commented in their critical review of FDR's second term in 1940, "these years have seen no return of the conditions of 1932 or 1933, to be sure, but on the other hand no great or permanent improvement in national income, production or employment above the level already achieved in 1936."

Low prices defined the New Deal's other major economic problem. Indeed, the failure of farm, wholesale, and retail prices to climb back to 1929 levels is one of the principal reasons why we still think of the 1930s as "the depression decade" (see Figure 7.3). The character of the industrial price problem lay in the eye of the beholder. By 1933 many industrialists argued that overproduction and "cut-throat" competition had depressed prices for finished goods, and that exceptionally low prices discouraged new investment. Speaking through their trade associations, these businessmen wanted government to permit price-fixing and market sharing agreements. However, as long as annual incomes remained low and employment uncertain, union leaders and advocates for the poor saw prices as too high. These liberal "underconsumptionists" argued for redistributive policies that would raise working people's incomes while holding prices in check. Other liberals, including many of the lawyers who advised FDR after 1934, also argued that high prices discouraged recovery, but they urged more vigorous enforcement of existing anti-trust laws as a remedy. Obviously President Roosevelt could not satisfy all these groups simultaneously. As a result New Deal industrial recovery policy was inconsistent over time. The dilemma was not overcome until the early 1940s when, in the pursuit of victory in World War II, the federal government was able make itself both principal investor in, and chief consumer of, the nation's industrial output.

Low prices for agricultural commodities created similar difficulties for the Roosevelt administration. The agricultural price problem also lay in the eye of the beholder. Consumers, particularly those with substandard diets, saw food prices as too high. But poor consumers, though numerous, lacked political clout. Only occasionally when represented by liberal appointees did their views influence policy. On the other hand, farm

Year	Consumer price index (1926 = 100)[1]	Wholesale price index (1926 = 100)	Farm price index	Farm price parity Ratio[2]
1929	100	92	105	92
1930	97	85	88	—
1931	88	75	65	—
1932	79	70	48	58
1933	75	71	51	64
1934	78	78	65	75
1935	80	78	79	88
1936	81	80	81	92
1937	73	85	86	93
1938	82	82	69	78
1939	81	81	65	77
1940	81	83	68	81

Sources: *Historical Statistics of the United States: Colonial Times to 1957*, 1961; and Susan Previant Lee and Peter Passell, *A New Economic View of American History*, 1979.

[1] Excludes prices of farm products and food.
[2] The farm price parity ratio was a crucial component of the New Deal's agricultural adjustment policy. It expressed the relationship between the prices farmers received for what they produced and the prices they paid for manufactured goods. The base period chosen for the parity ratio (= 100) was 1910–14.

Figure 7.3   The Depression Decade: prices

owners were well represented in Congress. Farm organizations had been trying to enact federal programs to combat what they saw as dangerously low commodity prices since the mid-1920s. By the time Franklin Roosevelt took office there was no shortage of ideas about what the government might do to raise farm incomes. There was, however, no consensus on answers to such basic questions as: what caused low agricultural prices, and how was the agricultural depression related to the depressed condition of the rest of the economy?

When unsold surpluses mounted in government warehouses, clearly supply and demand were not balanced, but what caused this imbalance? Did drastically lower farm prices result from overproduction, as FDR's Secretary of Agriculture Henry Wallace always believed? And if so, did collapsed rural demand for the output of the cities then spread the depression from rural to urban areas? Or did weak demand from urban and foreign consumers cause low farm prices as proponents of underconsumptionist ideas thought? If the underconsumptionists were right, Henry Wallace's domestic allotment plan to raise farm prices by reducing agriculture's output might actually compound the overall national recovery problem.

For us the struggle between advocates of overproduction and underconsumption theories of the Great Depression remains an interesting intellectual contest. But for Franklin Roosevelt, his advisors, and the Congress these problems posed tremendous *political* difficulties. Unlike the Nazi regime in Germany, to which it was often compared, the Roosevelt administration could not count on rubber stamp approval from the legislature, nor could it impose economic policy on the nation using the threat of detention to silence opponents. Conscription of labor at low wages – the Nazi formula for full employment – was simply not an option in democratic America. FDR had to build and sustain a diverse national coalition of supporters for his administration's economic policies. Especially during the early New Deal years he struggled to define policies that incorporated the views of powerful established lobbies and the views of liberals who raised the concerns of the least powerful Americans. That FDR's political balancing act produced ineffective economic policies seems clear to us, but was it so clear to contemporaries? After all, they were the ones who voted to return Franklin Roosevelt to office in 1936, 1940, and 1944.

A Complete Failure?

Economic conditions improved markedly during Roosevelt's first term, yet in 1936 Republicans led by former President Hoover described the recovery as anemic and "delayed for two years." They blasted New Deal policies for inhibiting the business confidence necessary to restore full employment. Were these Republican critics right? Did the so-called "Roosevelt recovery" occur *despite* the New Deal? Or to put the question differently, was New Deal economic policy really a complete failure?

To answer this question, we must consider the view from the 1930s. A majority of Franklin Roosevelt's contemporaries rejected the Republican assertion that his New Deal prevented economic recovery. We know this because the issue was twice put to a popular vote. By mid-1934, most Republicans, major newspapers and business organizations, and the American Liberty League (a newly formed bi-partisan organization of wealthy conservatives) had turned against the New Deal on the grounds that it was destroying economic freedom and preventing real recovery. President Roosevelt responded to this criticism in a fireside chat on September 30th, claiming that the New Deal had "brought order out of the old chaos" and re-employed "more than four million persons." FDR then concluded, "We are moving forward to greater freedom, to greater security for the average man than he has ever known before in the history of America." On this platform, Democrats added to their already large congressional majorities in the mid-term elections in November. The 74th Congress followed up on the President's promise by enacting the most liberal legislation of the New Deal era including the Social Security Act and the National Labor Relations Act in 1935.

During the next election year conservative opposition to the New Deal became even more strident. In 1936 Herbert Hoover claimed the New Deal was "stifling private enterprise." Al Smith, the leading spokesperson for the American Liberty League, said there was no difference between socialism and the New Deal, warning "There can only be one capital, Washington or Moscow." Even the once moderate Republican presidential nominee, Governor Alfred Landon of Kansas, joined the growing conservative chorus. He closed his campaign by condemning the New Deal as "a dictatorship" and predicting "Business as we know it is about to disappear." Franklin Roosevelt responded by proudly defending the achievements of his New Deal and improvements in the economy since 1933. "There is no question but that things are better in every part of the country," he told a huge cheering crowd in Utica, New York in mid-October. Elsewhere his exact words differed, but the message and the size of the crowds were same. On election day FDR won a second term with the greatest electoral majority since 1820. The result was a ringing endorsement of the New Deal and the "Roosevelt recovery."

The New Deal was in fact responsible for the economic revival of the mid-1930s. But most voters probably did not understand which policies were responsible for the improvement. The Roosevelt administration's most visible recovery efforts, the Agricultural Adjustment Administration (AAA) and the National Recovery Administration (NRA), had failed to promote self-sustained economic growth. Both AAA and NRA were intended to raise prices and incomes by planning production, but neither ever achieved the recovery goals set for them (see Chapter 8). In fact their demise at the hands of the Supreme Court in 1935–36 seemed not to disturb the recovery trend in the economy.

The New Deal is often equated with a policy of massive deficit spending, but prior to 1938 Franklin Roosevelt resisted the idea that federal deficits were necessary to promote recovery. Nonetheless, his New Deal ran up what were then record peacetime deficits totaling $13,600,000,000 during the fiscal years 1934–37. This new federal debt resulted from borrowing required to cover shortfalls in tax collections and pay for the administration's many "emergency" programs. All together, new debt financed 46 percent of federal spending during FDR's first term. The mounting federal debt worried the President. Deficit spending was something he hoped to eliminate, not part of a deliberate macro-economic recovery policy.

Liberal Democrats and progressive Republicans had long advocated increased spending on public works to combat unemployment in the labor-intensive construction industry and spur recovery in all the industries that produced construction supplies. Although FDR had doubts about the economic efficacy of this so-called "pump-priming" strategy in 1933, he could not ignore its political popularity. Thus the President seemed to violate his own budget-balancing promises when he agreed to Title II of the National Industrial Recovery Act. Title II authorized borrowing and spending up to $3,300,000,000 on "public construction" projects under the supervision of a new Public Works Administration (PWA). Large-scale borrowing and spending for CCC and FERA relief programs also contributed to budget deficits during the early New Deal.

The federal budget deficit soared as soon as recovery stalled in the winter of 1933–34 because tax revenues fell while relief costs increased sharply. To prevent a repeat of the mass deprivation and disorder of the previous winter, Harry Hopkins asked President Roosevelt to approve a new temporary work relief program devised by his staff. On November 9, 1933, FDR issued an executive order creating the Civil Works Administration (CWA). CWA demonstrated Hopkins' ability to quickly mobilize the resources of the federal government. Financed with the unspent balances of other relief programs and administered by federal relief officials already in place in the states, Hopkins had 1,500,000 unemployed people enrolled in CWA construction projects by the end of the month. At its peak in early January 1934, CWA employed 4,264,00 workers who in turn supported another 12,000,000 people. CWA imposed no means test and it paid wages that approximated local minimums. For these reasons, working people demonstrated enormous enthusiasm for CWA even though Hopkins could not create CWA jobs for all who wanted them. The president of the Bricklayers Union in Birmingham, Alabama spoke for many working people when he thanked Harry Hopkins for the "speed of the CWA . . . making it possible for our members to have employment in time to earn some Christmas money and provide some pleasure for loved ones." But CWA was also attacked by conservatives who accused the agency of wasting money on useless "make work" jobs for people who were not truly destitute. In mid-January, FDR and Hopkins responded to this criticism by cutting back the maximum CWA work week from 30 to 24 hours, and by scrapping plans to extend the program. CWA closed its doors in March 1934 after spending approximately $1,000,000,000.

In 1934–35 only drastic reductions in the New Deal's "emergency" relief programs could have balanced the federal budget, but such cuts would have caused widespread human suffering and further depressed aggregate demand. More than two million people were enrolled in the Federal Emergency Relief Administration's urban and rural work relief programs during 1934. Most of these people were destitute workers who labored part-time on roads, sewers, parks, and the repair of public buildings for wages that usually equaled and sometimes exceeded (especially in the rural South) local minimum rates. In August 1934 Budget Director Lewis Douglas, who had tried hard to maintain a fiscally conservative New Deal, resigned in protest of FDR's refusal to scale back FERA programs and wage rates. His resignation cleared the way for even larger "emergency" expenditures on public works and work relief projects.

FDR proclaimed, "The Federal Government must and shall quit this business of relief," in his annual message to Congress on January 4, 1935. It was an ambiguous proclamation. Roosevelt wanted Congress to abolish FERA and the dole and replace them with unemployment insurance and permanent social security programs for those who could not work. These programs would be funded by new taxes. FDR also asked Congress to approve funding to extend the CCC and PWA, as well as create a new works program that would put millions of unemployed people to work on projects in their communities. FDR signed the Emergency Relief Appropriation Act in April 1935. It authorized $4,000,000,000 in new borrowing – a staggering sum by contemporary standards – and the spending of an additional $880,000,000 in previously authorized but not yet appropriated funds. The President defended this deficit-financed initiative in his seventh fireside chat on April 28th. The New Deal would now, in his words, "put men and women now on the relief rolls to work and . . . assist materially in our already unmistakable march toward recovery." Despite these last words, FDR was not announcing a new policy of deliberate deficit-financed stimulation of the economy. Instead he presented expanded work relief as "a great national crusade, a crusade to the destroy enforced idleness which is an enemy of the human spirit generated by this depression."

Franklin Roosevelt was torn between his conviction that sound government required balanced budgets and what Frances Perkins described as his wanting "to do the right thing by his unemployed fellow citizens." "It was," Perkins wrote, "one of the conflicts in Roosevelt's nature and in his thinking." This conflict expressed itself in the continued incoherence of his administration's fiscal policy. In 1935, he asked the same session of Congress that approved massive borrowing for work relief to raise income taxes on wealthy Americans and corporations, as well as impose new taxes on employers and employees to fund social security pensions and unemployment insurance. He also blocked for a year the enactment of the veterans' bonus bill with a long and strongly felt veto message which dismissed as "ill-conceived" the idea "that spending the money is the most effective means of hastening recovery."

When economic conditions continued to improve in 1936 conservative criticism of the New Deal's unbalanced budgets mounted. FDR was especially sensitive to this criticism because deep down he still believed balanced budgets were the hallmark of successful government. During a presidential campaign stop in Pittsburgh, Roosevelt once again promised to balance the budget "within a year or two." As it turned out, he actually moved much more quickly to fulfill this campaign promise.

Strange as it may seem to us today, fears of inflation arose within the Treasury and the Federal Reserve in late 1936. When communicated to the President by Federal Reserve chairman

Marriner Eccles and Treasury Secretary Henry Morgenthau, these fears hastened FDR's promised budget-balancing initiative.[2] Rising prices alone, a sign of recovery, would not have had this result. However, higher prices were accompanied by a rapid flight of capital and gold to the United States. European investors who feared war and were seeking a safe haven for their assets threatened an uncontrolled expansion of circulating dollars. So the President followed recommendations to curb gold imports, while the Federal Reserve sharply raised the reserve requirements of member banks (thus reducing the funds banks could use for loans).

Treasury Secretary Morgenthau also tried to convince FDR that the time was right to cut "emergency" borrowing and spending so as to balance the whole federal budget. He was opposed by the Federal Reserve chairman who believed high levels of deficit spending remained necessary as long as millions of workers remained unemployed. Marriner Eccles knew that Morgenthau had underestimated the depressing effects of the new social security taxes that would be collected for the first time in 1937. Those taxes (which totaled $2,000,000,000 in 1937 alone) would reduce aggregate demand because collection started in January 1937, five years before the first scheduled pension payouts.

On December 17th, Marriner Eccles sent the President an urgent memorandum explaining that "it would be unsafe to slash federal expenditures until the expansion of private enterprise took up the whole slack of employment." FDR hesitated, but finally announced his decision to follow Morgenthau's recommendations in a message to Congress in April 1937. He ordered huge reductions in work relief programs and public works "to eliminate this deficit during the coming fiscal year." Instead of marking the final success of New Deal recovery efforts as Roosevelt and Morgenthau hoped, the budget balancing policy of 1937 contributed to the steepest economic downturn in American history.

By March 1938 another 4,000,000 people had been added to the unemployment rolls. Recovery from this "Roosevelt recession" only began in mid-1938 after FDR had completely reversed himself. In a fireside chat on April 14, 1938 Roosevelt told the nation that it was up to government "to create an economic upturn." Without ever acknowledging the part his budget balancing orders had played in the recession, FDR embraced what economists call compensatory fiscal policy. He promised increased government borrowing and spending would be "a trigger to set off private [investment] activity," and that once real recovery was achieved debt would be retired because "government expenditures will go down and government tax receipts will go up."

President Roosevelt's decision to embrace compensatory fiscal policy marked the triumph of Marriner Eccles, and of many less visible liberal economists in the administration who had been absorbing the ideas of British economist John Maynard Keynes. Nonetheless, growing conservative opposition to the New Deal (including the opposition of many Congressional Democrats) limited the administration's ability to implement the new policy. Only after the United States began its massive armaments buildup was Roosevelt's fiscal "trigger" sufficient to eliminate mass unemployment. The federal government borrowed $200,000,000,000 to finance America's role in World War II. At its wartime peak federal spending accounted for more than half the nation's GNP. Victory over fascism and imperialism legitimized what remained politically impossible when the Great Depression was America's only enemy.

The way federal borrowing and spending promoted complete economic recovery during the war led many contemporaries (and many historians) to assume that New Deal fiscal policy must have had an equally strong economic impact in the 1930s. Recent studies cast doubt upon this reasoning. Although New Deal deficit spending undoubtedly augmented aggregate demand, this fiscal stimulus amounted to just 1 or 2 percent of GNP, certainly not enough to promote the growth recorded from 1934–37. Likewise, the reductions in federal borrowing and spending that FDR ordered in 1937 were not in themselves sufficient to create the sharp contraction of 1938. But New Deal monetary policy did strongly influence economic trends in the 1930s.

promoted the rapid expansion of GNP in the mid-1930s that felt like recovery to most Americans. In retrospect it is relatively easy to identify many shortcomings of New Deal economic policies. We have learned from those mistakes. We recognize that New Deal economic policies could have been more coherent, consistent, and effective. What is harder for us to grasp are the difficulties that confronted economic policymakers in the 1930s. These included lack of information, inadequacy of economic theory, and perhaps most importantly, numerous political complications that arose when so many different groups wanted the administration and Congress to adopt their policy ideas. Political pressures compounded FDR's own uncertainty about economic policy. To make unprecedented interventions in the nation's economy the President needed to hold a broad coalition of supporters together. Thus he sometimes had to incorporate conflicting recommendations into the New Deal's overall recovery effort. Nonetheless, the Roosevelt administration still managed to reverse the Great Depression and spur significant economic growth. As the great majority of Americans who voted in 1934 and 1936 understood, the New Deal was far from a total economic failure.

FURTHER READING

Primary Sources

Eccles, Marriner S. *Beckoning Frontiers: Public and Personal Recollections.* New York: Alfred A. Knopf, 1951.

Hopkins, Harry L. *Spending to Save: The Complete Story of Relief.* New York: W. W. Norton, 1936.

Hoover, Herbert. *American Ideals versus the New Deal.* New York: Scribner, 1936.

Ickes, Harold L. *The Secret Diary of Harold L. Ickes, Volume II: The Inside Struggle 1936–1939.* New York: Simon and Schuster, 1954.

Jones, Jesse. *Fifty Billion Dollars: My Thirteen Years With the RFC.* New York: Macmillan, 1951.

Leuchtenberg, William ed. *The New Deal: A Documentary History.* New York: Harper & Row, 1968.

Lowitt, Richard and Beasley, Maurine eds. *One Third of a Nation: Lorena*

Hickok Reports the Great Depression. Urbana: University of Illinois Press, 1981.

Louchheim, Kate ed. *The Making of the New Deal: The Insiders Speak.* Cambridge, Massachusetts: Harvard University Press, 1983.

McElvaine, Robert S. *Down and Out in the Great Depression: Letters from the Forgotten Man.* Chapel Hill: University of North Carolina Press, 1983.

Roosevelt, Elliot. *F. D. R.: His Personal Letters 1928–1945.* New York: Duell, Sloan and Pearce, 1950.

Roosevelt, Franklin Delano. *The Public Papers and Addresses of Franklin D. Roosevelt, Volume Four: The Court Disapproves, 1935.* New York: Random House, 1938.

Roosevelt, Franklin Delano. *The Public Papers and Addresses of Franklin D. Roosevelt, 1937 Volume: The Constitution Prevails.* New York: Macmillan, 1941.

Roosevelt, Franklin Delano. *The Public Papers and Addresses of Franklin D. Roosevelt, 1938 Volume: The Continuing Struggle for Liberalism.* New York: Macmillan, 1941.

Secondary Sources

Bernstein, Michael A. *The Great Depression: Delayed Recovery and Economic Change in America, 1929–1939.* New York: Cambridge University Press, 1987.

Bordo, Michael D.; Goldin, Claudia; and White, Eugene N. eds. *The Defining Moment: The Great Depression and the American Economy in the Twentieth Century.* Chicago: University of Chicago Press, 1998.

Blum, John Morton. *From the Morgenthau Diaries: Years of Crisis, 1928–1938.* Boston: Houghton Mifflin, 1959.

Brinkley, Alan. *The End of Reform: New Deal Liberalism in Recession and War.* New York: Alfred A. Knopf, 1995.

Brown, Clair. *American Standards of Living 1918–1988.* Oxford: Blackwell Publishers, 1994.

Davis, Kenneth. *FDR: Into the Storm 1937–1940.* New York: Random House, 1993.

Eichengreen, Barry and Hatton, T. H. *Interwar Unemployment in International Perspective.* Dordrecht: Kluwer Academic Publishers, 1988.

Kindleberger, Charles. *The World in Depression, 1929–1939.* Berkeley: University of California Press, 1986.

Rose, Nancy E. *Put to Work: Relief Programs in the Great Depression.* New York: Monthly Review Press, 1994.

Romasco, Albert U. *The Politics of Recovery: Roosevelt's New Deal.* New York: Oxford University Press, 1983.

Schlesinger, Arthur Jr. *The Age of Roosevelt: The Politics of Upheaval.* Boston: Houghton Mifflin, 1960.

Schwarz, Jordan A. *The New Dealers: Power Politics in the Age of Roosevelt.* New York: Random House, 1993.

Temin, Peter. *Lessons From the Great Depression.* Cambridge, Massachusetts: MIT Press, 1989.

8

Reconstructing Capitalism

> "It is childish to speak of recovery first and reconstruction afterward. In the very nature of the process of recovery we must avoid the destructive influences of the past."
>
> Franklin Roosevelt, *Message to Congress, June 4, 1934*

The Politics of Agricultural Adjustment

The men and women who developed the New Deal were convinced that weaknesses in the economy of the 1920s had created the poverty and social disorder of the early 1930s. New Dealers often differed sharply over the definition of particular problems and over measures designed to solve those problems, but none of them desired a return to the *status quo ante*. The Roosevelt administration and its supporters in Congress wanted federal economic reforms to promote recovery and prevent a recurrence of the Great Depression.

Economic collapse and widespread social disorder both facilitated and complicated the New Deal's reconstruction efforts. In 1933 New Dealers had the advantage of a unique national consensus for government intervention in the economy. Franklin Roosevelt did not exaggerate when he claimed in his first inaugural address a mandate for "direct, vigorous action." But what type of action? The intertwined economic and social crises of early 1933 raised a welter of voices, each seeking to have its particular economic remedy included in the New Deal. In these circumstances, only a dictator could have imposed a single ideologically coherent program on the country, and FDR was no dictator. What he later described as "the recovery of confidence in our democratic processes, our republican institutions" was as important to him as economic recovery. After the banks reopened Roosevelt knew that Congress would act swiftly only if he compromised with powerful interests and politicians. His administration's initial compromises imbedded ideological incoherence in the New Deal. Thereafter, Supreme Court rulings against the New Deal and increasing political pressure brought by previously marginalized groups further complicated the Roosevelt administration's reconstruction of the economy. A brief history of one of the New Deal's most enduring programs, agricultural adjustment, illustrates these patterns.

Agricultural reconstruction was written into law under duress. On March 16th FDR asked Congress to stay in special session to pass a farm bill that he admitted was "a new and untrod path." The President wanted to resolve the farm crisis before spring planting. He knew that millions of farmers were desperate, and that stabilizing the banks had so far done nothing to address their problems. Mass demonstrations and defiance of property laws continued in the most distressed areas. FDR realized that government inaction would provoke even greater disorders. Milo Reno, leader of the Farm Holiday Association, had said as much when he called on the federal government to guarantee "the cost of production" or confront a national farm strike in May. Crisis conditions inspired FDR's call "for the trial of a new means to rescue agriculture." The extraordinary bill he sent to Congress on March 16th asked for a grant of power to plan the nation's output of food and fiber.

To prepare the political ground for this unprecedented step, representatives of the nation's oldest farm organizations, cooperatives, farm journals, and agricultural colleges had been called to Washington on March 10th. They met for two days with congressional leaders and officials from the Department of Agriculture. For years most of these men had offered, and Congress had debated, various schemes for raising farm prices. But without strong presidential leadership none had become law. Export subsidies, cooperative marketing agreements with processors, government purchase and storage of surpluses, domestic allotment plans to reduce output, and various inflationary schemes all had their adherents. With Franklin Roosevelt's full support, Agriculture Secretary Henry Wallace and his new Assistant Secretary Rexford Tugwell presented a plan for voluntary domestic allotment – a scheme that would pay farmers who agreed to reduce production of specified commodities. Wallace and Tugwell feared a knockdown fight with proponents of other ideas; instead they found the agricultural establishment nervous and compliant. The farm leaders were easily persuaded to support a delegation of broad authority to the Secretary of Agriculture after he promised to include in the bill a variety of policies to raise commodity prices. Only inflation was counted out. Thus the proposal that emerged on March 16th temporarily pleased almost all of the agricultural establishment.

A huge majority of the House passed this bill on March 22nd, but it stalled in the Senate when proponents of inflation introduced amendments not wanted by the President. Driving up prices by putting more money into circulation had been agrarian Democrats' preferred solution to depression since the 1890s, and it was still extremely popular in the West and South. As we have already seen, FDR was quietly considering ways to increase the money supply, but at this time he did not want to lose the support of congressional conservatives who opposed inflation on principle. The impasse over inflation gave lobbyists for food and fiber processors (who would be taxed to pay for the output reduction features of the bill) time to organize resistance to the whole measure.

To prod the Senate, as well as to respond to a swelling tide of farm protest, on April 3rd FDR sent Congress additional legislation authorizing the federal government to "provide for the refinancing of mortgage and other indebtedness" to bring "an end to the threatened loss of homes and productive capacity now faced by hundreds of thousands of American farm families." When the Senate failed to move with dispatch on this latest proposal, violent demonstrations spread across the upper Midwest. Six counties in Iowa were placed under martial law and at least 150 farmers were jailed after collection agents, sheriff deputies, and a judge were attacked by angry mobs. A general farm strike in the corn and wheat belts now seemed imminent. Although we cannot be sure how much this unrest influenced events in Washington, it seems more than a coincidence that the Senate logjam broke up at this time. First, the Thomas amendment gained the support of all inflationists after FDR made clear he would accept language leaving the timing and method of adding to the money supply up to the President's discretion. While the Senate tied together authorization for adjusting commodity prices, the farm mortgage assistance measure, and presidential control of monetary policy into a single omnibus bill, Governor Floyd Olson of Minnesota persuaded Farm Holiday leaders to postpone their threatened strike. Congress passed the Farm Relief Act on May 10th and the President signed it two days later. This first significant reform of the Hundred Days marked a true turning point in federal agriculture policy.

The Farm Relief Act delegated broad powers to the Executive branch, allowing it to develop policies rather than imposing a single approach to recovery. This type enabling of legislation, typical of the early New Deal, reflected the politics of the moment. Crisis conditions mandated quick actions not the slow and difficult task of building a majority for a single policy. Through Title I, usually called the Agricultural Adjustment Act, Congress gave the President and his Department of Agriculture power to intervene in commodity markets, leaving the details of interventions in particular markets up to the administration. Hoping to preserve the national unity that had emerged during the banking crisis, FDR and Henry Wallace opted to give all those who had politically powerful voices at least something of what they demanded. As a result, contradictory policies were imbedded in the Department of Agriculture's new Agricultural Adjustment Administration (AAA). When farm prices failed to reach recovery levels quickly these contradictions created conflicts within the administration and among farm state representatives in Congress. For these reasons, historians have focused most of their attention on the price adjustment aspects of the New Deal agriculture policy.

The more successful Title II of the legislation, also known as the Farm Mortgage Assistance Act, deserves more attention. It granted the newly created Farm Credit Administration power to refinance farmers' mortgages at low interest rates. Henry Morgenthau, the first director of the Farm Credit Administration, quickly used this power to restore financial stability to the areas hit hardest by the foreclosure crisis. In its first seven months Morgenthau's agency arranged over $100,000,000 in mortgage refinancing. It also began a program of rescheduling farmers' other debts through local farm debt readjustment committees. In time, with the approval of Congress, this often forgotten agency established regional banks to make mortgage, crop, and marketing loans and provide credits to cooperatives. As a result, interest rates plunged all across rural America. Farmers who wanted to reacquire foreclosed property with new mortgages adjusted to lower prices and interest rates could do so under regulations spelled out in the Farm Bankruptcy Act that Congress passed in June 1934. This law and its successor, the Farm Mortgage Moratorium Act of 1935, also allowed hard-pressed farmers to suspend bankruptcy proceeding for five years while they worked out new financing to cover their old debts.

Another agricultural support program was established in the fall of 1933 after crop prices began slipping and farm groups in the South and Midwest threatened new protests. On October 16th FDR issued an executive order which created a price-support loan program administered by a new Commodity Credit Corporation. Using financing initially provided by the RFC (which was fast becoming a bank for New Deal agencies), the Commodity Credit Corporation could loan farmers whom the President designated as eligible a sum equal to what they would have received for their crop at a specified target price. Initially this program was available to just two groups of farmers: cotton growers who borrowed against a 10-cents-a-pound target price, and corn farmers whose target was 45 cents a bushel. These farmers could sell their crops and pay back the government if prices rose above their targets, or they could just keep what they had borrowed leaving the government holding the surplus. The Farm Credit Administration and the Commodity Credit Corporation helped to defuse the farm crisis in the rural regions hit hardest by the Great Depression. They did this by greatly reducing the financial risks faced by the families who owned most of America's farms. Small wonder that even traditionally Republican farm states in the Midwest voted for Franklin Roosevelt in the presidential election of 1936.

Whereas Title II of the Agriculture Act of 1933 was both a practical and political success, agricultural adjustment had a more troubled history. The trouble began when FDR selected George Peek, a manufacturer of agricultural equipment and protege of conservative Democratic financier Bernard Baruch, as AAA's first director. Peek was appointed to maintain the President's broad coalition of support, but he was completely out of step with Wallace, Tugwell, and the liberal economists and lawyers they had brought into the Department of Agriculture. George Peek did not believe farmers suffered from overproduction which required government-directed crop reduction. Instead Peek had long advocated export subsidies and cooperative agreements with food processors as the best ways to reduce the huge farm surpluses that depressed domestic prices. During the summer and fall of 1933, Peek and Wallace battled over the right mix of programs for specific commodities. At the same time the AAA's Legal Division headed by Jerome Frank and its Consumer Division led by Frederic Howe held up marketing agreements negotiated by Peek because these agreements would have allowed processors to pass the price increases received by farmers directly on to consumers. Peek resigned under duress in December 1933. His replacement, Chester Davis, a strong proponent of crop reduction, confirmed the central place of planned output reductions in New Deal agricultural policy.

During 1933, the AAA had started up voluntary domestic allotment programs for cotton, wheat, corn, hogs, rice, tobacco, and milk. Production control measures for nine other commodities were added during the next two years. AAA administrators for each crop worked through existing the Agriculture Exten-

banks should not be permitted to underwrite securities."
Aldrich and many other big city bankers also supported authorization of limited branch banking within individual states,
and reforms that gave the Federal Reserve greater power to
prevent speculative loans by member banks. Small banks liked
federal deposit insurance, something FDR tried to block by
arguing that it would be too expensive and ineffective in panic
situations. The President actually threatened a veto until Congressman Steagall agreed to scale back the deposit insurance
program.

The Glass–Steagall Banking Act approved in June 1933
strengthened the Federal Reserve's regulatory powers, separated commercial and investment banking, and secured private deposits with a government-run insurance program. The
Federal Deposit Insurance Corporation (FDIC) began operations on July 1, 1934 and was made permanent by the Banking Act of 1935. All banks in the Federal Reserve system had
to join FDIC and pay assessments according to size; other banks
had two years to become members. The FDIC offered insurance coverage ranging from 100 percent for deposits up to
$10,000 to just 50 percent for deposits over $50,000. It was a
complete success for exactly the reasons big Eastern banks
had opposed it. FDIC forced those banks to contribute to the
security of smaller banks. In combination with stricter regulation, FDIC eliminated the kind of bank panics that had plagued
the country since the early nineteenth century. Franklin
Roosevelt was quick to take full credit for FDIC, even though
he had done his best to block its creation.

FDR actually deserves more credit for initiating another
extremely popular financial security program, the Home
Owners Loan Corporation (HOLC). Sent to Congress in April
1933 at time when thousands of homeowners were being foreclosed each week, the bill authorizing HOLC had few opponents in Congress. HOLC did for urban homeowners what
the federal farm mortgage refinancing did in rural areas. The
agency made direct low interest, long-term loans to homeowners who were in default or in danger of default. In 1934,
HOLC issued three-quarters of all the home mortgages in the

sion Service to initiate the process of establishing county production control committees. In the South, Extension Service agents simply picked committee members; in the Midwest they supervised elections. County production control committees had responsibility for enlisting farmers and assigning their acreage reductions. Farmers who signed contracts with the AAA received benefit payments estimated as fair compensation for their reduced crop. Under the original legislation these payments were financed out of taxes imposed on middlemen such as processors and elevator operators. Regardless of how they were selected, county committees were almost always dominated by large landowners who used the program to their best advantage. Although they were supposed to pass on benefit payments to tenants and sharecroppers who suffered acreage reduction, landlords were not forced to do so. Nor were they restrained from evicting tenants on land withdrawn from production. So the initial burdens of domestic allotment fell most heavily on the poorest segments of the farm population.

Resentment against the unfairness of domestic allotment took months to surface, but the methods used to reduce 1933 cotton and pork production aroused immediate public protest. By the time the Senate passed the Farm Relief Act, cotton farmers had already planted 4,000,000 more acres than in 1932, despite the fact that unsold cotton stored in the United States could satisfy world demand for a year. This expanded cotton acreage dramatically confirmed Henry Wallace's argument that unlike manufacturers who cut back production in the face of falling demand, unorganized agricultural producers increased output, thus further depressing prices. Wallace admitted that "to destroy a standing crop goes against the soundest instincts of human nature," but he was still determined to reduce output before cotton prices fell further. In June, AAA asked cotton farmers to plow under 10,304,000 acres in return for $100,000,000 in government payments. Facing a similar problem among pork producers by September, AAA ordered production control committees to allocate the destruction of 6,200,000 young pigs and 200,000 farrowing sows in return for $200,000,000 in payments. These actions raised prices and farm incomes, but they also appalled non-farmers who could not understand the logic of destroying food and fiber when so many people were poor. Leading newspapers including the Chicago *Tribune* and the chain owned by William Randolph Hearst conveyed the idea that these drastic actions typified AAA policy. And though AAA never again initiated such actions, many Americans continued to believe agricultural adjustment and crop destruction were synonymous.

Controversies involving AAA policies continued during the next two years. The most important of these arose after organization of a Southern Tenant Farmers Union among Arkansas sharecroppers in early 1934 forced AAA officials to confront class and racial inequality in the Cotton Belt. Within the agency, Jerome Frank's lawyers took up the cause of the neglected tenants and sharecroppers. When the Legal Division inserted a clause into acreage reduction contracts that insured 1934 benefit checks would go directly to tenants, howls of protest arose from the representatives of plantation owners. One of AAA's young lawyers, Alger Hiss, later recalled how Senator "Cotton" Smith of South Carolina came directly to his office to tell him "Young fella, you can't do this to my niggers, paying checks to them. They don't know what to do with money." On this point Jerome Frank retained the backing of AAA director Chester Davis. But in early 1935 Frank took advantage of Davis' absence from Washington to issue directives requiring landlords to retain tenants. Much to the satisfaction of the cotton state delegation in Congress, this time Chester Davis asked Secretary Wallace to fire Jerome Frank and a half dozen of his staff. Although Henry Wallace knew the Legal Division had been trying to carry out the best intentions of the New Deal, he also understood that poor tenant farmers had no political clout in Washington in 1935. By "purging" AAA's Legal Division of its leading liberals, the New Deal retained the support of most Southern Democrats in Congress.

The power of this regional group was also demonstrated in other ways. AAA's original domestic allotment programs were all voluntary. In most places at least eight of every ten eligible farmers had enrolled in crop reduction programs. But reports that many small cotton farms planned to plant "up to the fence rails" to cash in on higher prices in 1934 led Senator John Bankhead of Alabama to propose modification of the AAA's production control plan. Over the objections of Secretary Wallace, but in accordance with the views of the vast majority of planters signed up with the AAA, Congress passed the Bankhead Cotton Control Act in April 1934. This law imposed a punitive tax on farmers who produced above their allotted share of a state's quota. It thus ended voluntary domestic allotment in the Cotton Belt. Voluntarism was eliminated by similar legislation affecting Southern tobacco farmers in late 1934. Taking a cue from their Southern colleagues, congressional delegations from Idaho and Maine pushed through a Potato Control Act in 1935. Slowly Congress was replacing voluntary domestic allotment with mandatory controls and price supports.

In the fall of 1933 the Roosevelt administration responded to farmer protests against low pork prices and public outcry over the hog reduction program with government purchase of surpluses. In September 1933, the Federal Emergency Relief Administration had announced it would buy surplus pork from the AAA. Under this program approximately one-tenth the total weight of hogs killed by the AAA reached relief recipients as salt pork. Two weeks later, FDR established a Federal Surplus Relief Corporation "to purchase directly from farmers, whenever desirable, in such a way to carry out the purposes of the Agricultural Adjustment Act." In subsequent years, government purchases and storage of surpluses were integrated into Henry Wallace's attempt to stabilize prices through an "ever-normal" supply plan under which government would store crops in bumper years and sell them off when yields fell. Stored surpluses shrunk in 1935–36 when the continued mid-continent drought reduced yields and drove up prices of cotton, wheat, and corn; but in the late 1930s the federal government added to its stockpiles of agricultural commodities.

In January 1936 the Supreme Court decided six to three that a suit brought by former Republican national committee chairman William Butler on behalf of Hoosac Mills, a cotton cloth manufacturer, correctly identified the AAA tax on processors as an unconstitutional effort to control agricultural production. The Court's action did not alter the Roosevelt administration's commitment to raising farm prices by controlling output. Four days after the Butler decision, FDR told reporters he favored a new acreage reduction program that would "retain and regain soil fertility." Two months later Congress approved the Soil Conservation and Domestic Allotment Act, which continued production control efforts in the name of promoting sound agricultural practices. Sharply falling farm prices during the "Roosevelt recession" forced Congress to consider a new AAA that included Henry Wallace's "ever-normal granary" ideas, crop insurance, and expanded Commodity Credit Corporation loans. The Agricultural Adjustment Act of 1938 also reflected the continued ability of major farm organizations to achieve their goals within the framework of the New Deal. The new law moved the power to set price support goals from the Agriculture Department crop to the Congress. As a result, in subsequent years, specific price support levels became a test of the political power of well-organized producers.

Poor farmers never received comparable assistance from the New Deal. After the AAA "purge," their principal advocate within the Agriculture Department was Undersecretary Rexford Tugwell. Tugwell thought a separate agency was needed to consolidate and expand programs aimed at raising the living standards of sharecroppers, tenants, and subsistence farmers who made up nearly half the nation's farm population. President Roosevelt gave Tugwell an opportunity to tackle rural poverty problems by naming him director of a new Resettlement Agency (RA) in May 1935. Unfortunately the RA and its successor, the Farm Security Agency (FSA), could not overcome two related problems: the enormous extent of rural poverty, and resistance from Congressional conservatives including many Southern Democrats who did not want to undermine the political power of large landowners (see Chapter 10). Perhaps the most enduring achievement of the RA and FSA was the work done by their photographers under the direction of Roy Stryker, a former Tugwell student. Stryker hired Dorothea Lange, Walker Evans, Ben Shahn, Arthur Rothstein, and other photographers to document rural poverty and New Deal efforts to alleviate it. Many RA/FSA photographs were used in contemporary newspaper and magazine features, as well as government publicity. Even more importantly, some images such as Dorothea Lange's famous photograph of a migrant mother and her children became cultural icons which still tell us the Great Depression was that moment in American history when the pioneers' dream of independence on the land finally collapsed.

Although conservative critics slammed agricultural adjustment for its alleged "regimentation" of agriculture, and liberals attacked it for failing to adequately address the problems of poor farmers, most farm owners approved of the New Deal because it raised farm income. Prices of controlled commodities more than doubled after 1933. Admittedly, the increases never amounted to full recovery. However, eligible farmers could now supplement what they received from the market with AAA benefit payments and retained price support loans. Total farm income doubled during the New Deal years. In some years as much as half this increase was derived from federal support programs. Agricultural adjustment never came close to equalizing rural and urban incomes, but it did keep millions of farm families on their land. This was extremely important because the New Deal's principal industrial recovery measure failed to eliminate mass unemployment in the cities.

The Politics of Industrial Recovery

During the early months of the special session of 1933, President Roosevelt was unable to submit an industrial recovery bill for congressional approval. FDR's own uncertainties about how to proceed, and serious divisions among the many people who wanted to contribute to the bill created the delay. On one hand, anti-trust Democrats and progressive Republicans were convinced that big business had stifled recovery by keeping prices up while laying off workers and slashing wages. But most of FDR's advisors, as well as most of the big business community, thought too much competition had driven prices, wages, employment, and profits down past the point of recovery. FDR had hoped to postpone consideration of industrial recovery until after Congress returned from its summer recess. However, pressure from business groups and organized labor, and the fear that Congress might act independently finally forced him to put the issue on his agenda for the special session.

On April 6, 1933 the Senate voted 53 to 30 for a bill sponsored by Senator Hugo Black of Alabama that aimed to lower unemployment by setting a maximum work week of five 6-hour days. First proposed at the American Federation of Labor's national convention in November 1932, the 30-hour bill was uncomplicated and thus very appealing. It would have simply prohibited from interstate commerce anything produced by workers who exceeded its maximum hours provisions. Senator Black and his supporters argued that a shorter work week would force employers to hire more labor. Just as importantly, they also saw the bill as fulfillment of business boosters' longstanding promise that industrial progress would improve everyone's life. As Senator Black explained to his colleagues, "at this very time, with more than 12,000,000 people helpless and hopeless in the grip of unemployment . . . we find people in every State of this Nation . . . working from 10 to 16 hours a day in order to earn a mere pittance." Why not, Hugo Black argued, spread the work and bring to Americans "the benefit of that leisure which comes from machinery and efficiency."

Senator Black's 30-hour bill garnered widespread support. Union leaders and workers from all over of the country wrote Congress urging its passage. President Roosevelt abhorred the Black bill, and he feared the House would approve it. To Labor Secretary Perkins, FDR complained that the measure was flawed because it contained no minimum wage provisions and because it failed to recognize that some industries might require longer hours. He also thought the bill was unconstitutional. But Franklin Roosevelt recognized the shorter-hours movement was a potent political force. So despite his personal belief that there was no harm in a 48-hour work week, FDR promised congressional leaders that he would present an industrial recovery measure which included provisions for a shorter work week.

President Roosevelt set several different groups to work on the problem of industrial recovery. This method, also used to prepare other administration measures, gave FDR a range of options as well as opportunities to test political responses to particular ideas before including them in proposed legislation. But FDR's method left him open to the charge of being devious, since he encouraged everyone who worked on the legislation whether or not he used their ideas. Moreover, FDR's method often led to legislation that cobbled together potentially divisive policies. This last problem was especially manifest in the National Industrial Recovery Act.

The three groups that worked on the administration's bill disagreed among themselves on what had caused the collapse of industry, and therefore about how the federal government could revive production and create jobs for the unemployed. But they agreed with FDR that this was no time for vigorous anti-trust action. So anti-trust liberals and progressives were simply excluded from the bill-drafting process. The most influential group working on the bill included Raymond Moley, labor lawyer Donald Richberg, and former General Hugh Johnson, most recently an associate of George Peek at the Moline Plow Company. Johnson had served on the War Industries Board that Bernard Baruch directed in 1918, and thought its form of business-government partnership should be revived to combat the Great Depression. He was not alone. Several influential businessmen including the president of General Electric and the chairman of the United States Chamber of Commerce had been publicly pushing this idea for at least a year. All these men were mainly concerned with raising prices. They wanted the nation's anti-trust laws suspended so that each industry could establish "codes of fair competition" bestowing cartel-like powers on private trade associations.

The two other drafting committees also favored limited competition, but their recovery strategies stressed income redistribution to raise consumer demand, which would in turn lift prices. One group comprised Undersecretary of Commerce John Dickinson, Frances Perkins, and Rexford Tugwell proposed industrial boards that would implement flexible plans to raise real wages and reduce the work week while allowing firms to stabilize prices. Another larger group working under the direction of Senator Robert Wagner wanted to limit the number of boards to just a few big industries that would also agree to recognize independent labor unions as a counterweight to corporate power. Wagner's group also insisted the legislation include a massive "pump-priming" public works appropriation to reduce unemployment.

The Dickinson and Wagner groups combined forces and presented a single draft bill to the President at the end of April about the same time the Johnson–Richberg group presented its draft legislation. Neither side compromised until May 10th when FDR told the leaders of each group to "lock themselves in a room" and settle their differences. The resulting industrial recovery bill reflected the ideas of both groups. Title I suspended the anti-trust laws for two years and established a new National Recovery Administration (NRA) to supervise the implementation of "codes of fair competition" approved by the President. FDR signaled the influence of the Johnson–Richberg group in his message to Congress which condemned "cut-throat underselling" and "selfish competition." But the Dickinson and Wagner groups also left a strong imprint on the bill. Section 7(a) of Title I included a vaguely worded guarantee of labor's right to organize unions and more explicit language requiring each industry's code to ban child labor while setting minimum wages and maximum hours. Moreover, as we have already seen Title II authorized massive borrowing to fund a new Public Works Administration.

The House quickly approved the measure, but in the Senate many opponents charged the bill was triumph for big business. Progressive Republican William Borah of Idaho led the opposition, crying out at one point in the debate, "Stabilization, what crimes are to be committed in they name?" Borah prophetically argued that small businesses would be hurt by the industrial codes while already large companies would increase their market shares in the biggest industries. Robert Wagner responded that "the bill does not abolish competition," instead it merely targeted "competition that was wasteful, blind, and destructive." Wagner insisted the bill's sole purpose was "the restoration of employment at wage scales sufficient to provide comfort and a decency level of living." But as events soon proved many businesses had different ideas about what the industrial recovery program was supposed to achieve.

On June 13th, the Senate approved the National Industrial Recovery Act by a narrow seven vote margin. FDR called it "the most important and far-reaching legislation ever enacted by the American Congress." He was right in one respect; the law did have a long reach. The NRA eventually negotiated 541 different codes of fair competition that covered, in Huey Long's words, "everything from a peanut stand to a powerhouse." NRA codes were given the force of law by executive order. Most of them followed guidelines announced in mid-July that included the abolition of child labor, a 40-hour work week, and minimum wages no less than 30 cents an hour. Nearly 80 percent of the codes explicitly prohibited selling below cost. Other common price stabilization provisions included open pricing and cost plus specified mark-up formulas.

FDR appointed Hugh Johnson NRA director, while the new Public Works Administration was placed under the authority of Interior Secretary Harold Ickes. Johnson, a man with enormous energy but also a heavy drinker subject to wide mood swings, got NRA off to a rousing start. He came up with the idea of having businesses display a Blue Eagle symbol and the slogan "We Do Our Part" to signify their participation in the industrial recovery program. Johnson organized a nationwide campaign complete with mass rallies and enormous parades that made compliance into a test of patriotism. NRA's 12-hour long parade in New York City included 500,000 marchers who were cheered on by several million spectators. Yet

Johnson was a poor administrator who usually caved into business demands while resisting efforts by liberals and unions to strictly enforce the labor provisions of the industrial codes.

When recovery stalled in the winter of 1933–34, NRA came under fire from several different quarters. Consumers and farmers argued it had driven up prices but done nothing for incomes and employment. Small businesses complained about burdensome paperwork. By 1935 FDR's critics relentlessly attacked this aspect of the recovery program. Huey Long mocked, "It would take 40 lawyers to tell a shoeshine stand how to operate and be certain he didn't go to jail." Progressive Republicans weighed in against NRA too. As early as January 1934, Senators Borah and Nye held hearings that showed large firms benefited most from non-price competition. A National Recovery Review Board chaired by Clarence Darrow found especially rapid concentration of market shares in steel and movie production.

The NRA also increased tensions between management and workers. By establishing labor's right to organize, but not providing for any effective enforcement or disputes resolution, Section 7(a) invited trouble for the Roosevelt administration. John L. Lewis sent United Mine Workers' staff into the coal fields carrying the message, "The President wants you to organize." Elsewhere, including the critically important steel, auto, and electrical equipment industries, long repressed local union activists set up organizations that demanded recognition from management for the purposes of bargaining over wages, hours, and working conditions. At the time, precious few American companies recognized the rights of labor. Most ignored section 7(a) proclaiming it a violation of their own "right to manage." In the fall, strikes designed to force recognition of unions spread in the coal and steel industries. On October 5th 21 people were shot by sheriff's deputies intent on breaking up a steel workers picket line in Ambridge, Pennsylvania. Franklin Roosevelt intervened, calling the president of U.S. Steel to the White House. Still anxious to maintain business support for the New Deal, FDR did not insist that companies follow the intent of the law. Instead he set up a National Labor Board to hear disputes, and also permitted companies to sponsor in-house "employee representation plans" instead of recognizing independent unions. This arrangement bought time for management and the Roosevelt administration, but all over the country an unstoppable movement of workers into independent unions had begun to change the political balance of power in the industrial economy.

By the summer of 1934, when mass strikes erupted in many places across the country, NRA had few important supporters outside the White House. Hugh Johnson was eased out of his position in August after a series of publicly embarrassing speeches and private temper tantrums. He was replaced by a five-person NRA board effectively dominated by an increasingly pro-business Donald Richberg. Labor problems increasingly bedeviled the administration's efforts to garner support for continuation of the recovery program. Then on May 27, 1935, a day memorialized as "Black Monday" in New Deal mythology, the Supreme Court ruled unanimously against the Roosevelt administration in three cases including *A.L.A. Schecter* v. *United States.*[1] In the *Schecter* case, the Court decided that the National Industrial Recovery Act had violated the interstate commerce clause of the Constitution by giving the President the power to interfere with what was essentially intrastate business.

NRA was dead, just a month before its authorization was due to expire. Few people in Washington really believed the disappearance of NRA was a serious setback for the country, but the ruling infuriated FDR. He told reporters, "We have been relegated to the horse-and-buggy definition of interstate commerce." Then for the next year Roosevelt remained silent on the subject of the Supreme Court, even though it continued to strike down New Deal measures using a *laissez-faire* logic that seemed to him both dangerously outdated and out of step with the desires of the electorate.

The administration's industrial recovery program had probably contributed to the rising trend in prices in 1933–34. The NRA raised wage rates in some industries, and it made considerable progress in reducing child labor and establishing a standard 40-hour work week. But FDR had promised NRA and PWA would together "*put people back to work*, to let them buy more of the products of farms and factories, and to start our businesses at a living rate again." The National Industrial Recovery Act fell far short of these goals. In fact, as we have already seen, the most vigorous phase of the "Roosevelt recovery" actually occurred after the demise of NRA.

At least two reasons explain the failure of the National Industrial Recovery Act. First, President Roosevelt's selection of Harold Ickes as PWA administrator frustrated the "pump-priming" intent of Title II. Ickes was an inexperienced administrator and very cautious spender. Instead of spending PWA's budget quickly to jump-start the nation's construction and building supply industries, Ickes proceeded very slowly. He personally reviewed all proposals PWA received from other federal agencies, the states, and local governments, approving only those he judged to be financially sound and of long-term value. By early 1934, Ickes had signed PWA contracts totaling one-fourth of the agency's two-year budget, but spent only 3 percent of its appropriation. Consequently PWA did almost nothing to reduce mass unemployment in 1933–34. What PWA eventually built – including dams, schools, hospitals, sewer systems, bridges, tunnels, and lighthouses – were scandal-free projects, and of great use to the nation. But as a recovery program PWA was ineffective.

Even more importantly, as Senator Borah had warned, NRA's whole recovery strategy was flawed by its preference for what was called at the time "self-government in industry." NRA codes could be enforced in capital-intensive industries that already had effective trade associations, but not in industries made up of thousands of small labor-intensive firms. Where they were effective, the NRA code authorities acted like cartels, raising prices while restricting output. This strategy enabled many big firms to make profits without risking significant new investment in plants and equipment. Thus, where it worked best, NRA worked against what the nation really needed: an investment-driven recovery that would have dramatically expanded production and employment.

Stability through Regulation

The "associationist" hope that the federal government could supervise the behavior of industries for the mutual benefit of management, workers, and the public did not die with the *Schecter* decision. The Emergency Railroad Transportation Act of 1933 remained in effect for another year. This law had created a special federal office to coordinate operations among companies in the same regions while also mandating employment stabilization. Moreover, as soon as NRA's fate was sealed several other so-called "sick industries" immediately began lobbying Congress for special legislation to prevent a return to "cut-throat" price and wage competition.[2] Cotton textile producers, lumber companies, and northern coal mine owners all called for "little NRAs" to continue price stabilization and production control programs.

Only the bituminous coal industry got what it wanted. There were two reasons for its success. First it could couch its demands in terms of conservation of a valuable natural resource. And more importantly, the powerful voice of United Mine Workers president John L. Lewis also demanded a "little NRA." Lewis threatened a national coal strike if the Congress did not replace NRA's bituminous coal code with a substitute authority that would safeguard the gains made by workers and their union since 1933. His political pressure was effective. FDR put a coal bill sponsored by Pennsylvania's Senator Joseph Guffey on his "must legislation" list in June 1935. Two months later Congress passed the Bituminous Coal Conservation Act. The Guffey Act and its successor (the Bituminous Coal Act of 1937) authorized a national commission to oversee price maintenance and labor standards.

Congress also used conservation arguments in shaping a "little NRA" for crude oil producers. After the opening of massive new fields in East Texas brought on a near total collapse of crude oil prices in 1931, established oil companies had persuaded state governments to limit production. But neither Texas' famed Rangers nor Oklahoma's National Guard were able to stop the interstate shipment of "hot oil" (oil produced in excess of state mandated limits). Section 9-C of the National Industrial Recovery Act gave the President power to regulate the interstate oil business. FDR delegated this power to Harold Ickes who had just about solved the "hot oil" problem when the Supreme Court declared Section 9-C unconstitutional in January 1935. Within a month, Congress passed a law sponsored by Texas Senator Tom Connally that restored federal control of interstate oil shipments. Ickes used this new authority to negotiate an Interstate Oil Compact that effectively regulated production and stabilized prices for the remainder of the decade.

Transportation companies also received federal protection from competition in the aftermath of the *Schecter* decision. On June 7, 1935, President Roosevelt sent a message telling Congress it was "high time to deal with the Nation's transportation as a single, unified problem." Although Congress never went this far, it did eventually enact most of the legislation that FDR called for in this message. Effective lobbying by the American Trucking Association insured quick passage of the Motor Carrier Act. This law gave the Interstate Commerce Commission power to use licenses to control entry into the industry. Licensed trucking companies were required to file rates, use common financial practices, and adhere to common labor practices.

In June 1936, Congress approved the administration's Merchant Marine Act. It established a five-member Maritime Commission to oversee a program of subsidies designed to protect shipbuilders and shipping companies from foreign competition. The commission's first chairman, Joseph Kennedy, established a program designed to modernize America's fleet by sponsoring 50 new ships a year. Shipyard subsidies were calculated to make up the difference between higher U.S. materials and labor costs and what foreign yards would charge. Shipping company subsidies were designed to keep an American fleet operating on what were deemed essential trade routes.

Mail subsidies had been used to make the airline industry into a government-sponsored cartel in the late 1920s. In 1934 Congress imposed competitive bidding on the industry after investigations revealed corruption in the awarding of mail contracts. This new system threatened financial disaster when new firms rushed into the field often making bids below costs. Pressure from the leading companies (Trans World, United, Eastern, and American airlines) led Congress and the administration to regulate the industry. The Civil Aeronautics Act of 1938 abandoned all pretexts of competitive bidding for mail subsidies and price competition between companies. It established a Civil Aeronautics Authority that controlled entry, set routes, prescribed rates, and set labor standards for the airline industry.

Similar regulated markets were set up for the broadcasting, telephone, and telegraph industries after Congress approved the administration's communications bill in February 1934. The stated purpose of the Communications Act was "To make available . . . to all the people of the United States, a rapid, efficient, nation-wide, and world-wide wire and radio communications service with adequate facilities at reasonable charges." Under this law, a new seven-member Federal Communications Commission (FCC) was given power to license broadcasters and allocate radio (and later television) frequencies, and regulate the facilities and rates charged by companies offering "wire communications." The new FCC accepted the argument of American Telephone and Telegraph's president that "Telephone is a monopoly, and competition is against the public interest," making policy that certainly benefited the company, but that also gave most Americans access to reliable telephone service.

New Deal legislation imposed regulated markets on agriculture and the energy, transportation, and communications industries. The underlying rationale for the transformation of these economic sectors was clearly explained by Franklin Roosevelt in a fireside chat on September 30, 1934. "Private enterprise in times such as these," FDR explained, "cannot be left without assistance and without reasonable safeguards lest it destroy not only itself but also our processes of civilization." The New Deal's reconstruction of the economy was neither socialism nor fascism. It helped save American capitalism by promoting stability for private companies and greater economic security for farmers and workers.

The Politics of Financial Regulation

Reforming America's banking and financial sectors created different practical and political problems than agricultural and industrial reconstruction. In his first inaugural address FDR had proclaimed, "The money changers have fled from their high seats in the temple of our civilization. We may now restore that temple." At the time virtually everyone in the administration and the Democratic majorities in Congress thought a weak banking structure and speculative investment behavior were primary causes of the Great Depression. The Emergency Banking Act had been just a first step towards reconstruction of the banking industry. Senator Carter Glass provided the next step in the form of legislation that addressed problems inherent in a system made up of thousands of mostly small single unit banks, as well as problems created by commercial banks that operated speculative investment subsidiaries. Glass' bill had been approved by the Senate in January 1933, but had failed in the lame duck House. Senator Glass reintroduced it on March 9th, the same day that Congress passed the Emergency Banking Act. Congressman Henry Steagall sponsored a similar bill in the House, but added a controversial section establishing comprehensive federal deposit insurance.

The Glass–Steagall bill was supported by some very prominent bankers who wanted federal regulation to restore public confidence in their shattered industry. Winthrop Aldrich, president of New York's Chase National Bank (the nation's largest), stated "The spirit of speculation should be eradicated from the management of commercial banks, and commercial

country. By the end of the decade when private mortgage lending finally picked up, HOLC was actually forced to foreclose on some of its borrowers. But by that time it had refinanced and made secure almost one-fifth of all the private homes in America.

HOLC also allowed lenders to trade defaulted mortgages for government bonds, thus saving many private institutions from financial ruin. In 1934 the newly established Federal Housing Administration (FHA) began issuing mortgage insurance; 10 years later nearly half of all new mortgages were secured by FHA insurance. Both HOLC and FHA made mortgage lending less risky and home ownership more secure. In the long run these programs built up America's middle class by opening the possibility of home ownership to millions of families who would have been deemed ineligible for home loans before the New Deal. Still the programs were not without flaws. Neither agency did anything to change the longstanding industry practice of maintaining residential segregation by denying mortgages to minorities who wanted to live in predominately white neighborhoods.

In November 1934, FDR picked Marriner Eccles to head the Federal Reserve Board. FDR knew the liberal Eccles wanted to eliminate the decentralized features of the existing Federal Reserve system. The Banking Act of 1935 authored by Eccles created the modern Federal Reserve. It gave power to presidential appointees in Washington, not private bankers in New York and other reserve cities. The new law replaced the old Federal Reserve Board with a Board of Governors consisting of seven members appointed by the President for staggered 14-year terms, and a chairman who served 4-year terms. The Board of Governors was given power to confirm the regional bank presidents, as well as system-wide power over interest rates, discounting, reserve requirements, and open market operations. Thus for the first time the Federal Reserve became a true central bank capable of exercising effective control over the nation's monetary policy.

New Deal regulation of the securities industry and financial markets was designed to create greater stability by reducing risk and increasing public confidence in private institutions. When he submitted the "Truth-in-Securities" bill on March 29, 1933 FDR told Congress, "This proposal . . . puts the burden of telling the whole truth on the seller. It should give impetus to honest dealing and thereby bring back public confidence." However, the measure was so poorly drafted that even its sponsor, Congressman Sam Rayburn of Texas, asked for a complete revision.

At Rayburn's and Raymond Moley's request, Harvard law Professor Felix Frankfurter and three of his former students, James Landis, Benjamin Cohen, and Thomas Corcoran, rewrote the bill in three days in early April. Frankfurter and the younger lawyers he called to Roosevelt's attention would help change the character of the New Deal in 1934–35. Unlike the Brains Trust and most others in FDR's original inner circle, these men were all disciples of anti-trust theorist Louis Brandeis. They distrusted big business, and believed concentrated economic power threatened democracy. The Securities Act of 1933 which they authored rightly presumed that investment fraud was a fairly commonplace occurrence. Their law was designed to prevent fraud by requiring companies to register all new issues of stocks and bonds with the Federal Trade Commission. It compelled issuing corporations to make "full and fair" disclosure of all relevant financial information about the new issues and the companies involved in them. Franklin Roosevelt wrote one worried friend in Boston, "it will not hurt any honest seller of securities," but this unprecedented intervention into financial markets distressed investment bankers, sending the first really strong signal that the New Deal might act in ways contrary to wishes of the business community.

President Roosevelt had postponed exchange regulation during the Hundred Days because he feared it would arouse a storm of protest among the nation's financiers. FDR's fears were justified. In December 1933 Ben Cohen and Tom Corcoran drafted a securities exchange bill which gave the Federal Trade Commission the power to separate brokers and dealers, regulate margin requirements, and force the disclosure of detailed financial information on all publicly traded securities. FDR sent this bill to Congress on February 9, 1934, saying "it should be our national policy to restrict . . . the use of these exchanges for purely speculative operations." Richard Whitney, president of the New York Stock Exchange, responded immediately by setting up committees opposed to the bill in cities around the United States, and by moving to Washington to personally direct the operations of this *ad hoc* organization. Other prominent businessmen who had supported the New Deal until now, including Sears Roebuck chairman Robert Wood, also registered immediate opposition.

Hoping to appease these opponents of exchange regulation, FDR asked Cohen and Corcoran to redraft the bill in early March. The new bill shifted jurisdiction over margin requirements to the Federal Reserve and weakened some mandatory disclosure requirements, but it was greeted by even more strident opposition. Richard Whitney's committees bombarded Congress with letters and telegrams opposing the measure. A group of 28 leading industrialists proclaimed the bill would put American business "under the strangling regulation of a Federal bureau." James Rand, chairman of Remington Rand, went even further, telling Sam Rayburn's House Commerce Committee that the bill was a step "down the road from Democracy to Communism."

Big business' ferocious campaign against the securities exchange bill backfired. FDR sent a letter to congressional committee chairmen emphasizing the bill's importance and his unwillingness to make any more compromises. The President also intervened when significant discrepancies between the House and Senate versions of the bill threatened to hold up passage. The Securities Exchange Act which FDR signed on June 6, 1934 established strict federal regulation of the securities industry. It set up a five-person Securities and Exchange Commission (SEC) to enforce the new regulations as well as those set forth in the Securities Act of 1933.

The President outraged his liberal advisors when he named millionaire Democrat Joseph Kennedy (who had given him great assistance during the 1932 campaign) first chairman of the SEC. FDR joked that he was going to "set a thief to catch a thief." But Kennedy rewarded the President's confidence in him. He used his insider knowledge to educate the commission's staff. Kennedy encouraged fellow commissioner James Landis to develop the SEC's administrative law, and supported staff lawyer William O. Douglas' investigation of corporate reorganizations. He also tried to convince Wall Street that it had nothing fear from federal regulations which built public confidence in the securities business.

A bitter fight over the administration's public utility holding company bill undermined Kennedy's public relations campaign in 1935. Franklin Roosevelt had long believed high rates charged by private companies were discouraging rapid electrification. Already he had championed public hydroelectric power development in New York and the Tennessee Valley. FDR was particularly gratified that TVA was forcing private companies to lower their electric rates. By 1935 the President was ready to abolish public utility holding companies which he believed imposed unnecessary charges upon the consuming public.

Sixteen giant utility holding companies controlled more than 90 percent of the nation's electric power output in 1929. The largest of these, Associated Gas & Electric, itself controlled 40 other smaller holding companies. Holding company pyramids had been the subject of FTC and congressional investigations since 1930. Tom Corcoran and Ben Cohen used material from these investigations when they wrote the administration's regulatory bill. President Roosevelt himself insisted that Title I instruct the SEC to dissolve all holding companies unless they proved, in his words, "absolutely necessary to the continued functioning of a geographically integrated operating utility system." Title II ordered the Federal Power Commission to work with private companies to set up regional power systems based on efficiency, not financial speculation.

The industry waged an all-out campaign to prevent federal regulation by focusing their attention on the so-called "death sentence" provision in Title I. Once again, Wendell Wilkie, chairman of Commonwealth and Southern, led the opposition to the New Deal's electric power policy. In May Wilkie charged the administration was trying "to 'nationalize' the power business in this country." Wilkie's remarks set the tone for the remainder of this fierce political battle. Power companies pulled out all the stops, sending 660 lobbyists to Washington and paying for hundreds of thousands of telegrams to individual Congressmen. This massive lobbying effort rallied the business community, but failed to block the bill. Hugo Black chaired a Senate investigation of the power lobby that revealed widespread fraud in the telegram barrage. Soon after these revelations, the President speeded passage of the measure by compromising on the "death sentence" provision. The compromise exempted holding companies controlling power systems that the government judged to be well integrated, and it postponed the deadline for compliance from 1940 to 1942.

The Public Utilities Holding Company Act (PUHC) took effect in August 1935, but the industry continued to resist it. All across the country, utility companies initiated lawsuits to block SEC regulation. This strategy delayed enforcement for several years, but after the Supreme Court upheld the constitutionality of PUHC, the SEC proceeded to regulate and reduce the size of holding companies in the power industry. Industry lawsuits designed to thwart this process were still working their way through the courts in the late 1940s.

The activities of the SEC epitomized the rise of anti-trust liberals within the administration. After Joseph Kennedy stepped down as SEC chairman in September 1935, a series of liberal lawyers including James Landis, William O. Douglas, and Jerome Frank filled the post. These men directed the SEC's fight to regulate public utilities. They also forced reform upon America's securities industry. After 1935, SEC investigations and prosecutions initiated by Landis, Douglas, and Frank served as constant reminders of the new more liberal character of the New Deal. William O. Douglas proclaimed "the time is past when the country's exchanges can be operated as private clubs," and he meant it. The SEC imposed uniform rules and accounting procedures, and cracked down on in-

sider trading and the use of fraudulent information in securities dealings.

Securities exchange and public utilities regulation marked a
turning point in the political history of the New Deal. Never
again would FDR be able to count on the kind of broad cross-
class coalition that had helped him during his first year in
office. But equally important, after 1934 FDR no longer had
to rely on business class support to continue the New Deal's
reconstruction of American capitalism. Voters sent more
Democrats, including unprecedented numbers of urban liberals, to Washington in November 1934. Those urban liberals
made the 74th Congress more willing than its predecessor to
fulfill Franklin Roosevelt's promises to redistribute income,
promote the workers' rights, and provide economic security
for all Americans.

FURTHER READING

Primary Sources

Dudley, William. *The Great Depression: Opposing Viewpoints*. San Diego:
    Greenhaven Press, 1994.
Eccles, Marriner S. *Beckoning Frontiers: Public and Personal Recollections*.
    New York: Alfred A. Knopf, 1951.
Fleischauer, Carl and Brannan, Beverly W. *Documenting America 1935–
    1943*. Berkeley: University of California Press, 1988.
Freedman, Max ed. *Roosevelt and Frankfurter: Their Correspondence, 1928–
    1945*. Boston: Little, Brown and Company, 1967.
Ickes, Harold L. *The Secret Diary of Harold L. Ickes: The First Thousand
    Days 1933–1936*. New York: Simon and Shuster, 1954.
Louchheim, Katie ed. *The Making of the New Deal: The Insiders Speak*.
    Cambridge: Harvard University Press, 1983.
Moley, Raymond. *After Seven Years*. New York: Harper & Brothers, 1939.
Perkins, Frances. *The Roosevelt I Knew*. New York: Viking, 1946.
Roosevelt, Eliot. *F. D. R.: His Personal Letters 1928–1945*. New York:
    Duell, Sloan and Pearce, 1950.
Roosevelt, Franklin Delano. *The Public Papers and Addresses of Franklin
    D. Roosevelt, Volume Two: The Year of Crisis 1933*. New York, Ran-
    dom House, 1938.
Roosevelt, Franklin Delano. *The Public Papers and Addresses of Franklin*

D. Roosevelt, Volume Three: The Advances of Recovery and Reform 1934. New York: Random House, 1938.

Roosevelt, Franklin Delano. *The Public Papers and Addresses of Franklin D. Roosevelt, Volume Four: The Court Disapproves 1935.* New York: Random House, 1938.

Roosevelt, Franklin Delano. *The Public Papers and Addresses of Franklin D. Roosevelt, Volume Five: The People Approve 1936.* New York: Random House, 1938.

Seligman, Lester G. and Cornwall, Elmer E. *New Deal Mosaic: Roosevelt Confers with his National Emergency Council, 1933–1936.* Eugene: University of Oregon Books, 1965.

Zinn, Howard ed. *New Deal Thought.* Indianapolis: Bobbs-Merill, 1966.

Secondary Sources

Bellush, Bernard. *The Failure of the NRA.* New York: Norton, 1975.

Blum, John Morton. *From the Morgenthau Diaries: Years of Crisis, 1928–1938.* Boston: Houghton Mifflin, 1959.

Burns, Helen M. *The American Banking Community and New Deal Reforms, 1933–1935.* Westport: Greenwood, 1974.

Gordon, Colin. *New Deals: Business, Labor, and Politics in America, 1920–1935.* New York: Cambridge University Press, 1994.

Irons, Peter H. *The New Deal Lawyers.* Princeton: Princeton University Press, 1982.

Hawley, Ellis. *The New Deal and the Problem of Monopoly.* Princeton: Princeton University Press, 1966.

McConnell, Grant. *The Decline of Agrarian Democracy.* Berkeley: University of California Press, 1953.

Perkins, Van L. *Crisis in Agriculture: The AAA and the New Deal.* Berkeley: University of California Press, 1969.

Parrish, Michael. *Securities Regulation and the New Deal.* New Haven: Yale University Press, 1970.

Schwarz, Jordan A. *New Dealers: Power Politics in the Age of Roosevelt.* New York: Random House, 1993.

9

Mass Movements and New Deal Liberalism

"During this period in 1934 and 1935 . . . countless voters were in the ugly frame of mind brought on by the hardships of the depression. They were ready for rash action under a reckless leader."

James A. Farley, Behind the Ballots (1938)

From National Unity to Social Justice Politics

In March 1933 President Roosevelt had defined the Great Depression as a national emergency which could be resolved only if Congress united behind his legislative proposals. FDR's immediate aims – to restore economic stability and social order – were basically conservative. Nearly everyone in Congress shared these goals so compromises between liberals and conservatives were achieved swiftly. The first New Deal of 1933 saved American capitalism by rescuing banks and property owners, rushing relief to the poor, and imposing risk reduction programs on agriculture, industry, and finance. At a uniquely frightening moment in their nation's history, the vast majority of Americans had rallied behind these unprecedented federal interventions in the economy.

Yet national unity soon gave way to bitter partisan politics which divided the country along ideological and class lines. By mid-1934 widespread business resistance to federal regulation of financial markets and NRA-mandated labor standards had heartened conservative politicians, newspaper editors, and political commentators. During the summer months preceding that year's congressional elections, conservatives attacked the New Deal for promoting budget deficits, wasteful relief programs, regimentation of economic markets, and labor policies that crippled American business. Many conservative spokesmen also accused FDR of harboring dictatorial ambitions. The rise of this well-financed and widely publicized conservative opposition to the New Deal gradually convinced Franklin Roosevelt to abandon his national unity political strategy. During those same months, rapidly growing mass movements for what contemporaries called "social justice" influenced the President's new strategy and agenda. By early 1935 FDR had committed himself to a New Deal that pitted the interests of urban working people and farm families against America's wealthiest individuals and most powerful corporations.

President Roosevelt first spoke of a new more liberal agenda in a fireside chat on June 28, 1934. He told Americans that "the security of the men, women and children of the nation" was the guiding principle for the development of new legislation. The President promised the New Deal would provide "social insurance," measures to guarantee "the means of livelihood of our citizens may be more adequate to meet their daily needs," and "added means of providing better homes." This fireside chat signaled a change of course for the New Deal away from the economic stabilization issues that dominated FDR's first year in office, and towards the momentous social justice legislation of 1935 that historians call "the second New Deal."

The political circumstances of 1934–35 created a golden opportunity for ardent liberals in Congress to advance their agenda. Franklin Roosevelt also wanted to enact liberal legislation, but he was reluctant to abandon national unity politics. FDR recognized the political risks involved in pushing a social justice agenda which included an economic security program, steeply progressive taxes, and federal protection for labor unions. He was sure Republicans and the nation's overwhelmingly conservative press would charge him with inciting class conflict. Roosevelt also feared splitting his Democratic Party. If he pressed too hard for liberal legislation extending federal authority over issues previously reserved to the states and private employers, FDR knew conservative Democrats (especially numerous in southern delegation in Congress) would rebel against his leadership.

President Roosevelt tried to minimize these risks by claiming he had the support of "the people" while his opponents remained a tiny anti-democratic elite. "It is true that the toes of some people are being stepped on and are going to be stepped he on," he admitted in his June 1934 fireside chat. "But these toes belong to the comparative few who seek to gain position or riches or both by some shortcut which is harmful to the greater good." In that same speech Roosevelt also anticipated the conservative charge that he had embraced radicalism. "A few timid people who fear progress, will try to give you new and strange names for what we are doing," he told his radio audience,

> Sometimes they will call it "Fascism," sometimes "Communism," sometimes "regimentation," sometimes "Socialism." But in doing so, they are trying to make very complex and theoretical something that is really very simple and practical.

This fireside chat reveals FDR's continued wariness of ideologically divisive politics. Yet even as he spoke, political developments in the country beyond his control were converging to establish the conditions necessary for enactment of a more liberal New Deal.

The improving economy still left tens of millions of Americans poor and insecure. In these circumstances retirees, poor farmers, and working people organized around demands for economic security, income redistribution, and federal protection for unions. FDR realized that if he did not assume leadership of this potential majority, someone else might do so. In this sense, mass movements for social justice had a much greater influence over the content and timing of the second New Deal of 1935 than they had exercised over the first New Deal.

Older Americans formed the core constituency of one of the most influential new social justice movements. Dr. Francis Townsend, the health commissioner of Long Beach, California, founded Old Age Revolving Pensions Limited in January

1934. Townsend wanted the federal government to impose a 2 percent gross income tax on all workers in order to finance monthly payments of $200 to all retired persons over 60 years old. Payments would be continued as long as recipients spent every dollar received within 30 days. Townsend thought his plan would both end the Depression and promote greater social equality. Older Americans who lived in small cities and towns flocked to meetings organized by his supporters. By the summer of 1935, there were 4,500 local Townsend clubs with perhaps 2,000,000 dues paying members. The movement's political lobbying insured inclusion of an old-age pension plan in the administration's economic security bill. FDR told Frances Perkins, chair of his Committee on Economic Security, "We have to have it [pensions]. The Congress can't stand the pressure of the Townsend Plan unless we have a real old-age insurance system."

The Townsend movement was just one of many social justice movements that flourished during the mid-1930s. Each of these movements challenged New Dealers to make good their promise of a more democratic capitalism. West Coast campaigns to put unemployed people to work in empty factories and on deserted farms so that they could sell their production in their own stores attracted millions of voters. "Production-for-use" was a central tenet of the Commonwealth Builders who controlled Washington State's Democratic Party, and of novelist Upton Sinclair's campaign for California's governorship. Sinclair shocked party leaders when he won the 1934 Democratic primary on a platform called EPIC (End Poverty in California). Like most social justice reformers, Upton Sinclair believed "the present depression is one of abundance, not scarcity." Thus he favored steeply progressive taxes as well as state operation of idle industrial plants where unemployed workers could produce goods "for their own use."

Production-for-use had some support among New Dealers. Harry Hopkins' FERA enrolled 30,000 people in small production-for-use projects that turned out such things as mattresses, brooms, and maple syrup in 1934–35. Moreover FDR was charmed by Upton Sinclair when the two met at

Hyde Park. Nonetheless, after Raymond Moley denounced production-for-use as "a call for a blessed retreat – back beyond industrial civilization" in an editorial in *Today* magazine, the President refused to support his party's nominee for governor in California. Without FDR's help, Upton Sinclair's campaign floundered. Movie mogul Louis B. Mayer, California's Republican Party chairman, delivered a fatal blow to EPIC in a media blitz featuring fake newsreels, fake photographs, and forged affidavits portraying Sinclair as an atheistic communist who favored "free love" and the opening California to America's homeless people.

FDR's refusal to aid Upton Sinclair reflected his usual political caution. The President also adopted a circumspect response to the tumultuous campaigns of labor unions for social justice. Union-organizing drives inspired by Section 7(a) of the National Industrial Recovery Act gained momentum as the national economy improved during the spring of 1934. Older industrial unions such as the United Mine Workers, Amalgamated Clothing Workers, and International Ladies Garment Workers rebuilt memberships that had disintegrated during the 1920s. At the same time, worker-activists (including many veterans of the Unemployed Councils) began building new organizations in the automobile, rubber, electrical equipment, steel, and other major industries. Hundreds of thousands workers signed up with these newly formed industrial unions hoping to win from employers recognition that would include the right to bargain for wage increases, greater control over working conditions, and an end to the arbitrary authority of foremen.

Strikes were initiated when employers refused to bargain with growing unions. Over 1,500,000 workers walked off their jobs in more than 1,800 disputes during 1934. The militancy of so many workers and the political radicalism of many industrial union organizers frightened most businessmen and editorial writers. Conservative craft unions leaders of the American Federation of Labor such as Metal Trades' vice-president John Frey and Carpenters' Union president William Hutcheson were also alarmed by the new militancy of industrial workers. But United Mine Workers' president John L. Lewis saw the growing workers' revolt a great opportunity to build up the power of organized labor. By 1935 he was ready to split from the AFL and lead a new labor federation which would support industrial unionism and mass strikes.

Divisions among labor's leaders and anti-union news stories that highlighted the radicalism of union organizers made Franklin Roosevelt especially cautious. Throughout 1934 he tried to preserve NRA's cooperative model of industrial relations rather than endorsing a collective bargaining system which presumed conflict between bosses and workers. In March the President prevented a threatened strike against General Motors by establishing an Automobile Labor Board to "pass on all questions of representation, discharge, and discrimination." FDR described his action as "charting a new course in social engineering in the United States," but it merely won a little time for a cooperative approach which neither management nor unions really wanted. Two months later the failure of FDR's automobile labor policy was demonstrated when pickets and a huge crowd of supporters battled more than 1,000 police and Ohio National Guardsmen in the streets outside a struck auto parts plant in Toledo.

In 1933–35 most strike-related violence occurred because employers defied Section 7(a) of the National Industrial Recovery Act. FDR's refusal to insist on compliance with NRA's unprecedented guarantee of the right of workers to form independent unions abetted corporate resistance to labor's organizing campaigns. American companies spent tens of millions of dollars hiring labor spies and private police, and stockpiling small arms and tear gas during the NRA years. Workers who struck to gain union recognition were frequently fired and replaced by strikebreakers. When this occurred picketing workers and their supporters tried to stop the introduction of strikebreakers. More often than not, as was the case in Toledo, police and/or the National Guard intervened to break picket lines and protect strikebreakers.

During the summer of 1934 newly organized workers and anti-union employers battled in increasingly violent strikes.

Street fighting between striking truck drivers and strikebreaking forces repeatedly paralyzed the city of Minneapolis. The worst incident occurred on July 20th when police shot 67 strike supporters in a downtown ambush. That same month a long walkout by West Coast longshoremen brought violent class conflict to San Francisco. Two pickets and a bystander were shot dead and at least 115 other people were wounded by police and strikebreakers who forced open the port on July 5th. The next day angry workers convinced the city's Labor Council to endorse a general strike. The following Monday, tens of thousands of strike supporters walked through downtown San Francisco in a funeral procession for the slain workers. At least 130,000 workers stayed away from their jobs during the next week. The city's leading newspapers applauded strikebreaking efforts of employers' associations, vigilante groups, police, and the National Guard while accusing strike leaders of fomenting revolution. Hugh Johnson, the soon-to-be-fired head of NRA, endorsed this conservative reaction in speech at the University of California, but a vacationing FDR followed the advice of his cool-headed Labor Secretary Frances Perkins and remained silent.

On September 1, 1934 over 400,000 textile workers struck hundreds of mills in New England and the South. National Guardsmen and thousands of special deputies were deployed in mill towns in every New England state except Vermont and New Hampshire, as well as in every Southern state from Virginia to Mississippi. During the first week of the strike, at least 16 pickets were shot dead and scores of others were wounded by this strikebreaking army. FDR had no choice but to intervene in what was the biggest interstate strike since 1919. On September 5th, he appointed a Board of Inquiry headed by New Hampshire's Governor John Winant. The textile workers' walkout and repressive violence continued for two weeks while the Winant Board investigated the dispute. The Board finally recommended creation of a special labor relations commission for the industry, but refused to endorse union recognition or condemn employers for failing to abide by Section 7(a). Questions involving the rehiring of strikers, wages, and improvements to working conditions were all deferred. As a result, the great textile workers' strike of 1934 failed completely, and the new United Textile Workers union collapsed. Once again FDR had avoided a confrontation with the business class over federal support for collective bargaining while allowing employers to destroy a popular new union.

It was Senator Robert Wagner of New York, not Franklin Roosevelt, who took the lead in trying to fashion an effective liberal response to the latest round of America's labor wars. As chairman of the NRA's impotent National Labor Board Wagner realized that bloody labor conflict would continue, and most unions would fail, unless the federal government established and enforced workers' rights and strict rules for channeling industrial relations into orderly collective bargaining. Wagner wanted to create a new regulatory agency to achieve these goals. Senator Wagner and his chief of staff, Leon Keyserling, also believed strong unions would promote economic recovery by redistributing corporate income, putting more of it in the hands of workers who had a high propensity to consume.

In March 1934 Robert Wagner introduced his national labor relations bill in the Senate. Although FDR told reporters off the record on May 25th, "I am in favor of this legislation and hope it will go through," he really feared the Wagner bill would increase business opposition to the New Deal. The President asked Wagner to support a weak substitute proposal. Wagner demonstrated his loyalty to the President by withdrawing his bill and supporting FDR's substitute. That curiously named Public Resolution Number 44 was enacted on June 18th. Although the National Labor Relations Board (NLRB) it created could hold elections to certify unions as representing a majority of a company's work force, Public Resolution Number 44 did not force employers to respect workers' rights or accept collective bargaining. Just as Robert Wagner expected, it failed to diminish the intensity of labor conflict in America.

Franklin Roosevelt refused to support Senator Wagner's labor relations bill in 1934 because he had not yet given up on the NRA. He also thought strong pro-union legislation would hurt

Democrats in the upcoming November elections. Republicans and conservative Democrats were already describing the Wagner bill as a capitulation to labor violence and radicalism. In truth, what Robert Wagner proposed – establishment of the workers' right to join unions, the unions' right to represent workers in collective bargaining, the right to strike employers who failed to bargain in good faith, and penalties for companies who interfered with these rights – was indeed a radical change in America's labor law. Franklin Roosevelt recognized the potentially disruptive significance of the Wagner bill, and for more than a year he refused to endorse its passage.

FDR also worried about other mass movements in 1934–35. Democratic Senator Huey Long seemed to pose the most direct political threat to the President. Huey Long had supported the New Deal in 1933, but made no secret of his presidential ambitions. Louisiana's "Kingfish" announced formation of his Share Our Wealth Society in the first of many nationally broadcast speeches in February 1934. Long's campaign was based on the simple premise that the Depression had been caused by a gross maldistribution of the nation's wealth. Its slogan was "Every Man a King." Huey Long claimed he could end the Depression and guarantee every family an American standard of living (including a home of their own) by redistributing wealth and income. He proposed taxes that would prevent families from owning more than $5,000,000 in wealth and individuals from earning more than $1,000,000 a year.

Long's Share Our Wealth movement grew swiftly in Louisiana and Arkansas, and then spread through the rest of the South. It also established significant memberships in the upper Midwest, New York and California. Share Our Wealth clubs were usually led by local politicians who spoke for the lower middle class, small farmers, and skilled workers. By mid-1935, more than 27,000 Share Our Wealth clubs claimed over 4,600,000 members. Although this membership figure was undoubtedly exaggerated, the still-impressive growth of the Share Our Wealth movement demonstrated that many Americans now favored redistributive tax policies. The Share Our

Wealth movement also created a springboard for Huey Long's expected presidential bid in 1936.[1]

Huey Long's redistributive message was amplified by the amazing rise of Detroit's radio priest, Father Charles Coughlin. Although he too had been a Roosevelt supporter, Father Coughlin turned against the New Deal after Roosevelt ignored his advice. In series of weekly broadcasts in November 1934, Coughlin began telling his mostly Catholic listeners in the Northeast and Midwest that the New Deal was not sufficiently committed to social justice. "It may boast that it has driven the money changers from the temple," Coughlin exclaimed, "but it permits industry to cling tenaciously to the cast-off philosophy of the money changers." The radio priest announced formation of a National Union for Social Justice, pledging he would organize millions of men and women to force the government to guarantee "an annual wage system that is just and equitable and thus permit American workmen to preserve the American standard of living."

By early 1935, when up to 30,000,000 Americans were tuning into his weekly radio speeches, Father Coughlin appeared ready to join forces with Huey Long and oppose FDR's re-election. The potential power of a Long–Coughlin alliance was demonstrated when FDR sent to the Senate a proposal to have the United States join the World Court. Since World Court membership required ratification of treaties that isolationists had blocked since 1920, Roosevelt anticipated considerable opposition. But he also believed the huge Democratic majority in the upper House assured ratification. FDR's expectations were confounded by Senator Long's outspoken opposition and the extraordinary influence of the radio priest. On Sunday January 27th, just two days before the vote on the World Court, Father Coughlin vehemently denounced the initiative in a broadcast sermon that invoked the psalms, George Washington, the specter of communism, a conspiracy of international bankers, and fear of war. "Instead of guaranteeing a just and living wage to every laborer who is willing to contribute honest work," Coughlin warned,

America is ready to join hands with the Rothschilds and Lazere Freres, with the Warburgs and Morgans and Kuhn and Loebs to keep the world safe for the inevitable slaughter.

After Coughlin's diatribe, senators received 50,000 telegrams denouncing U.S. membership in the World Court. When they voted on Tuesday, a 52 to 36 majority approved FDR's proposal, seven short of the two-thirds needed for ratification.

A few days after the World Court vote, in a letter to Henry Stimson, a Republican supporter of World Court membership who had served as both Secretary of War and Secretary of State, Roosevelt observed "these are not normal times; people are jumpy and very ready to run after strange gods. This is so in every other country as well as our own." FDR's comments reflect his recognition that the strong political forces currently on the rise in America might not move the country in a democratic direction, and that it was part of his responsibility as President to lead people away from the "strange gods" who seemed to be gaining ever-larger followings.

The Right Moment for Reform

President Roosevelt took an extraordinary 10,000 mile journey in the summer of 1934. He began by sailing on the *U.S.S. Houston* from Annapolis across the Caribbean to Colombia where he extolled his administration's "Good Neighbor" policy towards Latin America. The *Houston* then took the President through the Panama Canal to Hawaii and back to Portland, Oregon. Joined there by Louis Howe, Eleanor, and three sons, FDR returned by rail to Hyde Park via the northern tier of states and Chicago. On that return trip, Roosevelt toured the monumental new federal hydroelectric dam projects at Bonneville and Grand Coulee on the Columbia River and Fort Peck on the Missouri River, proclaiming them "Government yardsticks so that the people of this country will know whether they are paying the proper price for electricity." He also visited areas devastated by drought, promising "If it is possible for us to solve the problem, we are going to do it." Everywhere FDR was greeted by wildly enthusiastic crowds. He seemed to be reviving his image as the leader of a united America. However, when he stopped in Green Bay, Wisconsin, FDR described a businessman's letter calling for a return to *laissez-faire* government as evidence that a deep ideological divide now separated his administration from business class conservatives. "My friends, if we were to listen to him and his type," Roosevelt explained, "the old law of the tooth and the claw would reign in our Nation again."

The formation of the American Liberty League that summer emphasized the class character of the New Deal's most outspoken opponents. The Liberty League was created by a group of conservative Democrats including former presidential candidates Al Smith and John W. Davis and some of the country's leading businessmen – among them Alfred P. Sloan of General Motors, Sewell Avery of Montgomery Ward, oil magnate Howard Pew, and Pierre and Irenee Dupont. With the generous support of wealthy Americans the Liberty League disseminated anti-New Deal propaganda throughout the nation. The League claimed it had a non-partisan mission "to teach the duty of government to protect individual and group initiative and enterprise." However, its publications and principal spokesmen attacked the Roosevelt administration for its economic failures and alleged radicalism.

Privately Liberty League members expressed what reporter Marquis Childs described as "a consuming personal hatred of President Roosevelt and, to an almost equal degree, of Mrs. Roosevelt." In fact Eleanor Roosevelt's feminist independence, and her highly publicized visits to factories, coal mines, working class neighborhoods, and African-American communities especially offended high society's matrons. By 1936 Childs found false rumors about heavy drinking and dissipated living at the White House, and even insanity among the Roosevelts were regular cocktail party fare among East Coast and Midwest elites. Although the Liberty League never had more than 125,000 active members, for two years it sustained high profile attacks on the New Deal which left no hope of restoring the coalition politics of 1933.

The Liberty League's heavily advertised appeal to "Save the Constitution" seemed to have little impact on the 1934 congressional elections. An unusually large number of citizens cast ballots that November, confounding pundits who had expected low turnout and something like the usual gains for the party out of power in a mid-term elections. Instead voters sent many new liberal Democrats as well as ten Left-leaning independents to Congress. Overall Democrats established a better than three-to-one margin over Republicans in the House, and won nine new seats in Senate. The results were a ringing endorsement of the New Deal and FDR's promise of more liberal reforms.

By early 1935 FDR's administration had also been infused with new liberal blood. Although the Cabinet was unchanged, key administrators who had done so much to contain New Deal liberalism – especially Budget Director Lewis Douglas, NRA's Hugh Johnson, and AAA's George Peek – had all departed. Raymond Moley, the most conservative member of the original Brains Trust, still wrote occasional speeches for FDR, but he had returned to New York disillusioned by the rise of anti-big business liberals within Roosevelt's inner circle. Adolph Berle also had returned to New York, however, he remained more active as a special advisor who favored income redistribution. Of the original Brains Trust, only Undersecretary of Agriculture Rexford Tugwell stayed on in Washington. Finally Louis Howe, FDR's oldest and most trusted political advisor also remained in Washington, but as invalid confined at first to a room upstairs in the White House and then to a bed in Walter Reed Hospital (where the President often visited him before his death in April 1936).

A new inner circle of presidential advisors formed at the White House in 1934–36. Their agenda was far more liberal than the group they replaced. Lawyers Tom Corcoran and Ben Cohen were especially interested in curbing the power of big corporations, while former social workers Harry Hopkins and Frances Perkins wanted to create more work relief jobs and a comprehensive economic security program. Samuel Rosenman, the liberal New York judge who had been FDR's counsel in Albany, also returned as the President's chief speech writer and a trusted legal advisor. Perhaps most importantly, Eleanor Roosevelt increasingly appeared in speeches, magazine articles, and her own newspaper column as the New Deal's most visible advocate for working women, poor children, and racial minorities.

Eleanor Roosevelt was the President's liberal conscience, and his emissary to America's working people. "Our country as a whole and each one of us as an individual cannot be secure until we have taken care of our less fortunate brothers and sisters," she wrote in 1933. The First Lady acted on these beliefs. She spent many months each year visiting "less fortunate" Americans wherever they lived and worked, spreading the message that government in Washington cared about them. When in residence at the White House, she invited reporters, trade unionists, and reformers to dinners with the President to make sure he knew the real conditions of working people's lives. In short, Eleanor Roosevelt never let her husband forget that the New Deal was committed to economic security and social justice for all Americans.

Thanks largely to the efforts of Eleanor Roosevelt and Harold Ickes, and to the increasingly effective National Association for the Advancement of Colored People and the Urban League, black Americans established a presence within the administration at this time. Responding to criticism that the New Deal "was not always fair to the Negro race," Eleanor Roosevelt told an Urban League convention that racial discrimination "is not the intention of those at the top, and as far as possible I hope that we may work together to eliminate any real injustice." By 1936 over 50 African-Americans, including future Housing Secretary Robert Weaver and future UN ambassador Ralph Bunche, had been appointed to important positions in Cabinet departments and New Deal agencies. To increase their influence these officials formed the Federal Council on Negro Affairs, a group reporters dubbed "the black cabinet." The black cabinet met on Friday nights at the home of Mary McLeod Bethune, an educator, founder of the National Council on Negro Women, and assistant director of the

National Youth Administration (an agency set up in June 1935 to provide work and educational opportunities to unemployed young people). At the invitation of her friend Eleanor Roosevelt, Mary Bethune visited the White House six or seven times a year, bringing specific suggestions for making federal programs non-discriminatory to the President's attention. As Robert Weaver later recalled, "My younger associates and I developed and analyzed program proposals. She articulated and dramatized them." This process was still a long way from the direct exercise of policy-making power. Nonetheless Mary Bethune and the black cabinet helped prompt the Roosevelt administration to make the first genuine effort to establish racial equality in the federal government since Reconstruction.

The results of the congressional elections of 1934 energized both liberal New Dealers and their supporters in Congress. Harry Hopkins told his staff, "Boys – this is our hour . . . Get your minds to work on developing a complete ticket to provide security for all the folks of this country up and down and across the board." Hopkins presented his ideas about expanded work relief and resettlement programs to Franklin Roosevelt at Warm Springs just after Thanksgiving. As winter approached, the President's special Committee on Economic Security, appointed in June, finished its proposal for comprehensive national social insurance. At the same time Treasury Secretary Morgenthau's staff was working out the details of a much more progressive tax code, while Ben Cohen and Tom Corcoran put the final touches on the public utilities holding company bill. November's election results had also encouraged the Senate's leading urban liberal, Robert Wagner of New York. During the winter months his staff redrafted the national labor relations bill and a new proposal to replace urban slums with low-cost government-built housing.

By 1935 millions of citizens had demonstrated their desire for federal programs that would mitigate the insecurities and inequalities of American capitalism. Advised by ardent liberals within his own administration, Franklin Roosevelt prepared to welcome a very liberal Congress to Washington. FDR recognized that he might never again have such supportive majorities in Congress. Yet Roosevelt also knew that pushing hard for federally guaranteed economic security for everyone risked setting middle class moderates as well as conservatives against him when he stood for re-election. Thus as the new year dawned FDR found himself ready to propose a second New Deal, but not quite ready to fight hard for its enactment.

FURTHER READING

Primary Sources

Buhite, Russell D. and Levy, David W. *FDR's Fireside Chats*. Norman: University of Oklahoma Press, 1992.

Coughlin, Charles. *Series of Lectures on Social Justice*. Royal Oak, Michigan: Shrine of the Little Flower, 1935.

Dudley, William ed. *The Great Depression: Opposing Viewpoints*. San Diego: Greenhaven Press, 1994.

Farley, James A. *Behind the Ballots: The Personal History of a Politician*. New York: Harcourt Brace, 1938.

Long, Huey Pierce. *My First Days in the White House*. Harrisburg: Telegraph Press, 1935.

Perkins, Frances. *The Roosevelt I Knew*. New York: Viking, 1946.

Roosevelt, Eleanor. *What I Hope to Leave: The Essential Essays of Eleanor Roosevelt*. Brooklyn: Carlson Publishers, 1995.

Roosevelt, Elliot. *F. D. R.: His Personal Letters 1928–1945*. New York: Duell, Sloan, and Pearce, 1950.

Simon, Rita James. *As We Saw the Thirties: Essays on Social and Political Movements of a Decade*. Urbana: University of Illinois Press, 1967.

Secondary Sources

Bernstein, Irving. *Turbulent Years: A History of the American Worker, 1933–1941*. Boston: Houghton Mifflin, 1971.

Brinkley, Alan. *Voices of Protest: Huey Long, Father Coughlin, and the Great Depression*. New York: Random House, 1982.

Davis, Kenneth S. *FDR: The New Deal Years 1933–1937*. New York: Random House, 1979.

Irons, Peter. *The New Deal Lawyers*. Princeton, Princeton University Press, 1982.

Mitchell, Greg. *The Campaign of a Century: Upton Sinclair's Race for Cali-*

fornia Governor and the Birth of Media Politics. New York: Random House, 1992.

Schlesinger, Arthur M. Jr. *The Politics of Upheaval.* Boston: Houghton Mifflin, 1960.

Sitkoff, Harvard. *A New Deal for Blacks: The Emergence of Civil Rights as a National Issue.* New York: Oxford University Press, 1978.

Williams, T. Harry. *Huey Long.* New York: Alfred A. Knopf, 1970.

Wolfskill, George. *The Revolt of the Conservatives: A History of the American Liberty League.* Boston: Houghton Mifflin, 1962.

10

The Second New Deal

"Dear President . . . Know you are the one & only President that ever helped a Working Class of People."

A Paris, Texas furniture maker, 1936

Rural Relief

The second New Deal included all of the reforms enacted during the long first session of the 74th Congress including reorganization of the Federal Reserve and the Public Utilities Holding Company Act. But as it is most commonly used today the term "second New Deal" refers especially to the new work relief programs, more progressive taxes, Social Security Act, and National Labor Relations Act that Congress approved between April and August 1935. This social justice legislation comprised the supreme liberal reform achievement of Franklin Roosevelt's presidency.

President Roosevelt asked Congress to create a *permanent* economic security program and greatly expanded but *temporary* federal work relief projects in his Annual Message on January 4, 1935. "The stark fact before us," he admitted, "is that great numbers still remain unemployed." FDR explained that legislation prepared by his Committee on Economic Security would provide a permanent safety net for "those unable to maintain themselves independently." He also recommended work relief instead of the dole for the much larger number of "able-bodied but destitute workers." The President made his case for work relief in terms with which both liberals and conservatives agreed. "Continued dependence upon relief induces a spiritual and moral disintegration fundamentally destructive of the national fiber," he explained.

Calling the dole "a narcotic" and "a subtle destroyer of the human spirit," Roosevelt asked Congress "to make it possible for the United States to give [temporary] employment to all of these three and a half million employable people now on relief, pending their absorption in the rising tide of private employment."

FDR suggested putting the able-bodied unemployed to work clearing slums, building low-cost rural housing, bringing electricity to rural areas, improving highways, and assisting local governments. Yet the work relief bill sent to Congress on January 21st was merely a two-page long request for authority to borrow and spend $4,880,000,000 on relief in a manner to be decided by the President.[1] Neither Harry Hopkins nor Harold Ickes had been consulted during the bill's drafting, nor were they able to clarify the President's intentions when answering questions during congressional committee hearings in late January. Nonetheless, a big majority of House Democrats passed the measure after very little debate on January 24th.

During the next two months senators unwilling to give unlimited authority over so much money to the President amended the bill. The revised measure contained an explicit preference for private over public employment, and a provision setting work relief wages below prevailing local minimums. These conservative amendments insured work relief programs would be temporary, and that their "security wages" would be insufficient to eliminate poverty. Fears that FDR would turn work relief into a new form of presidential patronage inspired another amendment requiring Senate approval of all relief administrators paid more than $5,000 a year. The majority of the Senate also expressed its strong anti-war sentiment by prohibiting work relief agencies from building ships for the Navy (as the Public Works Administration had been doing since 1933).

Franklin Roosevelt signed the Emergency Relief Appropriation Act on April 4th. It took nearly six months to get all the new work relief programs up and running. FDR acted first to consolidate programs to alleviate rural poverty. In early May he transferred existing rural relief programs from the jurisdic-

tion of the FERA, AAA, and the Interior Department to a new
Resettlement Administration (RA). Undersecretary of Agriculture Tugwell was put in charge of the new agency. Dubbed
"Rex the Red" by conservatives who despised his preference
for planned economic development, Tugwell was a favorite
target of congressional opponents of the New Deal. He also
disagreed with presidential advisors like Tommy Corcoran and
Ben Cohen who believed increased competition, not planning,
would solve the nation's economic problems. As a result
Tugwell found it doubly difficult to obtain support for the
kind of resettlement programs he believed would permanently
reduce rural poverty.

Although the Resettlement Administration was supposed
to expedite movement of sharecroppers, tenants, and subsistence farmers from poor land to more productive acreage,
Tugwell actually thought the solution to rural poverty lay in
moving poor farmers into non-agricultural forms of employment. He wanted the RA to build model communities that
would demonstrate the promise of planned suburban and rural development. His staff drew up ambitious proposals during the summer of 1935, but Tugwell could not muster enough
political support to implement them. Only three of nine proposed model suburban towns (Greenbelt, Maryland; Green-
hills, Ohio; and Greendale, Wisconsin) and only one model
rural community were ever built. The RA's model communities received extensive publicity and academic attention, yet
they helped very few people escape rural poverty. Rural resettlement on the land, the RA's major anti-poverty program,
was equally ineffective. The RA and its successor eventually
retired 9,000,000 acres of marginal land from production, but
moved fewer than 5,000 families onto better land.

In February 1937, a few months after a frustrated Rex
Tugwell had left Washington, FDR passed onto Congress the
recommendations of a special committee he had set up to study
the problem of farm tenancy. Southern Democrats took charge
of this legislation, pushing the Bankhead-Jones Farm Tenancy
Act through Congress. It replaced the RA with a new Farm
Security Administration (FSA). The FSA shifted the New Deal's

primary rural relief effort from relocation of sharecroppers and tenants to the provision of credits to these same groups. Tugwell later wrote that the change amounted to giving notice "that the class structure of the South must not be disrupted by federal assistance to sharecroppers and tenants." This assessment of FSA was only partly true. The Farm Security Administration continued to be run by liberals who wanted to improve the lives of the rural poor. But like its predecessor, the FSA never received sufficient funds from Congress to accomplish its mission. By 1941 only 21,000 sharecroppers and tenants – fewer than one in every 20 applicants to the program – had received FSA loans enabling them to purchase their farms.

Both the RA and FSA also provided controversial assistance to migrant farm workers. These agencies built camps in California and other Western states to provide shelter, medical care, cooperative stores, and recreational programs for migrants from the Dust Bowl. By 1942, FSA's 95 California camps housed 75,000 people. Although the FSA's Western migrant camps often served only white "Okies," they were strongly supported by California's liberals. Both the book and film versions of *The Grapes of Wrath* portrayed the FSA camp as a humane alternative to the ramshackle and sometimes brutal compounds run by fruit and vegetable growers. The growers' associations and the state's Republicans strenuously objected, countering with accusations that the government camps were fostering socialism and radical unions. These red-baiting criticisms helped build congressional support for closing down the Farm Security Administration in 1943.

Unlike the RA and FSA, Franklin Roosevelt's other major rural relief initiative, the Rural Electrification Administration (REA), was a huge practical and political success. Using authority established by the Emergency Relief Appropriation Act, President Roosevelt established the REA in May 1935 "to initiate, formulate, administer, and supervise a program of approved projects with respect to the generation, transmission, and distribution of electric energy in rural areas." At the time, nearly 90 percent of America's farms had no electricity because private power companies refused to extend their lines into thinly settled areas. The industry, already up in arms over the administration's public utilities holding company bill, insisted the high costs of bringing electricity to relatively few customers prevented them from ever turning a profit on rural power delivery. FDR had been a public power advocate since 1928, and he now aimed to prove the industry wrong.

The President called on Morris Cooke to direct the REA. Cooke was a wealthy Philadelphia engineer on whom FDR had long relied for advice on public power issues. Cooke soon found REA's standard work relief rules (especially the requirements that at least 25 percent of spending go to labor, while 90 percent of the labor be drawn from local unemployment rolls) to be impossibly restrictive. In late 1935 Cooke convinced the President that REA would have to become more of a lending agency if it were ever going to deliver electricity to rural areas. But most private companies still wanted no part of rural electrification, even when the REA offered them 40-year loans at very low interest rates. So Cooke adopted the method that TVA already had used to solve a similar problem in the Tennessee Valley. He had REA promote farmer-owned, non-profit electric cooperatives. The cooperatives borrowed from REA the funds they needed to bring electricity to their members. In May 1936, Senator George Norris of Nebraska and Congressman John Rankin of Mississippi pushed legislation through Congress to formalize these changes.

During the next 15 years scores of REA-sponsored rural cooperatives either built lines to distribute electricity from their own hydro-stations or power purchased at wholesale rates from private producers. Although it did not function for long as a work relief program, REA still vindicated FDR's faith in public power development. Congressman Clyde Ellis' whole family gathered at his mother's house in Arkansas' Ozark hills one day in 1940 to see the lights come on. "I remember my mother smiling," he recalled.

> When they came on full, tears started running down her cheeks . . . It was a day of celebration. They had all kinds of parties – mountain people getting light for the first time.

By that year nearly 40 percent of America's farms had electric power. A decade later nine in ten farms were wired for electricity. Thanks to the New Deal, rural America finally entered the age of electricity.

The second New Deal's biggest work relief program, the Works Progress Administration (WPA), also contributed greatly to the modernization of rural America. WPA workers recruited from local relief rolls constructed or renovated thousands of public buildings, water systems, and recreational facilities in small towns across the continent. WPA workers also built or repaired 572,000 miles of rural roads before the program was terminated in 1943. The WPA's "farm to market" road program improved connections between rural families and towns while simultaneously providing desperately needed income to poor farmers. "It was a job, a job for money," recalled Conrad Torso, a farmer in Otter Creek County, Minnesota whose family survived the drought of 1936 because he found work on a WPA road-building crew. All across America's vast hinterland, the story was the same. WPA modernized rural and small town infrastructure while it helped feed millions of poor people. "Farm-to-market roads and the REA changed the life of Texas farmers and ranchers," Congressman Sam Rayburn explained. Rayburn's words were applicable in nearly every agricultural region. The New Deal never eliminated rural poverty, but it offered substantial material assistance to poor people while laying the foundations for vast improvements in rural living standards after 1940.

Urban Relief

Franklin Roosevelt stated the underlying liberal principles which informed all of the New Deal's work relief programs in a fireside chat on September 30, 1934. "No country, however rich, can afford the waste of its human resources," FDR proclaimed.

> Demoralization caused by vast unemployment is our greatest extravagance. Morally, it is the greatest menace to our social order . . . I

stand or fall by my refusal to accept as a necessary condition of our
future a permanent army of the unemployed.

Like his most influential advisors on this issue – Eleanor
Roosevelt, Harry Hopkins, and Frances Perkins – the President clearly believed relief programs should do more than simply prevent starvation. FDR advanced two compelling reasons
why government should act as an employer of last resort in
the mid-1930s. First, work relief could prevent the social problems – alcoholism, domestic violence, broken families, and
crime – that resulted from the "demoralization" of those people who could not find private sector jobs. And secondly, work
relief could put to productive purposes the creative human
labor that would otherwise be wasted by unemployment.

The CCC and all of the second New Deal's work relief programs embodied these principles, but they found their most
imaginative expression in the Works Progress Administration
(WPA). Harry Hopkins, WPA's first director, knew from experience that small public works projects would employ the
largest number of unemployed "breadwinner" males, and that
such projects would be most widely appreciated if they both
originated with, and were visible in, local communities. From
May to September 1935, Hopkins and PWA administrator
Harold Ickes fought a nasty turf battle over what type of
projects WPA would be permitted to build, and who would
control the largest share of the new relief appropriation. FDR
finally decided to fund just 10 percent of the PWA projects
proposed by Ickes, while directing billions of dollars to
Hopkins' WPA.

The WPA replaced FERA but retained its decentralized administration. A small Washington staff and 53 "state" offices
reviewed proposals from local governments and directed funding to approved projects.[2] Unlike the Public Works Administration, the WPA did not use private contractors. WPA hired
(and fired) workers and supervisors for its projects. This feature made WPA vulnerable to Republican charges that WPA
was a gigantic patronage scheme. Democratic bosses such as
Memphis' Edward Crump and Jersey City's Frank Hague did

reward their minions with positions in WPA's state-level administrations, and political favoritism by Democrats undoubtedly influenced some local WPA employment decisions. But this kind of problem cut both ways. Hopkins' office also received complaints about local discrimination against Democrats from places where Republicans remained dominant. What really mattered was the overall efficiency of WPA; it more than offset this kind of predictable political problem. WPA administrative costs averaged just 4 percent of total spending during its first five years. Eighty-nine percent of WPA's 1935–43 expenditures were paid out as wages to people hired off local relief rolls.

The WPA is probably best remembered for the work relief opportunities it provided to unemployed artists. Harry Hopkins had wanted to assist this group ever since the early 1930s when he had witnessed terrible poverty among friends in the arts community of New York City. The special WPA arts programs that Hopkins established in 1935 assisted unemployed artists while simultaneously encouraging their continued creativity. By 1943 tens of thousands of impoverished painters, sculptors, musicians, actors, and writers had earned WPA security wages. Unlike most WPA programs, the Federal Arts, Music, Theatre, and Writers Projects were run directly from Washington. WPA artists, including Jackson Pollock, William Gropper, and Willem de Kooning, produced thousands of murals and pieces of sculpture, and many more paintings, photographs, and posters (which advertised New Deal programs and other government activities). WPA's art teachers taught classes to children and adults at over 100 community arts centers located all around the country. The Federal Music Project also had a national presence. It supported free dances and performances by jazz bands, choral groups, and over 30 orchestras, including an ensemble of all blind performers in Vicksburg, Mississippi. The Federal Writers Project employed about 10,000 people including Saul Bellow, Richard Wright, and Nelson Algren. WPA writers produced a series of state guidebooks which John Steinbeck judged "the most comprehensive account of the United States ever got together," as well as hundreds of government-issued pamphlets. WPA writers also assembled a portrait of American folklife from interviews done with ethnic Americans, poor white Southerners, and former slaves.

The Federal Theater Project (FTP), directed by Hopkins' old friend Hallie Flanagan, was perhaps the New Deal's most controversial program. Previously Flanagan had run experimental theaters at Grinnell and Vassar Colleges. She initially hoped FTP would support five regional theater groups, but the program grew beyond all expectations. At its peak in 1936, FTP plays drew as many as 350,000 people a week to theaters in 28 cities. Ticket prices for performances ranged from 10 cents to a dollar. Federal Theater goers saw productions of classic plays by Shakespeare, Marlowe, Shaw, and O'Neill; children's plays such as *Pinocchio*, and new musicals such as *Sing for Your Supper*. Conservatives in Congress hated the FTP because it financed radical new plays such as Marc Blitzstein's unabashedly Marxist *The Cradle Will Rock*, and a stage adaptation of Sinclair Lewis' anti-fascist novel *It Can't Happen Here* which opened simultaneously in 22 different cities. FTP players also presented "Living Newspapers" which critiqued social conditions and current politics. Swayed by conservative critics who argued it was spreading radical propaganda, Congress terminated the Federal Theater Project in 1939.

While political controversy swirled around the WPA's arts projects, the vast majority of its workers labored to improve local infrastructure. WPA administrators applied three criteria to proposals submitted by local governments for approval. The project had to be clearly useful to the community; the community had to be suffering a high level of unemployment; and sufficient numbers of appropriately skilled unemployed workers (including engineers, supervisors, clerks, and typists as well as laborers and craftsmen) had to be locally available. Local governments picked up most non-labor costs for projects which usually involved the repair, renovation, or construction of roads, water systems, and public buildings (see Figure 10.1). Seventy-seven percent of the 8,500,000 Americans who

Between 1935 and 1943 the Works Progress Administration built
or improved:

- 572,000 miles of rural roads, 67,000 miles of urban streets, and
  31,000 miles of sidewalks.
- 122,000 bridges and 1,000 tunnels.
- 1,050 airfields and 4,000 airport buildings.
- 500 water treatment plants, 1,800 pumping stations, 19,700 miles
  of water mains, 4,000 municipal wells, 3,700 water storage tanks,
  1,500 sewage treatment plants, and 24,000 miles of sewers and
  storm drains.
- 3,300 stadiums, 5,000 athletic fields, 12,800 playgrounds.
- 36,900 schools, 1,000 public libraries.
- 2,552 hospitals, 2,700 firehouses, 900 armories, 760 prison buildings.
- 19,400 other state, county, and local government buildings.
- 416 fish hatcheries and 7,000 miles of firebreaks.

Source: U.S. Federal Works Agency, *Final Report on The WPA Program
1935–43*. Washington: Government Printing Office, 1947.

Figure 10.1   WPA's contribution to infrastructure, 1935–43

had received WPA security wages by 1943 worked on these
kinds of labor-intensive public works projects. Without the
federal funds that WPA provided, most of these permanent
improvements to local infrastructure would never have gotten
off the drawing board.

Republicans attacked WPA projects as "make work"
boondoggles, but supporters greatly outnumbered opponents
in the mid-1930s. Just as Roosevelt and Hopkins had hoped,
WPA helped poor workers to feed their families while also
countering the demoralizing effects of unemployment. Thousands of workers wrote the White House directly to express
their gratitude. "Please continue this W.P.A. program," a man
from Battle Creek, Michigan wrote FDR in 1936, "It makes
us feel like an American citizen to earn our own living." For

many Americans, gratitude for WPA lasted a lifetime. Jane Yoder, who had come close to starving in a central Illinois mining town, remembered "my father immediately got a employed in this WPA. This was a godsend. This was the greatest thing. It meant food, you know. Survival, just survival." Even Ronald Reagan retained a soft spot in his heart for WPA. In his autobiography, *An American Life,* Reagan recalled, "The WPA was one of the most productive of FDR's alphabet soup of agencies because it put people to work building roads, bridges, and other projects."

The political benefits of the WPA were enormous. Edward Santander, a Midwestern teacher, explained that before WPA his "county had been solidly Republican from the Civil War. And then it was Democratic until the end of Truman's time." There is no doubt that WPA played a critical role in what political historians call "the Roosevelt realignment" of the mid-1930s. Tens of millions of Americans saw work relief as the primary example of the federal government doing good things well. Improved roads, bridges, parks and playgrounds, sewers, and water systems made a real difference in people's everyday lives. "I feel in those days they spent every dollar for something they got a dollar's worth out of," recalled Laura Dunlap of Fergus Falls, Minnesota. Conservative Democratic Senator Josiah Bailey of North Carolina, a critic of what he saw as excessive and irresponsible spending on relief, summed up the political implications of this widespread public perception in 1938. "There are just millions of complaints [an exaggeration] . . . about the W.P.A. and other alphabet agencies," Bailey wrote. "Nevertheless large numbers of people are in love with them . . . at present any criticism of them is interpreted as being opposed to the Administration and as disloyalty to our great President."

African-Americans, who moved as a bloc into the Democratic Party in 1936, greatly appreciated the WPA, especially after Harry Hopkins issued instructions implementing FDR's order that people "qualified by training and experience to be assigned to work projects shall not be discriminated against on any grounds whatsoever." Blacks continued to suffer unemployment in far greater numbers than whites, so their participation in WPA rose steadily in the late 1930s when they were still refused jobs in the fast-growing defense industries. By 1939 nearly one in three African-American households were receiving income from the WPA. "Roosevelt came to be a god," African-American sociologist Horace Cayton remembered, "It was really great. You worked, you got a paycheck and you had some dignity."

Black pride was also fostered by the WPA arts projects which supported individual African-American artists, musicians, and stage performers, and by the establishment of community theaters and art centers in African-American neighborhoods. During 1937 over 4,000 people a month came into Harlem's Community Art Center to study with resident artists, hear lectures, and view exhibits. "As a result," the Center's director Gwendolyn Bennett wrote, "the Harlem Community Art Center is becoming not only a cultural force in its particular locale, but a symbol in the culture of a race." Many white Americans gained their first non-stereotypical view of black artists in this era, attending the long-running performances of Shakespeare and Shaw by WPA's Harlem Theater project, or seeing the national tour of the musical *Jazz Mikado* produced by an all-black Federal Theater Project company from Chicago.

Of course the WPA was not free from the damaging influence of white supremacy. Many African-Americans sent letters to the President and Harry Hopkins detailing their complaints about discriminatory hiring, wages, and assignments in the WPA and other work relief programs. However, most of these same letters also conveyed the realization that discrimination originated in local administration not from the policies of New Dealers in Washington. For example, when confronted by segregation in a Chicago street repair project, a group of black WPA workers wrote Hopkins asking, "Will You take Care of this particular Matter at once?" Questions like this one reflected a widespread belief among African-Americans that New Dealers really cared about racial equality. In this sense, for all its shortcomings, WPA was an important step towards the inclusion of African-Americans in the nation's political life. In the late 1930s, Ralph Bunche led a team of investigators that found dramatic increases in black efforts to register and vote in the South were linked directly to participation in the WPA. As Peter Epps of Columbia, South Carolina reported at the time, "I been here twenty years, but since WPA, the Negro sho' has started talkin' 'bout politics." Years later Robin Langston, who grew up in Hot Springs, Arkansas during the Depression, agreed that WPA had emboldened African-Americans. "The WPA and other projects . . . made us feel like there was something we could do in the scheme of things," Langston recalled.

African-Americans also recognized the value of the second New Deal's special programs for poor youth. Before the Great Depression, the private economy had provided jobs to the large majority of young people who left school before receiving a high school diploma. However unemployment among people in the labor force aged 16 to 24 years soared during the early 1930s, prompting widespread worries about a lost generation. The Civilian Conservation Corps was the first New Deal's response to these concerns, but it only helped young men and did very little to encourage development of marketable job skills. During the "Roosevelt recovery" of the mid-1930s three in ten young people remained unemployed because most employers preferred experienced workers. Social workers warned that millions of young people were in danger of never entering the work force, while police departments complained of rising youth crime rates. Hollywood films such as *Crime School*, *Dead End*, and *Angels With Dirty Faces* expressed these fears, as well as the prevailing liberal idea that "juvenile delinquency" could be combated by effective education and anti-poverty programs.

President Roosevelt created the National Youth Administration (NYA) by executive order in June 1935 to provide educational assistance and work relief wages to poor young people. FDR placed the NYA under the Works Progress Administration's umbrella, and named Harry Hopkins' trusted assistant, Aubrey Williams, its director. Like his boss, the Alabama-born Williams was a former social worker who believed in decentralized control and racial equality. The National Youth Administration worked out of a small Washington office that approved funds for locally developed programs designed to reduce poverty and unemployment among young people. To insure that African-American youth got its fair share of NYA assistance, Williams created an Office of Minority Affairs. As head of this unprecedented office, Mary McLeod Bethune became the nation's most outspoken and effective advocate of equal education for blacks.

The National Youth Administration helped young people of all races. Over 4,500,000 Americans received some assistance from the NYA before it was closed down in 1943. The NYA's most successful program helped keep young people in school by providing money for hiring students to do on-campus work in offices, libraries, cafeterias, maintenance, and janitorial services. A woman from Cleveland later recalled the experience.

> I was about fourteen when I joined the NYA. I used to get about $12.50 every two weeks. Making footlockers. I gave half to my mother. This was the first time I could buy some clothes.

At its peak in the 1939–40 school year, the NYA's work-study program distributed checks to students at 28,000 high schools and 1,700 colleges.

The National Youth Administration also tried to reach unemployed youth who were not in school. Developing work relief programs for young people in their home communities posed special problems. Aubrey Williams did not want to approve "leaf-raking" jobs that could be criticized as "make-work," but local government officials often had no idea about how to employ unskilled young people. So many NYA state offices took the initiative and "sold" programs to local governments. Texas' Lyndon Baines Johnson, the NYA's youngest state director, helped show the way by developing programs which built roadside parks and graveled turnouts on rural roads. Yet these types of "pick-and-shovel" projects still failed to develop young people's skills. President Roosevelt resolved this problem in 1939 by directing the NYA to prepare machinists and other skilled workers for the nation's fast-growing defense industries. Within a year NYA had terminated almost all its non-defense programs so that it could concentrate on the recruitment and training of young defense workers. During the war years, the productive labor of hundreds of thousands of NYA-trained workers helped make the United States into the "Arsenal of Democracy."

Social Security

The WPA and NYA were imaginative, humane responses to the persistent mass unemployment of the Great Depression. But work relief programs were considered "emergency" solutions to an extraordinary unemployment problem. All of them were cut back as the national economy responded to military orders after 1938. By 1943 every federal work relief program had been shut down. Federal work relief has never been revived, even when unemployment climbed above 10 percent of the national workforce.

In 1935 the Roosevelt administration and its supporters in Congress knew permanent reforms were necessary to insure that American capitalism remain more humane after the Great Depression. New Dealers wanted to use federal power to more equitably distribute income, wealth, and economic power, and provide at least a minimum of economic security for all Americans. The social security system they created remains a monument to their genuine commitment to these goals. Its passage marked both the culmination of reforms begun in the early twentieth century and the beginning of a new "welfare state" era in American history.

Northern industrial states had considered various forms of social insurance during the Progressive Era before World War I, but only a handful of them actually passed workmen's compensation laws. The Great Depression revived political efforts to provide government insurance against what FDR called the unavoidable "hazards and vicissitudes of life" including unemployment, old age, sickness and injury, mental illness, and the poverty that befalls children born to poor parents. In early 1932 Governor Philip LaFollette, leader of Wisconsin's independent Progressive Party, convinced his state legislature to enact the nation's first unemployment insurance program. The 1932 national Democratic convention subsequently approved a platform plank that advocated "unemployment and old-age insurance under state laws," but Franklin Roosevelt came to Washington intending to establish federal programs.

In June 1934, President Roosevelt put Labor Secretary Frances Perkins in charge of a cabinet-level Committee on Economic Security (CES). Perkins recruited two experts from Wisconsin, Arthur Altmeyer and Edwin Witte, to direct the bill-drafting work of the committee. After seven months of often rancorous discussion, Altmeyer's and Witte's staff produced a four-part plan to establish "cradle to grave" economic security. Their original draft included a national health insurance program. Health insurance was dropped from the final CES report because the committee's Cabinet members believed Congress would reject it in 1935. The President sent the CES's final report to Congress as an urgent bill on January 17th. The bill contained recommendations for (1) a joint federal-state program of unemployment insurance to be funded by a permanent payroll tax paid by employers; (2) guaranteed retirement income to be paid out of a federally managed trust fund built up by taxes collected from both employees and employers; and (3) Aid to Dependent Children (ADC) – federal matching grants to states which established satisfactory programs to aid poor people under age 16 (who comprised 40 percent of all relief recipients in December 1934).

FDR wanted quick action but the original 63 page bill was, in the words of Labor Department lawyer Thomas Eliot, "a hodgepodge – not of unrelated subjects, but of drafts prepared by various people." The House Ways and Means Committee held hearings on the measure for four weeks. Committee chairman Fred Vinson of Kentucky and chief counsel Middleton Beaman of Vermont directed daily line-by-line questioning of the administration's proposal. After each session Beaman, Eliot, and the Senate Finance Committee's lawyers worked late into the night rewriting what had been examined that day. This process kept the CES' three basic recommendations intact while producing a completely new bill now called "the Social Security Act."

The rewritten bill finally came to the floor of the House for eight days of debate in mid-April. After Republicans tried and failed to remove the old age pension program, the social security bill was approved by a lopsided 371–33 margin. The Senate then considered the House bill. Its Finance Committee added a non-controversial section to provide special assistance to the blind (which was later amended to included other "unemployable" persons). But Senator Champ Clark of Missouri slowed final approval by introducing an amendment that would have allowed workers a choice of either federal pensions or annuities offered by private insurance companies. Hard lobbying by the insurance industry won enough votes to keep Clark's "contracting-out" proposal in the bill passed by the Senate on June 19th. As a result, the House–Senate conference committee found itself at loggerheads over the Clark amendment.

By this time the Supreme Court's "Black Monday" rulings against the administration had put President Roosevelt in a fighting mood. On June 4th he informed Democratic leaders in Congress that he did not want them to recess for the summer until they had passed nine priority bills including a Social Security Act without the Clark Amendment. To insure passage of the bill he wanted, FDR asked his most effective advocate, Tom Corcoran, to lead a three-man lobby on Capitol Hill. Thomas Eliot, a member of Corcoran's team, convinced insurance industry experts working for Senator Clark to agree that no workable plan for including a private annuity option could be developed before September. The conference committee then resolved to set up a joint House–Senate panel to report to the Congress on "contracting-out" before social security took effect in 1937. A weary but triumphant Eliot wrote in his diary, "the Senate at last receded and dropped the Clark [amendment]. So now the President has his bill." Congress quickly passed the conference committee's report without a roll call vote. President Roosevelt signed the Social Security

Act on August 14, 1935 saying, "If the Senate and House of Representatives in this long and arduous session had done nothing more than pass this Bill, the session would be regarded historic for all time."

Just before adjourning the Senate approved FDR's three nominees for the new Social Security Board: former New Hampshire governor John Winant (chairman), former CES staff director Edward Altmeyer, and Arkansas lawyer Vincent Miles. For the next two years these men struggled to set up the federally administered old age pension program, as well as initiate the joint federal–state unemployment insurance, ADC, and other categorical assistance programs for unemployables. The Board had to overcome many obstacles. Their funding was temporarily blocked by a Huey Long fili-buster. Then they were besieged by members of Congress hop-ing to secure jobs in the new Social Security administration for loyal supporters. Soon after they were criticized by Ways and Means Committee chairman Vinson for hiring "too many New York Jews." They also confronted lawsuits which chal-lenged social security's constitutionality.[3] The Board's techni-cal problems were just as daunting. In that pre-computer era the task of assigning social security numbers and setting up individual social security accounts required an enormous amount of human labor. Applications were not mailed out until late November 1936. Yet only six months later over 30,000,000 employees (including 294,000 named Smith), and 2,600,000 employers, had successfully registered with the So-cial Security administration.

By using state governments to administer unemployment benefits and categorical assistance, the Social Security Act made the New Deal's most important welfare state program more palatable to politicians who feared a big central government. However, just as liberal critics such as Rex Tugwell and Jerome Frank predicted, federal matching fund formulas which tied unemployment benefits and ADC payments to contributions made by 48 different state governments created wide discrep-ancies in coverage. For example, in 1939 recipients of Aid to Dependent Children received as little as $8.10 per month in

Arkansas or as much as $61.07 per month in Massachusetts. Liberal critics also denounced the regressive character of the payroll tax, and the exclusion of agricultural workers and domestic workers, two occupations dominated by minority workers, from social security coverage.

The President knew the original Social Security Act was flawed legislation. In the signing ceremony, FDR described the law as "a cornerstone in a structure which is being built but is by no means complete." In January 1939 FDR sent to Congress recommendations prepared by the Social Security Board which were designed to make the system more comprehensive and equitable. A congressional majority agreed to make a few administrative changes and to provide pensions to widows and surviving children. But a conservative coalition of Republicans and Southern Democrats blocked presidential proposals which would have brought millions of America's poorest workers and their families under the social security umbrella.

This effort to make the system more comprehensive and equitable in 1939 showed Franklin Roosevelt and his supporters were still committed to putting an economic security "safety net" under all citizens regardless of their occupation, race, or age. The New Deal's failure to achieve this goal in the late 1930s stemmed not from a dearth of ideas or a lack of political will on the part of the President or his supporters. What checked the New Deal's welfare state was the growth of an effective conservative opposition in Congress that eventually included many members of the President's own party.

Progressive Taxation

New Deal policies that aimed to redistribute income, wealth, and economic power alienated conservative Democrats. FDR recognized this risk to his power, but still embraced social justice politics in his Annual Message to Congress on January 4, 1935. President Roosevelt described November's elections as:

> . . . a clear mandate from the people that Americans must forswear
> that conception of the acquisition of wealth which, through excessive
> profits, creates undue private power over private affairs and, to our
> misfortune, over public affairs as well.

Unlike Republican presidents who had celebrated the creation of millionaires in the 1920s, Franklin Roosevelt now wanted to curb the accumulation of great personal fortunes. FDR was reviving the progressive liberalism which had distinguished his campaign for the Democratic presidential nomination three years earlier. Once again he presented himself as a champion of "the forgotten man" who articulated the interests of working people and poor farmers. Roosevelt proclaimed,

> We do assert that the ambition of the individual to obtain for him
> and his family a proper security, a reasonable leisure, and a decent
> living throughout life, is an ambition to be preferred to the appetite
> for great wealth and great power.

These words earned FDR high praise from liberal Democrats and progressive Republicans in Congress. Yet neither Treasury Secretary Morgenthau, whose staff had prepared a very progressive tax bill, nor Senator Wagner, who wanted to use federally protected labor unions to redistribute income, received immediate presidential encouragement.

In early February Roosevelt told Morgenthau that tax reform would have to wait until the taxes necessary for social security had been established. Later that month when Senator Wagner introduced his revised labor relations bill in Congress, the President simply ignored union leaders' requests to publicly endorse the measure. At that time Roosevelt still hoped for quick passage of the huge emergency appropriation for work relief and enactment of the social security legislation. He was also preparing to send Congress his public utility holding companies bill. The furor that proposal created in business circles and the press in March, both angered and alerted FDR to the political dangers ahead. That spring Roosevelt seemed to many around him unusually worried about losing congressional support. He knew that advocacy of the Treas-

ury's progressive tax plan and Wagner's labor relations bill
would further alienate the business community and most of
the nation's press. So for several months FDR left congressional liberals wondering whether he would ever fulfill the
redistributive promise of his Annual Message.

The Supreme Court's "Black Monday" decisions prompted
Roosevelt to abandon his go-slow political strategy. With NRA
gone and millions of workers demonstrating their eagerness
to join unions, FDR recognized that new rules for increasingly disorderly industrial relations had to be established
quickly. Roosevelt also realized that he had better counter Huey
Long's fast-growing Share-Our-Wealth movement with a
redistributive tax proposal of his own. Having convinced himself that he could win the political support of the millions of
voters in the rising labor and social justice movements, FDR
gave up trying to hold onto business backing for the New
Deal. Industry's fierce lobbying war against his public utilities
holding company bill, and the glee with which the business
press had greeted the demise of the NRA, were the final straws
for the President. America's business class was expressing what
seemed to be irreversible opposition to the New Deal, so
Franklin Roosevelt was ready strike directly at the wealth and
power of that class.

Secretary Morgenthau had asked the President to reconsider
the Treasury's tax plan because the government's revenues
were not keeping pace with the rising costs of its non-relief
programs. In early June Roosevelt accepted Morgenthau's recommendations for a steeply graduated corporate profits tax,
a tax on intercorporate dividends (aimed at holding companies), higher tax rates on the highest incomes and estates, and
new taxes on gifts and inheritances.[4] The tax bill was included
in the "must get this session" memo the President presented
to the Cabinet and congressional leaders on June 4th.

Before sending the tax measure to Congress, FDR invited
Raymond Moley and Felix Frankfurter to Washington to go
over the draft message prepared by Secretary Morgenthau's
staff. Frankfurter strongly approved of the redistributive
features of the tax plan. But Moley, a long-time advocate of

business–government cooperation, was appalled by both the specific tax proposals and the critical "soak-the-rich" tone of the message. On this occasion Moley rightly recognized that he had become an outsider in a White House very much influenced by Frankfurter and his proteges. Although Moley convinced Roosevelt to drop the undistributed corporate profits tax and scale back the corporate profits tax, he could not soften the President's message.

On June 19, 1935 President Roosevelt told Congress that for the tax code "to be just it must distribute the burden of taxes equitably." He presented the Treasury plan, as well as a constitutional amendment (never approved) that would have permitted federal taxation of income earned on state and municipal bonds. FDR barely mentioned Secretary Morgenthau's concern about a revenue shortfall in this tax message. Instead using progressive language that harkened back to his speech at Oglethorpe University in 1932, he framed the whole proposal as a reform designed to achieve greater social justice. "Our revenue laws have operated in many ways to the unfair advantage of the few, and have done little to prevent an unjust concentration of wealth and economic power," Roosevelt explained. Challenging the primary conservative justification for the accumulation of great fortunes, he asserted "Wealth in the modern world does not come merely from individual effort; . . . the people in the mass have inevitably helped to make large fortunes possible." Therefore, Roosevelt argued, the people's government has every right to expect the rich to bear the heaviest burden for necessary government programs.

> Whether it be wealth achieved through the cooperation of the entire community or riches gained by speculation – in either case the ownership of such wealth or riches represents a great public interest and a great ability to pay.

Five months after signaling his intention to redistribute income, wealth, and economic power, Franklin Roosevelt had introduced legislation to make good that promise.

Privately, Roosevelt told Harold Ickes that he thought this

message was "the best thing I have ever done." This progressive tax proposal was true to FDR's basic political instincts. It was also another of his famous "bombshells." FDR clearly delighted in the surprise and shock it created. Thousands of telegrams and letters that poured into the White House mailroom were favorable, as were a few editorials. But what most newspapers called the "soak-the rich" tax plan looked like a red flag to their conservative publishers. William Randolph Hearst sounded the alarm on June 19th when he wired his editors, "President's taxation program is essentially Communism." On Hearst's orders all of his newspapers launched an unceasing attack on what they called "the Raw Deal" and its "Soak the Successful" tax scheme. These themes resonated among America's economic elites, and helped revive contributions to the American Liberty League. Anti-New Deal politics now assumed the characteristics of class conflict. Within a year, Marquis Childs reported a "chant of hatred" of Franklin Roosevelt arose whenever the rich gathered, and that this hatred was frequently explained by the simple declaration that "the President is a traitor to his class."

Roosevelt's tax message also sharpened ideological divisions in Congress. Liberal Democrats and progressive Republicans welcomed the opportunity to vote for redistributive legislation, but they faced significant obstacles. The President's tax message had surprised everyone on Capitol Hill including three key Southern Democrats: Senate Majority Leader Joe Robinson, Senate Finance Committee chairman Pat Harrison, and House Ways and Means Committee chairman Robert Doughton. Raymond Moley later wrote that June 19th was the "day the split in the Democratic Party began." He was probably right. Robinson, Harrison, and Doughton had supported the New Deal up to this time, but they deeply resented the imperious way FDR had handled this and other legislative matters. They also opposed the redistributive philosophy that informed Roosevelt's tax message. These conservative Democrats wanted to adjourn without considering new taxes, but Senator Robert LaFollette pressured them to schedule committee hearings by gathering 22 signatures on a bi-partisan petition that said Congress should stay in session until it approved the President's tax bill. FDR conveyed a similar message to his party's congressional leaders at a White House meeting on June 24th.

The legislative process gave opponents of progressive taxation opportunities to chip away at the President's proposal. The steeply graduated corporate profits tax and new inheritance taxes were especially vulnerable. Congressman Doughton's House Ways and Means Committee opened three weeks of hearings on the tax bill on July 8th. Secretary Morgenthau appeared as the first witness. Rather than emphasizing the social justice thrust of President Roosevelt message, Morgenthau stressed the need for additional revenues. He admitted that higher taxes might slow the recovering economy. Morgenthau also explained the Treasury view of inherited wealth as inactive, and thus a revenue source which could be taxed without inhibiting recovery. Morgenthau's testimony opened the door for major revisions in the President's tax plan. Opponents of the graduated corporate profits tax used the recovery argument to scale down those rates. To replace lost revenues, the committee added a tax on undistributed corporate profits. The full House passed a bill which still contained the controversial inheritance tax on August 5th, but its fate seemed uncertain in the Senate.

The Senate continued to diminish the progressive character of the tax bill during its August hearings. Following chairman Harrison's lead, its Finance Committee ignored objections raised by administration witnesses, and eliminated the inheritance tax. The Senate bill also dropped the undistributed profits tax while further reducing the corporate profits levy. The final legislation worked out by a House–Senate conference committee was sent to the President at the end of the month. It raised estate taxes and hiked the surtax on the nation's highest incomes from 59 to 75 percent, but retained only symbolic taxes on corporate profits and intercorporate dividends.

In the short run the Tax Act of 1935 had few redistributive consequences. Huey Long claimed the measure Roosevelt signed on August 31st proved the President was "a liar and a fake." As usual, Long's view was extreme and self-serving. However, proponents of redistributive fiscal policy had good reasons to feel let down. President Roosevelt had argued "Creative enterprise is not stimulated by vast inheritances," but Congress left inheritances untouched. FDR had publicly criticized Americans who earned more than a million dollars a year and avoided paying taxes on the full amount, yet the new law did not close any significant tax loopholes. Throughout the summer Treasury officials had stressed the revenue-raising purposes of their bill, but the new taxes approved by Congress brought in just $250,000,000 in additional revenue.

Nevertheless, the Roosevelt administration's battle for tax reform marked an extremely important turning point in American political history. The Tax Act of 1935 decisively reversed the "trickle-down" economics that had governed federal fiscal policy since the early 1920s. After 1935, the annual tax debate in Congress turned on questions involving how progressive rates should be, not whether progressive taxes should be implemented at all. Until his death in April 1945, President Roosevelt continued to favor steeply graduated taxes on corporations and individuals. During World War II Congress refused to go along with FDR's request for a 100 percent tax on all personal income above $25,000 a year, but it did approve the most progressive taxes in the nation's history. By the mid-1950s national income was more equitably distributed than it had been before the Great Depression or has been ever since. The New Deal's progressive tax policy certainly was not the major cause of greater income equality; nor were social security transfer payments. Nevertheless both these New Deal reforms made important contributions to a new political-economy that encouraged a more equitable distribution of the nation's income.

Taking the Workers' Side

New Deal labor policies significantly changed the balance
of power in the economy. The Wagner (National Labor Relations) Act, Walsh-Healy Act, and the Fair Labor Standards
Act forced many employers to pay workers higher wages. Soon
other employers who hoped to prevent unionization of their
workforces recognized they also had to pay higher wages. In
the long run a greater share of corporate income went into
paychecks. This was main reason America experienced greater
income equality in the 1940s and 1950s. New Deal labor policies also gave unions a federally protected voice in corporate
decisions (such as setting work schedules and work rules) that
had previously been the sole prerogative of management. By
endorsing and enforcing new legislation that redistributed
corporate income and empowered unions, Franklin Roosevelt
thoroughly alienated the nation's business community from
the New Deal. But these same actions, along with the rest of
the second New Deal, also made him America's only working
class hero President.

At a meeting of his National Emergency Council in October
1934, President Roosevelt clarified his commitment to the two
principal ways in which income would be redistributed in the
years to come.[5] During a long discussion of work relief's impact
on wages in private industry, FDR told Harry Hopkins, "don't
break down the minimum wage, child-labor, and short-hour
provisions of the [NRA] code. It is essential to maintain that
part of the codes." Franklin Roosevelt clearly believed government had a duty to put a floor under wages, as well as regulate
hours, and child labor. When the Supreme Court knocked down
the NRA, the President encouraged Labor Secretary Perkins to
send to Congress two bills continuing federal labor standards.
The Walsh-Healy Act that forced federal contractors to pay prevailing union rates was passed over considerable conservative
opposition in June 1936. And the Fair Labor Standards Act that
set national minimum wage, maximum hours, and child labor
standards finally secured congressional approval in 1938.

FDR also recognized the fundamental importance of unions in shaping income distribution. He told his Emergency Council, "we do not want to go and tear down the wage standard which has been arrived at after a long period of struggle for organized labor."

Before May 1935 Franklin Roosevelt had relied on the NRA to protect unions and increase wages. However, the NRA failed to raise workers' incomes as intended. Business resistance and weak enforcement undercut NRA's higher wage policy. Moreover shorter hours mandated by NRA codes tended to reduce workers' weekly earnings even when their hourly rates were increased. In addition labor unions were usually too weak to raise wages during the NRA years. FDR's unwillingness to stand up to recalcitrant corporations and enforce the NRA's declaration of labor's rights created uncertainty and disorder whenever unions tried to bargain with management. In early 1935 Francis Biddle, chairman of NRA's toothless National Labor Relations Board, explained "the machinery under which we are operating makes inevitable the breakdown of legal enforcement." The NRA may have prevented wage cutting, but it did not significantly increase incomes or protect unionized workers.

Senator Robert Wagner intended to replace the administration's failed labor policy with his revised National Labor Relations Act. Wagner's legislation established federal protection for workers who joined unions, and encouraged unions and management to use collective bargaining to set wages, hours, and working conditions. Wagner and his chief aide Leon Keyserling believed these protections would reduce what they described in Section 1 of the bill as "strikes and other forms of industrial strife or unrest, which have the intent or necessary effect of burdening or obstructing commerce." Wagner and Keyserling also targeted underconsumption, a problem they believed had caused the Great Depression. Their legislation intended to increase consumption by encouraging unions to counteract "The inequality of bargaining power . . . [that] tends to aggravate recurrent business depressions by depressing wage rates and the purchasing power of wage earners in industry."

Federally protected unions, Wagner and Keyserling reasoned, would redistribute corporate income to workers who have a high propensity to consume what they earn; thus stronger unions would strengthen America's mass-consumer economy.

Senator Wagner guided his labor relations bill through Congress without President Roosevelt's support. "It was not part of the President's program," Frances Perkins recalled. "It did not particularly appeal to him [FDR] when it was described to him. All credit for it belongs to Wagner." When Secretary Perkins testified in the Senate Labor Committee in March 1935, she expressed approval for Wagner's goals, but objected to establishing a new quasi-judicial National Labor Relations Board (NLRB) outside of her Department of Labor. Perkins had earlier advised the President that unions would oppose the Wagner bill because it required them to win elections conducted by the NLRB before they could be certified as a workforce's bargaining agent. Much to her surprise, union leaders enthusiastically supported the measure in their testimony in Congress. In fact, the American Federation of Labor brought 400 union representatives to Washington in late April to lobby on behalf of the Wagner bill.

The National Association of Manufacturers (NAM) and other trade associations countered labor's lobby with a massive propaganda campaign against the proposed labor law. In radio spots and newspaper ads, in broadcast and in-person speeches, on posters and billboards, and in letters and telegrams to Congress, business organizations hammered away at the Wagner bill as unconstitutional, a barrier to economic recovery, and an incitement to disorders even greater than the mass strikes of 1934. NAM counsel James Emery told the Senate Labor Committee that Wagner's proposal violated long-standing judicial precedents which ruled manufacturing exempt from regulation under the Constitution's commerce clause, and that it violated the Tenth Amendment which gave states the power to regulate those activities not specifically described in the Constitution. He also claimed the powers granted the NLRB to hear and pass judgments in cases involving violations of labor's rights infringed upon the due process guarantees of the Constitution. Emery's testimony was endorsed by corporate lawyers and editorial writers all over the country.

That spring business lobbyists found few opponents of the Wagner bill in the exceptionally liberal 74th Congress. Senate Labor Committee approval of an extremely pro-labor amendment highlighted this weakness. To Section 8 which described prohibited activity, the committee added a provision suggested by Francis Biddle that read: "It shall be an unfair labor practice for an employer . . . To refuse to bargain collectively with the representatives of his employees." If this provision could be enforced along with the rest of Section 8's prohibitions against management interference with their workers' right to participate in unions, a revolution in American labor relations would result. On May 2nd, the Labor Committee voted unanimously to send the amended bill to the full Senate.

Senators Robinson and Harrison both informed President Roosevelt that they preferred to adjourn before considering the bill. FDR's old friend Robert Wagner asked only that the President say nothing so that his proposal could come up for a vote. Roosevelt agreed. At the last minute conservative Democrat Millard Tydings of Maryland tried to subvert the Wagner bill by offering an amendment that would have allowed company-dominated unions. It garnered only 21 votes. The Senate then approved the bill by a startling 63 to 12 margin. Just 12 Republicans and 4 Southern Democrats opposed it.

Co-sponsor Representative William Connery of Massachusetts had complicated passage in the House by agreeing to Secretary Perkins' request to locate the NLRB within the Labor Department. President Roosevelt was still unwilling to give unconditional support to the Wagner version of the bill on May 24th. Three days later, however, the Supreme Court struck down the NRA. FDR reconsidered his position. Felix Frankfurter advised Roosevelt, "the Wagner Bill . . . should be vigorously pushed to passage." On June 4th the President included it in his "must get this session" memo to congressional leaders. FDR's endorsement speeded final enactment. The House approved Connery's version of the bill on June

19th without a roll call vote. Eight days later Congress approved a conference committee report that followed Wagner's suggestions regarding the final language of Section 1 and independence for the NLRB. President Roosevelt signed the Wagner Act into law on July 5th saying,

> Accepted by management, labor and the public with a sense of sober responsibility and of willing cooperation . . . it should serve as an important step towards the achievement of just and peaceful labor relations in industry.

Roosevelt's words betrayed his uncertainty about the implications of this most radical New Deal reform. As it turned out, FDR's worries were fully justified.

On July 6th *Business Week* called for massive resistance to the Wagner Act in an editorial titled, "NO OBEDIENCE!" This leading journal denounced the new labor law as "tyranny" and "despotism," and declared "Business will not obey this edict." *Business Week* offered a remarkable rationale for defiance:

> Although the Wagner Labor Relations Act has been passed by Congress and signed by the President, it is not yet law. For nothing is law that is not constitutional.

Corporate counsels across the country endorsed this rebellious logic, and advised their clients to ignore the Wagner Act. Under banner headlines that read "Fifty-Eight Lawyers Agree," most newspapers reported that a sample of the nation's leading business lawyers selected by the American Liberty League unanimously concluded the Supreme Court would declare the Wagner Act unconstitutional. Bolstered by this kind of legal advice, leading industrial corporations continued to harass and fire union activists, employ spies, and stockpile weapons and tear gas. They also refused to hold representation elections or obey other orders issued by the new National Labor Relations Board. Their massive resistance strategy received an enormous boost from conservative federal district court judges who issued restraining orders and injunctions which put the NLRB in legal limbo.

Of course union leaders greeted the Wagner Act with jubilation. For the first time in American history, they could really argue that the federal government wanted workers to join unions. The Wagner Act also provided new energy to local union organizers who had been active since 1933. Yet for more than a year organizing proceeded slowly in most places. Chastened by recent defeats, intimidated by managers who ignored the new federal law, and made cautious by still high levels of unemployment, most older married workers took a wait-and-see attitude towards the newest appeals of union organizers. Still enough workers joined unions to challenge corporate America's now illegal anti-union policies.

The growing crisis in industrial relations was complicated by a split in the labor movement. During 1935–36 a long simmering feud within the American Federation of Labor about how mass production workers should be organized exploded into a full-fledged schism. Conservative craft union officials insisted that new members in these industries be channeled into existing unions according to the type of labor they performed. These conservatives were opposed by other union officials led by the fiery United Mine Workers president John L. Lewis. Lewis' faction wanted to create new industrial unions which would represent all workers in an industry regardless of their skill or job category. Lewis recognized that the power of his mineworkers in the AFL would be greatly enhanced if workers in the steel, automobile, rubber, electrical equipment, and other major industries also formed industrial unions. In October 1935, Lewis told the AFL's annual convention that they had a duty to support struggling industrial organizations in the mass production industries because "the labor movement is organized upon a principle that the strong shall help the weak." When this convention refused to support his motion in favor of industrial unionism, the mineworkers' president and ten other union presidents rebelled. They established the Committee for Industrial Organization (CIO). The CIO gradually transformed itself into a new labor federation; in 1938 it changed its name to the Congress of Industrial Organizations. The AFL and CIO were locked in a bitter feud for the loyalty of workers and political influence in Washington for the next 15 years.

The explosive power of the new industrial unionism was demonstrated in Akron, home of America's rubber tire industry. Employees at Goodyear started joining the CIO's United Rubber Workers union (URW) as soon as the company announced it would shift workers from six-hour to eight-hour daily schedules in January 1936. Defiant workers began shutting down whole departments to protest the new regimen. Departmental sit-down strikes spread to nearby Goodrich and Firestone where workers were also resisting management efforts to increase production while cutting wages. On Valentine's Day, Goodyear management fired 137 workers who had shut off the power in Plant Two. Management's reprisals precipitated an all-out strike against Goodyear, and a rush to the join the URW. CIO officials sent to Akron by John L. Lewis helped organize the 14,000 strikers into picket lines that surrounded Goodyear's huge plant. The strikers defied an injunction against the picketing, and they stood up to an Akron Law and Order League that assisted the company. The strikers also refused suggestions by federal mediators to submit their grievances to arbitration. The walkout, which assumed the character of a community uprising, continued until March 20th when Goodyear president Paul Litchfield agreed not to alter work schedules without approval of affected departments. The new URW–CIO won a victory in Akron, but the neither Goodyear nor the industry's other major firms formally recognized the union. In fact all the companies stepped up their intimidation of union organizers in the aftermath of the strike. Observers all around the country recognized that the Goodyear strike was just the beginning of corporate America's desperate battle to resist the CIO's new industrial unions.

Class conflict in industry and other class issues that had emerged in congressional battles over the second New Deal, influenced the presidential election of 1936. By the time Democrats re-nominated Franklin Roosevelt, he was cut off from the political resources of America's business class. Postmaster General James Farley, the President's campaign manager, summed up FDR's predicament in a memoir written shortly after this crucial election. "President Roosevelt had collided head-on in dispute after dispute with the most powerful economic groups in the country, and they had banded together against him," Farley wrote.

> The bankers were against him solidly because they disliked his bank reform program; the financial interests . . . were almost frenzied in their opposition; the manufacturing and commercial interests were strongly opposed to him; and last, and perhaps most powerful of all, the big metropolitan newspapers were almost a unit in the fight to bring about his overthrow.

As a result FDR recognized that he especially needed union support for his re-election campaign. At the same time AFL and CIO leaders recognized that successful implementation of the Wagner Act and federal protection for growing unions depended on Franklin Roosevelt's continued presence in the White House. In May 1936 AFL president William Green told the National Women's Trade Union League, "We have been inspired and thrilled by the leadership destiny has given us and we want to continue it without change." That same month three CIO leaders, Mineworkers' president Lewis, Sidney Hillman of the Amalgamated Clothing Workers, and George Berry of the Pressmen's Union formed Labor's Non-Partisan League (LNPL) to provide money and grassroots organization for FDR's campaign. Although AFL unions were not barred from this first-ever political action committee, few participated.

In 1936 FDR continued to show labor leaders that he was on their side in political conflicts with business interests. In late May the AFL's William Green beseeched the President to pressure the chairman of the Judiciary Committee to release the Walsh-Healy public contracts bill so it could come up for a vote in the full House. Roosevelt's intervention succeeded, and Congress passed the Walsh-Healy Act. In June, shortly after Majority Leader Robinson blocked Senate passage of a new coal stabilization plan, the President conferred with John L. Lewis.[6] During that private meeting Roosevelt promised to push Senator Guffey's new coal bill through the next Congress and support the CIO's organizing drive in the steel industry. Lewis left the White House eager to help the President.

He campaigned for Roosevelt in major coal-mining and steel-producing centers, and contributed $600,000 in Mineworkers funds (a huge sum for those days) to the LNPL's effort to re-elect the President.

Franklin Roosevelt accepted the Democratic nomination in a nationally broadcast speech before 100,000 people packed into Philadelphia's Franklin Field on June 27, 1936. In this speech FDR burned the last of the political bridges connecting him to America's business class. Invoking Philadelphia's history, FDR compared the patriots' struggle in 1776 against "royalists who held special privileges from the crown" to the current struggle his administration was waging against the new "economic royalists . . . who sought to regiment the people, their labor, and their property." Roosevelt declared, "the average man once more confronts the problem that faced the Minute Man." Explaining this analogy, the President said, "Private enterprise, indeed, became too private. It became privileged enterprise, not free enterprise." Addressing all those critics, including wealthy Democrats now arrayed against him in the American Liberty League, FDR continued, "These economic royalists complain that we seek to overthrow the institutions of America. What they really complain of is that we seek to take away their power." Franklin Roosevelt told millions of listeners, "This generation of Americans has a rendezvous with destiny." Finally he asked those listeners to join him in a New Deal that had become more than "a war against want and destitution and economic demoralization . . . it is a war for the survival of democracy." This kind of populist rhetoric had not been heard from a major party's presidential candidate since William Jennings Bryan's heyday at the turn of the century.

The Hearst newspapers and American Liberty League set the tone for the Republican campaign. Supporters of GOP nominee Governor Alfred Landon of Kansas extolled his credentials as a budget balancer, but spent most of their time accusing Roosevelt's New Deal of having subverted the Constitution. All summer long, while the President received free publicity attending to duties in Washington and touring the drought-stricken Great Plains, Landon's supporters hammered away at FDR in speeches, radio broadcasts, and paid advertisements that emphasized the alleged radicalism of the second New Deal. The nastiest campaign was waged in New York where Roosevelt's name appeared on the ballot twice, as a Democrat and as the nominee of an American Labor Party (ALP) which Sidney Hillman had put together to capture the votes of the state's many left-wing New Deal supporters. Republican Party chairman Melvin Eaton told a campaign kickoff rally, "American voters must choose between having their country faced with the prospect of becoming a Socialized state or preserved within the terms of the Constitution." New York Republicans focused special attention on three of Roosevelt's presidential electors, the Jewish union leaders Max Zaritsky, David Dubinsky, and Sidney Hillman who had fled Russia after the failed socialist revolution of 1905. In October desperate New York Republicans mangled these facts in ads that claimed "the New Deal needs, wants, and cherishes the Communist vote represented by these well-known un-American agitators," or simply asked "Do you want another Russia?"

Late in the campaign, Republicans attacked social security as what Landon called "a cruel hoax." The Republican nominee told workers that the new system was "unjust, unworkable, stupidly drafted, and wastefully financed." He warned that a vast new social security bureaucracy would violate privacy rights, and that the payroll taxes scheduled to be first collected on January 1, 1937 would never be returned in old age pensions. Many companies put similar messages in their workers' pay envelopes during October.

The Republican pay-envelope tactic infuriated Franklin Roosevelt. He had left Washington in late September for a nonstop five-week campaign tour which included hundreds of public appearances. Everywhere he spoke, FDR was greeted by throngs of well-wishers. The size and overwhelming enthusiasm of the crowds and the positive reports he received from party officials around the country all told Roosevelt he was winning. By mid-October he was in the finest form of his long political career, never tiring of the motorcades and the handshaking, conveying confident energy to all around him. The campaign gave FDR the opportunity to respond to all the abuse his opponents had heaped upon his New Deal since the nominating convention. The President reserved his sharpest remarks for the Republican's attack on social security. "Only desperate men with their backs to the wall would descend so far below the level of decent citizenship as to the current pay-envelope campaign against American people," he told a packed house at Madison Square Garden on October 31st. "It is the 1936 version of the old threat to close down the factory or the office if a particular candidate does not win."

By the time FDR spoke in New York City, he was clearly trying to realign the parties. FDR believed most working people and farmers would support a more liberal Democratic Party under his leadership, while a much smaller number of conservatives would migrate to the Republican Party. Franklin Roosevelt warmed to this task in his Madison Square Garden speech. After lambasting the forces of what he called "organized money," FDR exclaimed, "Never before in all our history have these forces been so united against one candidate as they stand today. They are unanimous in their hatred for me – and I welcome their hatred." The crowd at the Garden roared their approval, but Roosevelt quickly quieted them. He wanted to be sure they heard the following words,

> I should like to have it said of my first administration that in it the forces of selfishness and of lust for power met their match. I should like to have it said of my second administration that in it these forces met their master.

That night Franklin Roosevelt was confident of victory, and confident that he could achieve all of the goals he had set for the New Deal. On November 4th, a great majority of American voters vindicated FDR's confidence. But whether or not he could extend the New Deal remained to be seen.

FURTHER READING

Primary Sources

Eliot, Thomas H. *Recollections of the New Deal: When the People Mattered.* Boston: Northeastern University Press, 1992.

Freedman, Max ed. *Roosevelt and Frankfurter: Their Correspondence, 1928–1945.* Boston: Little, Brown and Company, 1967.

Hopkins, Harry. *Spending to Save.* New York: W.W. Norton, 1936.

Ickes, Harold L. *The Secret Diary of Harold L. Ickes: The First Thousand Days, 1933–1936.* New York: Simon and Shuster, 1954.

Loucheim, Katie. *The Making of the New Deal: The Insiders Speak.* Cambridge: Harvard University Press, 1983.

McElvaine, Robert S. *Down and Out in the Great Depression: Letters from the Forgotten Man.* Chapel Hill: University of North Carolina Press, 1983.

Moley, Raymond. *After Seven Years.* New York: Harper & Brothers, 1939.

Nash, Gerald ed. *Great Lives Observed: Franklin Delano Roosevelt.* Englewood Cliffs: Prentice-Hall, 1967.

O'Connor, Francis V. ed. *Art for the Millions: Essays from the 1930s by Artists and Administrators of the WPA Federal Art Project.* Boston: New York Graphic Society, 1973.

O'Connor, Francis V. ed. *The New Deal Art Projects: An Anthology of Memoirs.* Washington: Smithsonian Press, 1972.

O'Connor, John and Brown, Lorraine. *Free, Adult, Uncensored: The Living History of the Federal Theatre Project.* New York: Simon and Shuster, 1978.

Perkins, Frances. *The Roosevelt I Knew.* New York: Viking, 1946.

Roosevelt, Franklin D. *The Public Papers and Addresses of Franklin D. Roosevelt, Volume Four: The Court Disapproves 1935.* New York: Random House, 1938.

Roosevelt, Franklin D. *The Public Papers and Addresses of Franklin D. Roosevelt, Volume Five: The People Approve 1936.* New York: Random House, 1938.

Terkel, Studs. *Hard Times: An Oral History of the Great Depression.* New York: Random House, 1970.

Witte, Edwin. *The Development of the Social Security Act: A Memorandum of the Committee on Economic Security.* Madison: University of Wisconsin Press, 1962.

Zinn, Howard ed. *New Deal Thought.* Indianapolis: Bobbs-Merril, 1966.

Secondary Sources

Baldwin, Sidney. *Poverty and Politics: The Rise and Decline of the Farm Security Administration.* Chapel Hill: University of North Carolina Press, 1968.

Berkowitz, Edward D. *America's Welfare State: From Roosevelt to Reagan.* Baltimore: Johns Hopkins University Press, 1991.

Bernstein, Irving. *Turbulent Years: A History of the American Worker, 1933–1941.* Boston: Houghton Mifflin, 1971.

Blum, John Morton. *From The Morgenthau Diaries: Years of Crisis, 1928–1938.* Boston: Houghton Mifflin, 1959.

Davis, Kenneth S. *FDR: The New Deal Years, 1933–1937.* New York: Random House, 1979.

Dubofsky, Melvyn. *The State and Labor in Modern America.* Chapel Hill: University of North Carolina Press, 1994.

Fraser, Steven. *Labor Will Rule: Sidney Hillman and the Rise of American Labor.* Ithaca: Cornell University Press, 1991.

Huthmacher, J. Joseph. *Senator Robert F. Wagner and the Rise of Urban Liberalism.* New York: Atheneum, 1968.

Levinson, Harold. *Unionism, Wage Trends, and Income Distribution, 1914–1947.* Ann Arbor: University of Michigan Business Studies, 1951.

Lubove, Roy. *The Struggle for Social Security, 1900–1935.* Cambridge: Harvard University Press, 1968.

Mangione, Jerre. *The Dream and the Deal: the Federal Writers Project, 1935–1943.* Boston: Little, Brown and Company, 1972.

Plotke, David. *Building a Democratic Political Order: Reshaping American Liberalism in the 1930s and 1940s.* New York: Cambridge University Press, 1996.

Reiman, Richard A. *The New Deal and American Youth: Ideas and Ideals in a Depression Decade.* Athens: University of Georgia Press, 1992.

Rose, Nancy E. *Put to Work: Relief Programs in the Great Depression.* New York: Monthly Review Press, 1994.

Schlesinger, Arthur M. Jr. *The Politics of Upheaval.* Boston: Houghton Mifflin, 1960.

Sullivan, Patricia. *Days of Hope: Race and Democracy in the New Deal Era.* Chapel Hill: University of North Carolina Press, 1996.

Tweeton, D. Jerome. *The New Deal at the Grass Roots: Programs for the People in Otter Tail County, Minnesota.* St Paul: Minnesota Historical Society, 1988.

Zieger, Robert H. *The CIO, 1935–1955.* Chapel Hill: University of North Carolina Press, 1995.

11

The End of the New Deal

FDR and the Supreme Court

On November 3, 1936, 83 percent of America's registered voters went to the polls. The election was a referendum on President Roosevelt and the New Deal. The results were clear and decisive. FDR received over 60 percent of the popular vote. He won majorities in every state except Maine and Vermont. The President received nearly 11,000,000 more votes that his Republican challenger, the largest victory margin on record. Roosevelt's landslide was also a tremendous triumph for his party. In the new 75th Congress, Democrats outnumbered Republicans 76 to 16 in the Senate, and 331 to 89 in the House.[1] Democrats also won 26 of 33 races for governor.

Nearly 6,000,000 more people turned out at the polls in 1936 than had voted in 1932, and five of every six of them voted for FDR. Labor's Non-Partisan League and the new CIO unions helped to build up Franklin Roosevelt's huge victory margin among first-time voters in the industrial neighborhoods and mining towns of the Northeast and Midwest. Ethnic federations and urban political machines also contributed to the unprecedented Democratic vote cast by Catholics, Jews, and African-Americans. These mostly working class groups formed the backbone of a new national Democratic majority. Of course the South remained solidly Democratic. Every Southern senator and all but one of the South's representatives in the 75th

Congress were Democrats. But for the first time ever, the majority of Democrats in the Congress represented non-Southern states.

Franklin Roosevelt's second inaugural address was an eloquent appeal for more liberal reforms. Frankly acknowledging the unemployment, poverty, and economic uncertainty that still afflicted the nation, he pledged to "find practical controls over blind economic forces and blindly selfish men." That this would mean further enlargement of the federal government's role in American life seemed clear. FDR indicated that WPA, social security, and the Wagner Act were first steps, not the end of New Deal efforts to raise the incomes all working people, including the poorest minorities. He proclaimed, "The test of our progress is not whether we add more to the abundance of those who have much; it is whether we provide enough for those who have too little." The President promised to make "every American citizen the subject of his country's interest and concern," and to never regard "any faithful, law-abiding group within our borders as superfluous." FDR's second inaugural address assured the diverse groups of workers and farmers in "the Roosevelt coalition" that the New Deal would continue to concentrate on solving their problems. Like their President, most Americans expected the overwhelmingly Democratic Congress to swiftly enact the administration's newest proposals.

President Roosevelt revealed many of his legislative priorities in a series of special messages to Congress in January 1937. FDR wanted immediate enactment of a fair labor standards bill, authorization of special economic assistance for America's 2,865,000 tenant farmers and sharecroppers, and a new program to replace urban slums with low cost public housing along the lines of legislation being written by Senator Wagner. To manage the sprawling federal government more efficiently, the President also asked Congress to approve the creation of six new presidential assistants and the consolidation of more than 100 programs and agencies under existing Cabinet departments. FDR expected significant opposition to this reorganization plan because it shifted power from the Congress to the White House. Still in preparation were the administration's new agricultural adjustment bill, an ambitious proposal to establish seven regional natural resource planning agencies, and measures to make good on the President's promise to place more effective "curbs on monopoly, unfair trade practices and speculation."

If Congress had actually approved these proposed reforms quickly, we would today recall the first half of 1937 as a "second Hundred Days." Instead, the opening session of the 75th Congress is remembered solely for the political battle over FDR's attempt to enlarge the Supreme Court. Roosevelt surprised Congress and the Cabinet with a court reform bill on February 5, 1937. He and Attorney General Homer Cummings had devised the plan in secret. Their bill would have authorized the President to appoint a new member to *every federal court* for each judge over the age of 70 who had served at least ten years and refused to retire. Solicitor General Stanley Reed, Donald Richberg, and Samuel Rosenman were the only people besides Cummings to preview the bill and accompanying message. These three lawyers were appalled by the bill's details and by the secrecy which had shielded it from criticism and revision. But they could not dissuade FDR from making his surprise attack on the court.

Roosevelt's court reform bill had a long history. Since 1900 many reformers had criticized the power of appointed judges to overturn legislation, and the influence of older justices on those decisions. Robert LaFollette had proposed a constitutional amendment allowing a two-thirds' majority of Congress to overturn Supreme Court rulings during his Progressive Party campaign for the presidency in 1924. This idea was revived after the Supreme Court began striking down major New Deal programs. By early 1937 many of Roosevelt's advisors as well as many Democrats in Congress wanted him to push for ratification of just such an amendment.

President Roosevelt clearly preferred a legislative remedy designed to force older judges off the bench. This was not a new idea. Theodore Roosevelt, William Howard Taft, and even Chief Justice Charles Evans Hughes had all favored mandatory retirement for federal judges to allow the views of younger generations to influence current decisions. In 1916 then Attorney General, James McReynolds, who later became one of the Supreme Court's staunchest conservatives, actually drafted a bill giving the President power to appoint additional judges to all federal courts (except the Supreme Court) whenever a sitting judge refused to retire at the age of 70.

Franklin Roosevelt himself had long believed that courts needed frequent turnover to keep their rulings in tune with a fast-changing society. He had advocated judicial reform as a State Senator in 1911, and again as Governor of New York in 1929. But during his first term as President, FDR refrained from speaking out on the subject until the Supreme Court began its attack on the New Deal. Shortly after the Court's "Black Monday" decisions in May 1935, Roosevelt surprised reporters with a long learned lecture on the separation of powers. He made clear his belief that the Court's narrow interpretation of the interstate commerce clause threatened the entire New Deal. "The issue is this . . ." FDR told reporters, "Is the United States going to decide . . . that their Federal Government has no right under any applied power or any court-approved power to enter into a solution of a national economic problem." But this statement and the much longer discussion of which it was a part were not released to the public. Instead, reporters were allowed only direct quotation of Roosevelt's final sarcastic remark about the Court having used "the horse-and-buggy definition of interstate commerce." The public uproar created by this remark convinced Roosevelt to bide his time on judicial reform.

In 1936 FDR still hoped one or more of the Supreme Court's older justices would retire and give him his first appointment opportunities. Instead the Court continued to reject New Deal reforms. The AAA was nullified in January; the Bituminous Coal Stabilization Act and the Municipal Bankruptcy Act were struck down in May. In *Morehead* v. *Tipaldo*, the Court declared against New York's minimum wage law for women and children. After *Tipaldo*, many Republicans joined Democrats in the widespread condemnation of the Court's insistence that liberty of contract prevented state regulation of wages. Even Herbert Hoover called for a congressional amendment to restore legitimate regulatory power to the states. On June 2nd President Roosevelt spoke briefly on the subject, telling reporters the Court had now defined "the 'no-man's-land' where no Government – State or Federal – can function." But FDR refused to be drawn out when asked what he intended to do about this problem. He knew that the American Liberty League and other conservatives would attack any judicial reform he proposed as evidence of his dictatorial ambitions. During the campaign of 1936 Roosevelt simply refused to discuss court reform.

As FDR prepared for his second term he believed the Supreme Court would continue to overturn key components of the New Deal. Social security and the Wagner Act were already on the Court's docket, and other cases were sure to follow. Although Roosevelt realized a constitutional amendment checking the power of the Court would be more popular than a legislative remedy, he thought its ratification would take years. "The Nation cannot wait until 1941 or 1942 to obtain effective social and economic national legislation," he explained to Felix Frankfurter just a few days after sending his court reform bill to Congress.

Roosevelt decided early 1937 was the optimum moment to get congressional approval for court reform. Public criticism of the Supreme Court's many decisions nullifying state laws and New Deal legislation had grown steadily since 1935. Over 100 court reform bills had been introduced in the previous Congress. A best-selling critique of the Supreme Court, Drew Pearson's and Robert Allen's *Nine Old Men*, first published in October 1936, had focused public attention on the age issue in court politics. Most importantly, a supremely confident FDR was sure his party's huge majorities in the new Congress would support a quick fix for the Supreme Court.

An additional personal element shaped Roosevelt's court reform strategy. FDR knew the older conservatives on the Court had hoped he would lose to Landon so a Republican President could replace them. Thus it must have gratified him when he was informed right after the election that Justice McReynolds had been heard saying, "I'll never resign as long as that crippled son-of-a-bitch is in the White House." We also can only imagine how much McReynolds' remark must have angered Franklin Roosevelt, a paraplegic who still lived with his beloved mother in the White House. This incident, in combination with an inflated sense of his own post-election power, helps explain why FDR seemed to lose his political bearings in his fight to reform the Supreme Court.

Franklin Roosevelt clearly relished what he saw as the cleverness of his court reform strategy. In his Annual Message in January FDR had told Congress that "Means must be found to adapt our legal forms and our judicial interpretation to the actual present needs of the largest progressive democracy in the modern world." But he made no specific recommendations at that time, nor did he subsequently consult with congressional leaders on this issue. Instead the President waited a month before springing his plan upon the legislature. This surprise attack strategy proved to be the most costly political error of his presidency.

FDR's February 5th message claimed the federal courts had "insufficient personnel with which to meet a growing and more complex business" and problems with judges who "cling to their posts . . . far beyond their years of physical or mental capacity." He urged "systematic addition of younger blood" because "older men, assuming that the scene is the same as it was in the past, cease to inquire into the present and the future." In 1937 six of the nine Supreme Court judges were over 70 years old including Chief Justice Hughes, Justice Brandeis, and the four most conservative members: Justices McReynolds, Sutherland, Van Devanter, and Butler. FDR's proposal would have given him the power to appoint up to six new Supreme Court justices if these six men refused to retire. There was ample precedent for legislation changing the size of the Supreme Court. The Constitution does not stipulate the size of the Court; it does not even require an odd number of Justices. Congress had previously changed the size of the Supreme Court six times. Yet none of those changes had provoked anything like the tidal wave of criticism which followed Roosevelt's announcement of his court reform plan.

The President's surprise message insulted most of the Supreme Court and angered many in Congress. Although FDR received thousands of letters of support at the White House, Congress received tens of thousands of protests during the month of February alone. Congressional Republicans including all the progressives in the Senate who had previously supported the New Deal opposed FDR's court reform bill. Shrewdly, Republican leaders muted their criticism while the Democratic majority splintered. Although most Democrats in both Houses initially supported the President, conservative southerners in the Senate, as well as other Democratic Senators who resented Roosevelt's methods, announced their opposition. Democratic Senator Burton Wheeler of Montana (who had been ready to sponsor a constitutional amendment limiting the Supreme Court's veto power) emerged as the opposition's floor leader. Wheeler strongly condemned the President for using deceptive means to upset the constitutional balance of powers in government. "A liberal cause was never won by stacking a deck of cards, by stuffing a ballot box, or by packing a court," he explained. Wheeler's vehement criticism of FDR gave courage to other Democratic Senators and Congressmen who resented the President's presumption that they would simply rubber stamp all of his proposals. Democratic Party unity in Congress became the first and most important casualty of the Court fight.

Herbert Hoover condemned the court bill within an hour of its announcement, telling reporters its real aim was "to pack the Court" with Roosevelt's yes-men. "Court-packing" immediately displaced the word "reform" in public discussion of the plan. Editorial writers were quick to pick up the themes of Wheeler's and Hoover's denunciations. Within a few days most newspapers in the country had denounced the court-packing bill as nothing more than a thinly disguised attempt destroy the independence of the Court. Frank Gannett, publisher of a chain of anti-New Deal newspapers, set up a "National Committee to Uphold Constitutional Government" to sustain the attack on FDR's alleged unwillingness to accept the restraints imposed by the Founding Fathers' plan of government. Just a few months after his great triumph in November's election FDR's court reform message had breathed new life into the opposition's major theme: that he really was intent on subverting the Constitution.

The "court-packing" fight in the Senate dominated national politics for nearly six months. President Roosevelt's refusal to back down or accept compromise prolonged the struggle. In early March, FDR thought he could still win if he changed tactics and launched a straightforward political attack on the undemocratic character of the Supreme Court's five-to-four rulings against the New Deal. "Our difficulty with the Court today rises not from the Court as an institution but from the human beings within it," Roosevelt told a national radio audience on March 9th. He continued, "We cannot yield our Constitutional destiny to the personal judgment of a few men who, being fearful of the future, would deny us the necessary means of dealing with the present." Denouncing his critics as the same people who had used "pay-envelope propaganda against the Social Security law," FDR claimed his proposal would protect the Constitution by making the courts "unwilling to assert legislative powers by writing into it their own political and economic policies."

Although this change of tactics temporarily bolstered FDR's support in Congress and the country, his opponents countered by staging weeks of headline-making testimony against the court-packing plan in the Senate Judiciary Committee. The greatest blow came on the opening day of the hearings when Senator Wheeler read into the record a letter from Chief Justice Hughes explaining how the Supreme Court was functioning well, and that any increase in the number of justices "would impair efficiency so long as the Court acts as a unit." Although the ethics of this letter were questionable (Hughes seemed to be speaking for the Court even though he had not consulted the other Justices), it completely undercut FDR's original reasons for court reform.

On March 29th, the Supreme Court reversed its *Tipaldo* decision and upheld Washington State's minimum wage law.

Justice Owen Roberts, the swing vote in every previous five-to-four ruling against the New Deal, sided with the Court's liberals in this case. Justice Roberts' about face signaled a new direction for the Court. This change was confirmed on April 12th when Roberts again delivered the key vote in a decision upholding the Wagner Act. On that momentous day, Justice McReynolds clearly aimed his angry dissent at Roberts. "Every consideration brought forward to uphold the [Wagner] Act before us," McReynolds shouted, "was applicable to support the Acts held unconstitutional in cases decided within two years." Roberts turned a deaf ear to this logic. Six weeks later he provided the majority vote upholding the constitutionality of social security taxes. All over Washington lawyers joked that Owen Roberts' "switch in time had saved nine."

FDR had gained a momentous practical political victory over the Supreme Court while his reform bill remained stalled in the Senate. FDR won another victory in mid-May when Justice Van Devanter, one of the four conservatives who had so often ruled against the New Deal, indicated his intention to resign at the end of the Court's spring session. Now nearly everyone close to Roosevelt urged him to end the confrontation with the Senate, but FDR refused to back down. Under pressure from still loyal Democratic leaders in Congress he agreed only to amend the original bill.[2] The Judiciary Committee voted ten to eight to condemn this substitute court-packing plan as "in direct violation of the spirit of the American Constitution" because it "would subjugate the courts to the will of Congress and the President." Nevertheless Roosevelt insisted that Majority Leader Joseph Robinson try to push the amended bill through the Senate. Robinson died trying, struck down on July 14th by a heart attack that his colleagues attributed to ten days of futile debate in the sweltering heat of the Capitol. When Congressional Democrats returned to Washington from Joe Robinson's funeral, they informed the President that the Court fight was over. FDR had no choice but to accept their decision to bury the court-packing bill.

The Supreme Court's reversal – from rejection to affirmation of New Deal legislation – in the spring of 1937 was a great turning point in American constitutional history. Franklin Roosevelt's subsequent appointments to the Court made the "switch in time" permanent. In August FDR named Senator Hugo Black, an ardent New Dealer, to fill the seat left vacant by Justice Sutherland's resignation. Other resignations soon followed. By 1940, five of the Court's nine justices – Hugo Black, Stanley Reed, Felix Frankfurter, William O. Douglas, and Frank Murphy – were Roosevelt appointees. This new "Roosevelt Court" accomplished a liberal revolution in judicial interpretation. It established flexible interpretations of the interstate commerce clause of the Constitution and of contract law that allowed government broad powers to regulate business and make economic policy. As a result, the Supreme Court never again struck down an important New Deal measure. The "Roosevelt Court" also reformed the meaning of judicial liberalism, remaking itself into a defender of civil liberties and a proponent of equal rights for blacks and other minorities.

FDR later wrote in the introduction to the 1937 volume of his Presidential Papers, "the change would never have happened, unless this frontal attack had been made on the philosophy of the Court." Roosevelt was partially right. The fight over his court reform bill surely speeded up the emergence of a new liberal Supreme Court. But this constitutional victory was also Franklin Roosevelt's costliest political defeat. By stubbornly pushing his too-clever court-packing scheme against a bi-partisan opposition, FDR squandered his opportunity to exploit the results of the election of 1936.

Towards a Conservative Coalition in Congress

In 1933 only two Democratic Senators, Carter Glass of Virginia and Thomas Gore of Oklahoma, had consistently opposed the New Deal. Born in 1858, Glass was an old-fashioned southern Democrat, who believed in white supremacy, balanced budgets, states' rights, and a limited Presidency. Not surprisingly he hated the first New Deal and Franklin

Roosevelt's extraordinary exercise of executive power. Gore shared Glass' conservative convictions and was, if anything, even more outspoken in his denunciations of the early New Deal. In 1934 three other southern Democratic Senators – Harry Byrd of Virginia, Millard Tydings of Maryland, and Josiah Bailey of North Carolina – occasionally joined Glass, Gore, and the Republicans in votes against administration proposals, but they were careful not to make a permanent break with the President.

The second New Deal of 1935 strained the party loyalty of all conservative Democrats in Congress. Massive borrowing to support relief spending, a compulsory national economic security program, steeply progressive taxes on income and wealth, and federally mandated collective bargaining seemed to them a betrayal of ideals that had defined their party since Jefferson's presidency. In October 1935 Josiah Bailey expressed the thinking of many Democrats in a letter explaining why he was turning against the New Deal. Bailey wrote, "We must make the choice between the policy of [individual] liberty and the policy of [government] control . . . Once we abandon the voluntary principles, we run squarely into Communism."

The potential strength of conservative Democrats had been demonstrated in 1935 in voting on the public utilities holding company bill's "death sentence" provision (see Chapter 8). After the House heard an impassioned speech by Alabama's George Huddleston in defense of the "old-fashioned Southern Democracy of Thomas Jefferson," 166 Democrats deserted the administration on a "death sentence" vote. In the Senate, an amendment that would have gutted the "death sentence" failed by just two votes after receiving the support of 29 Democrats. These votes clearly signaled conservative disapproval with the more liberal direction of Roosevelt's second New Deal. In retrospect they appear as a harbinger of the split within the Democratic Party that would end the New Deal.

Franklin Roosevelt's landslide victory in November 1936 benefited conservative as well as liberal Democrats. In the 75th Congress, liberals gained a few seats in the House, but in the Senate conservative Democrats actually outnumbered Republicans. The Court fight which dominated the first session of 1937 shattered Democratic party discipline in both houses of Congress. The Court fight provided the catalyst and the occasion for conservative Democrats to openly criticize the President and his New Deal. Senator Bailey wrote Senator Glass shortly after the Court fight, "What we have to do is to preserve, if we can, the Democratic Party against his efforts to make it a Roosevelt Party." The sharp rhetoric of the Court fight also encouraged more extreme conservative voices in Congress and the country to once again declare FDR "a dictator," to label the New Deal "Communist," or call it a "Jew Deal." But the Court fight was not the sole context for the revival of Democratic conservatism and anti-radical nativism. The rapid growth of the CIO in the spring of 1937 and the rapid onset of the Roosevelt recession that fall also shaped the political reaction against the New Deal.

After the election of 1936, workers all over the country wanted to put into effect the labor policy mandated by the Wagner Act. By 1938 union membership had doubled to 8,000,000 workers. Most of this growth occurred among the CIO's new industrial unions. The CIO frightened conservatives and many moderate supporters of the New Deal. Its organizing committees and local unions freely elected many Socialists and Communists to leadership positions. CIO unions mobilized whole communities to support mass strikes aimed at winning from big corporations the bargaining rights guaranteed by the Wagner Act. Moreover the CIO, unlike its AFL rival, was constitutionally committed to racial integration. Many CIO union organizers tried, frequently without real success, to create a working class solidarity that displaced racial and ethnic loyalties.

The success of the CIO organizing drive of 1937 stemmed from the militancy of rank and file members. When confronting managements who refused to obey the Wagner Act, CIO unions often struck the company to gain recognition. All totaled there were 4,740 strikes in 1937. Most of these walkouts occurred during the first nine months of the year before the "Roosevelt recession" created a very steep rise in unemployment. Strikes to secure union recognition, not wage and hours disputes, predominated in this period. Some of these strikes involved tens of thousands of workers, and many involved tactics that conservatives saw as a radical assault on the rights of property owners. Of course, conservatives never acknowledged that companies resisting striker demands for union recognition were violating federal law.

In 1937 CIO industrial unions such as the United Automobile Workers, United Rubber Workers, United Electrical Workers, and Steel Workers Organizing Committee endorsed the militant tactics of their members. Local union activists supported by CIO organizers often set up massive picket lines that blockaded struck plants. CIO unions organized motorized "flying squadrons" and "women's brigades" that would rush to the assistance of pickets battling police and strikebreakers. Workers also staged nearly 500 sit-down strikes in 1937 during which they seized, albeit temporarily, control of company property. The most important of these sit-down strikes was also one of the first. It occurred in Flint, Michigan, hometown and largest production center of the world's biggest industrial corporation, General Motors.

Workers affiliated with the CIO's new United Automobile Workers union (UAW) occupied a key auto body plant in Flint for 44 days during the winter of 1936–37. General Motors' chairman Alfred Sloan contemptuously dismissed the sit-down strikers as "trespassers." He refused to bargain with union officers or CIO president John L. Lewis. In January, after a huge crowd of strike supporters had repulsed police attempts to enforce a local court's evacuation order, GM asked for military assistance. But neither Michigan's Democratic governor, Frank Murphy, nor President Roosevelt agreed to send troops to secure the company's property. Instead Murphy ordered over 3,000 National Guardsmen to act as a buffer between strikers and strikebreakers. FDR told Frances Perkins,

> shooting it out and killing a lot of people because they have violated the law of trespass somehow offends me . . . The punishment doesn't fit the crime. There must be another way. Why can't these fellows in

> General Motors meet with the committee of workers? . . . They would
> get a settlement. It wouldn't be so terrible.

Perkins invited Sloan, GM president William Knudsen, John
L. Lewis, and UAW president Homer Martin to Washington
on January 20th, inauguration day; but neither side was willing to talk to the other.

The General Motors sit-down strike, already a riveting news
story, now took on great political significance. The day after
Roosevelt's inauguration John L. Lewis framed the issue in a
way that infuriated Republicans and conservative Democrats
alike. Lewis' statement to the press denounced "the economic
royalists of General Motors . . . who contributed their money
and their energy to drive the President of the United States out
of the White House." The union leader continued,

> The Administration asked labor to repel this attack. Labor gave its
> help. Now the same economic royalists have their fangs in labor, and
> the workers expect the administration in every reasonable and legal
> way to support the auto workers.

For obvious reasons, most newspapers reported that John L.
Lewis had called in a political debt or demanded a reward for
his extraordinary efforts in Roosevelt's re-election campaign.
An angry Alfred Sloan left Washington refusing Perkins' invitation to return to talks with her. At a news conference on
January 26th, FDR gave the impression that he was above the
fray, but behind the scenes he was pressuring Perkins and
Murphy to bring the parties together. At just the right moment, shortly after the UAW members seized a critical Flint
engine plant, the President called William Knudsen. The GM
president told FDR he was ready to negotiate an end to the
strike. On February 11th, General Motors signed a recognition agreement with the UAW–CIO.

The CIO's breakthrough victory in the Flint strike encouraged workers to sign up with unions that were ready to strike
to gain recognition and bargaining power. By the end of 1937,
CIO unions claimed nearly 4,000,000 members. So many of
its employees had signed up with the CIO's Steel Workers'
Organizing Committee (SWOC) by March that U.S. Steel rec-

ognized the union to avoid a showdown strike. Several other so-called "Little Steel" corporations resisted SWOC even after the Supreme Court upheld the Wagner Act in April. SWOC's recognition strikes against the "Little Steel" companies turned violent in May and June. The worst repression occurred on Memorial Day when police opened fire on SWOC demonstrators outside Republic Steel's South Chicago plant. Forty working people were shot, most of them while trying to run away. Ten died and two others were permanently paralyzed. SWOC failed to force the "Little Steel" companies to the bargaining table in the summer of 1937, but buoyed by a series of favorable rulings by the NLRB and by the publicity surrounding Senator LaFollette's investigation of the arms, espionage, and intimidation that big corporations had used against unions, SWOC resumed its organizing efforts in the fall.

The tumultuous rise of the CIO and the unprecedented sitdown strikes of the first six months of 1937 compounded conservative worries about what the New Deal was doing to the country. So did the bitter rivalry between the AFL and the CIO. Although most historians still speak of a single "labor movement" in this period, there were actually two labor movements that engaged in unceasing struggles for power against employers, and against each other. This latter struggle led the AFL to launch its own organizing drive in 1937. It also led the older labor federation to seek help in Washington. During the same months as the Court fight, conservative AFL leaders who wanted to amend the Wagner Act and make the National Labor Relations Board more amenable to their organization began forging a political alliance with congressional conservatives. The AFL's widely reported denunciations of communist influence in the CIO and the NLRB gave the congressional conservatives powerful ammunition to use against the New Deal.

The coincidental convergence of the Court fight with the sit-down strikes and the AFL's attack on the CIO imparted a very hard anti-radical nativist edge to the emerging conservative coalition in Congress. "The most ominous thing in American life today is the sit-down strike . . . down that road lurks a dictatorship," Republican Hiram Johnson told the Senate. Republicans just nodded their heads when Democratic Senator Allen Ellender of Louisiana blamed John L. Lewis for the sit-down strikes, calling the CIO leader "a traitor to American ideals and a menace to the peace and prosperity of the nation." Many resolutions condemning the sit-downs and the CIO were introduced in Congress during April 1937. South Carolina Democrat James Byrnes, who once had been FDR's point man in the Senate, offered an amendment to the new coal bill outlawing sit-down strikes for which Vice-President Garner publicly thanked him. Shortly after, most Democrats in both houses of Congress voted for a resolution condemning the sit-down strikes. Also in April, conservative Democrat Martin Dies of Texas tried to establish an investigation of possible connections between the sit-down strikes, alien radicals, and New Dealers. Although his motion failed in the House, Dies' proposal got 155 votes, including 78 cast by Democrats.

There was no "third New Deal" in 1937. During the Court fight, Congress passed just one major administration bill: authorization for the Farm Security Administration. Before adjourning, Congress also approved the creation of the federal low-cost housing construction program long advocated by Senator Wagner. But in each case, conservative Democrats and Republicans joined forces to amend the original bills in ways that reduced program costs, and thus limited the assistance they actually provided to America's poorest families. Southern Democrats, who recognized in the 1936 election returns the rise of a significant African-American voting bloc in Northern cities, were especially effective in turning states' rights and urban versus rural arguments against Wagner's housing bill. "Upon what recognized theory of government [did] it ever become the business of the national government . . . to tax all the American people to clear up slums in certain parts of the country?" asked Senator Glass. Glass' argument appealed to many other Democrats from rural states who certainly never applied the same logic to legislation benefiting their own districts. In the end, Republicans and rural Democrats from the

South and West limited the new United States Housing Authority's budget to just half of what Wagner originally requested. Fearing the program might do too much to aid Wagner's hometown, New York City, conservatives imposed a strict limit on how much the new housing authority could spend in one state. Southern and Western Democrats in the House also approved an amendment that barred aliens from occupying federally funded housing. Senator Wagner, himself an immigrant, so strongly objected to this nativist amendment that it was dropped in the conference committee which reconciled House and Senate versions of the bill.

In September 1937 President Roosevelt again toured the northern tier of states from the West coast to the Great Lakes. Shortly before leaving Washington, he confided to Ambassador Claude Bowers that "the voters are still with us just as they were last fall." The large crowds that greeted FDR wherever he spoke in the West reinforced his optimistic assessment of the electorate. Roosevelt used this trip to focus public attention on the physical evidence of what the PWA and WPA were accomplishing in the construction of hydroelectric dams, irrigation projects, airports, rural roads, and urban infrastructure, as well as the conservation work the CCC was doing in national forests and recreation areas. The President also hoped the trip would generate support for his most recent reform proposals. At the Bonneville Dam, he again called on Congress to set up seven regional planning boards to do for other parts of the country what TVA was already doing in the Southeast. In Grand Forks he urged enactment of a new permanent agricultural adjustment program. In Minneapolis his subject was wages and hours legislation. When he finally returned to Hyde Park, President Roosevelt was ready to call Congress into special session to pass these and other New Deal proposals.

By the time this special session convened on November 15th, farm prices and industrial production had fallen sharply, and unemployment was increasing rapidly. FDR sounded reassuring in his message to Congress, saying "there is no reason why we should suffer any prolonged recession." But no one knew for sure when economic growth might resume, and conservatives in Congress were not going to give FDR the benefit of the doubt. With the recession just underway, President Roosevelt had not yet decided that counter-cyclical policies were necessary. Besides a vague reference to liberalizing FHA requirements "to encourage private capital to enter the field of private housing on a large scale," FDR's message contained nothing new. Roosevelt wanted the special session to enact four of the bills he had introduced earlier in the year as New Deal priorities: a new agricultural adjustment act, minimum wage and maximum hours standards, an Executive branch reorganization plan giving the President a larger staff and more control over regulatory agencies, and authorization for seven regional boards that would plan "for the conservation and the development of those natural resources which are the foundation of a virile national life."

In stark contrast to the special session which had inaugurated the New Deal in 1933, this special session resisted Franklin Roosevelt's legislative proposals. North Carolina's Josiah Bailey and 11 other senators quietly circulated a statement of conservative principles which they hoped would unite the opposition coalition. But when the press reported the story as if it were a coup attempt, the group backed down. Nonetheless Congress completely frustrated the President during the five weeks it met in special session. His agricultural adjustment proposal, propelled by the farm lobby and amended to give Congress more control over price support levels, made it only as far as a conference committee before adjournment on December 21st. Growing fears of a prolonged recession helped move FDR's proposed easing of FHA regulations to another conference committee. But no final bill reached the President's desk for signature into law.

Conservative Democrats were responsible for this dismal result, as a brief review of the fate of Secretary Perkin's fair labor standards proposal makes clear. Perkins' bill called for the abolition of child labor, an initial minimum wage of 25 cents an hour (scheduled to increase to 40 cents after seven years), a maximum standard work week of 40 hours (to be phased in over two years), and time-and-a-half pay for overtime work. During the first three weeks of the special session, conservative Democrat John O'Connor of New York kept this measure locked up in his House Rules Committee while liberal Democrat Mary Norton of New Jersey rounded up enough signatures for a discharge petition. Once it was sent to the full House, a vote on the administration bill was blocked by the introduction of a competing measure promoted by AFL president William Green. In the acrimonious debate that followed, Democrats from the South denounced the minimum wage standard as sure to increase already rising unemployment, and as a threat to the color line. Cheered on by many of his southern colleagues, Martin Dies proclaimed "you cannot prescribe the same wages for the black man as for the white man." A few days later, Republicans and 133 Democrats (including 81 of the South's 99 Democratic Representatives) joined together to reject the labor standards proposal. It was the first major defeat for the administration in the House since 1933.

When the Congress reconvened in January 1938, President Roosevelt still hoped to restore the New Deal's political momentum. After opening remarks in which he noted the growing danger of war and the need to "keep ourselves adequately strong in self-defense," the President's message presented unequivocal liberal arguments for enactment of his principal agenda items. For example, he said agricultural adjustment and natural resource planning were needed because there "is not an inherent right of citizenship" for "every free born American to do with his land what he wants." A fair labor standards act, he explained, was "only legislation to end starvation wages and intolerable hours; more desirable wages are and should be the product of collective bargaining." A balanced budget was desirable, Roosevelt conceded, but only if "we continue the policy of not permitting any needy American who can and is willing to work to starve because the Federal Government does not provide the work." The President admitted some recently passed taxes might need to be adjusted, but he also insisted that "speculative income should not be favored over earned income." FDR concluded,

Government has a final responsibility for the well-being of its citizenship. . . . those suffering from hardship from no fault of their own have a right to call upon the Government for aid; and a government worthy of its name must make a fitting response.

Clearly FDR was not giving up the New Deal, even if his own party no longer lined up solidly behind him.

The New Deal's Last Stand

In January 1938 the Senate finally brought to the floor a bill that would have made lynching a federal crime whenever state authorities failed to prosecute it. The Wagner–Costigan anti-lynching bill had been the focus of a highly visible lobbying campaign by the National Association for the Advancement of Colored People (NAACP) in 1934, and it still suffered from FDR's unwillingness to make it an administration priority. Although FDR had denounced lynching as "a vile form of collective murder" in 1933, he also feared southern Democrats in Congress would retaliate against the New Deal if he endorsed the anti-lynching bill. In 1934 he only permitted the bill's sponsors to privately inform Majority Leader Robinson "that the President will be glad to see the bill pass and wishes it passed." Under no real pressure, Robinson sat on the bill for a year. Then a brief southern filibuster led by Texas' Tom Connally sent the anti-lynching measure back to committee.

By 1937 the NAACP had brought an impressive number of churches, academics, labor unions, and other liberal groups into the anti-lynching lobby. Effective lobbying and reports of a particularly gruesome lynching of two black men in Mississippi inspired the House to pass the Wagner–Costigan bill in April. Every Southern Democrat except Maury Maverick of Texas voted against the measure. In the Senate, the Democrats' southern leaders wanted to ignore the anti-lynching bill. However, Robert Wagner's deft parliamentary maneuvering forced the new Majority Leader, Alben Barkley of Kentucky, to put it at the top of the Senate's agenda for 1938.

Contemporary polls showed most Americans, including a narrow majority of Southerners, favored passage of the Wagner–Costigan bill. By January 1938 14 of the Senate's 16 Republicans and a majority of its Democrats had also said publicly that they favored the measure. But all Southern Democrats were opposed. Once the debate started, they stood together ready to talk the anti-lynching bill to death. Reading what these Southern politicians said on the floor of the Senate during this long filibuster reminds us that public racism was still legitimate in the 1930s. Louisiana's Allen Ellender who spoke for six days, proudly proclaimed, "as long as I am in the Senate I expect to fight for white supremacy." South Carolina's James Byrnes explained that the South had "been deserted by the Democrats of the North," and that "the Negroes of the North" now controlled the Democratic Party. Mississippi's Theodore Bilbo, an extreme white supremacist, offered a plan to send all blacks to Africa. Pat Harrison, Mississippi's other Senator, worried that the anti-lynching bill was just the first step on a slippery slope. "The next thing . . . ," he declared, "will be a bill to provide that miscegenation of the races cannot be prohibited." Senator Connally speculated that race liberals, the Roosevelt administration, and communism were linked. Six weeks into the filibuster, Southern leaders promised to talk "until Christmas" unless the bill was withdrawn. By this time many members and the President were anxious to move on to other business. FDR remained unwilling to risk any political capital on behalf of the measure. On February 16th, a motion to close the filibuster failed, so the Wagner–Costigan bill was again sent back to committee.

The anti-lynching filibuster revealed a fundamental difference between conservative and liberal Democrats, and one of the most serious political difficulties Franklin Roosevelt faced as the head of an ideologically incoherent party. Roosevelt's silence during the anti-lynching filibuster frustrated many liberals, but it helped him get the support of key Southern leaders and committee chairmen in Congress during important legislative battles in 1938. Farm groups and the President had asked Congress pass the agriculture bill before planting began. As soon as the anti-lynching debate ended, congressional Democrats moved quickly to approve the conference committee's agriculture bill. The Agricultural Adjustment Act of 1938 re-established parity price supports and renewed conservation, crop loan, and surplus storage programs. Congressional Democrats also acted swiftly to increase spending on urban and rural relief. The recession which had thrown several million people out of work convinced most of them that additional spending was needed. After New Deal supporter Lister Hill won an easy victory in Alabama's Senate primary election in January, conservative Democrats also worried about their re-election prospects if they opposed still popular spending to ameliorate unemployment. FDR made an emergency request for additional $250,000,000 for WPA in February, and sent his even more important $3,750,000,000 fiscal stimulus package to Congress in April (see Chapter 7). Although a couple of conservative Democrats joined Republicans in trying to cut back these requests, both spending bills were approved by overwhelming Democratic majorities.

Before adjourning in June, Congress also approved FDR's last anti-trust initiative, a request for authorization of "a thorough study of the concentration of economic power in American industry." Administration liberals including presidential advisors Corcoran and Cohen, Interior Secretary Ickes, and Assistant Attorney General Robert Jackson had been spreading the idea that monopoly was the underlying cause of the recession. Although these men originally spoke without consulting FDR, he was soon persuaded that anti-trust action would be an appropriate policy complement to his fiscal stimulus proposal. Senator Joseph O'Mahoney of Wyoming, a longstanding critic of monopoly, directed the task of turning the President's request into legislation. Since it required little spending, and promised to take years before producing any legislative recommendations, a bill establishing a Temporary National Economic Committee (TNEC) sailed through Congress.

During the next three years, the TNEC produced 43 monographs on the practices of American business. But, aside from a few changes in patent law, no effective anti-trust action resulted from the TNEC's work. FDR's appointment of Yale's Thurman Arnold to head the Justice Department's anti-trust division was actually more effective. Arnold directed his staff to go after excessively restrictive patents and the monopolistic practices of big industrial corporations and housing contractors. Before wartime protests from military contractors forced him to curtail this work, Arnold had initiated more anti-trust suits than any of his predecessors.

On May 2, 1938 liberal Congressman Claude Pepper, who was publicly praised by FDR, easily won Florida's Democratic Senate primary. Pepper's victory struck fear in the hearts of many Democrats who had opposed the President's Fair Labor Standards bill. In fact enough of them signed Congresswoman Mary Norton's discharge petition on May 6th to finally bring the bill back to the floor of the House for a vote. Two weeks later, after an all-night debate on nearly 50 amendments designed to limit coverage or cripple enforcement, the House passed a Fair Labor Standards bill. Fifty-two Southern Democrats who still wanted a lower wage standard for their region voted against the bill. Senate approval for the legislation came quickly once concessions were made that would allow below national standard wages in the South for as long as seven years. President Roosevelt signed the Fair Labor Standards Act on June 25th. In a fireside chat the night before the signing ceremony FDR asserted "Except perhaps for the Social Security Act, it is the most far-reaching, far-sighted program for workers ever adopted."

Many of the FLSA's liberal supporters took these presidential words with a grain of salt. They knew conservatives in Congress had so limited the FLSA's coverage that its impact would be much less than FDR claimed. Agricultural workers, fishermen, seamen, intrastate transport workers, most construction workers, domestic servants, as well as most white collar, retail, and service workers were placed in exempted categories. Over time FLSA coverage would be expanded, and more workers would be covered when higher wage minimum standards took effect. But the Labor Department reported only

300,000 workers would actually see their wages raised to 25 cents an hour in 1938. For this reason, the much-amended FLSA, which most historians consider the last New Deal reform, may also be seen as a victory for the New Deal's opponents.

Conservative Democrats and Republicans showed their continued strength in other ways during the congressional session that ended with passage of the FLSA. The conservative coalition had already blocked passage of FDR's proposal for "seven little TVAs" in 1937. They were no more receptive to the proposal in 1938. Jurisdictional questions raised by the Agriculture and Interior Departments, Army Corps of Engineers, and the Bureau of Reclamation made the congressional conservatives' work easy. There were so many objections voiced against the President's regional planning bill, it never even came up for a vote.

FDR's Executive reorganization plan also failed to win approval in 1938. Over the winter Senator Byrnes had convinced the President to scale back the plan. When Congress convened, the Senate's Southern leaders agreed to push for passage of the revised bill. It was a difficult task. The downsized plan passed by just six votes on a day when three staunch conservatives were absent. By the time Executive reorganization reached the House in April, Father Coughlin had claimed the measure would set up a "financial dictatorship in the person of the President." Hundreds of thousands of telegrams and letters opposing the bill poured into congressional offices. Editorials all across the nation warned of the dire consequences of putting more power in FDR's hands. Responding to this unexpectedly strong show of public unease with his presidency, a defensive Franklin Roosevelt felt obliged to tell reporters,

> I have no inclination to be a dictator. I have none of the qualifications that would make me a successful dictator. I have too much historical background and too much knowledge of existing dictatorships to make me desire any form of dictatorship for a democracy like the United States.

Conservative Democrats in the House remained unmoved by this rather remarkable statement. Rules Committee chairman

John O'Connor of New York who led the Democratic opposition told his colleagues, "this is no time to further incense our people, who have gone through eight years of a depression and who since last fall have suffered a relapse." Despite FDR's personal lobbying efforts, 108 House Democrats deserted him on the final vote, enough to kill his Executive reorganization plan in 1938.

Shortly before the 75th Congress adjourned, the House approved conservative Democrat Martin Dies' request for a special committee to investigate subversive activity in the United States. To attract enough votes for the proposal, Congressman Dies and his supporters indicated that the hundreds of fascist and anti-Semitic groups which had appeared around the country since 1933 would be a major target of the committee's work. In fact, when the House Committee for the Investigation of Un-American Activities set up shop in August 1938, it virtually ignored domestic fascism. On the second day of hearings Dies called on AFL vice-president John Frey to testify. Frey immediately told the committee a story about Communist infiltration of the labor movement. The CIO, Frey charged, "became a carrier of the virus of communism." Frey, like hundreds of witnesses who would follow him in the years to come, gave the committee the names of CIO union officials whom he believed were either Communist Party members or dupes of the Communists. In this first series of hearings Dies' also targeted liberal Democrats who were supportive of the CIO, or who had failed to denounce the sit-down strikes. Witnesses from Flint, Michigan's police department and the American Legion provided the committee with the names of alleged Communists in the UAW, while Flint's city manager charged "members of the LaFollette committee and Governor Murphy" with "treasonable action." These charges were picked up by Republicans in Michigan, and played a major role in the unseating of Governor Murphy in November.

By the time the 75th Congress adjourned, Franklin Roosevelt was already working to bolster support for the New Deal. He tried two different strategies. First, Roosevelt worked quietly to heal the split in the labor movement. He realized that working people had given him his great election victory in 1936, and thought that unified labor support for him could restore the New Deal's lost political momentum. This reconciliation effort (which Roosevelt continued in 1939) proved to be an exercise in futility. Neither the AFL's William Green nor the CIO's John L. Lewis was ready to make any concession to unify the labor movement. In fact, as we have just seen, rather than coming to the rescue of the New Deal, AFL officials were working closely with some of its most outspoken opponents by the summer of 1938. Although sometimes overlooked by historians, the split in the labor movement played a major role in ending the New Deal.

Franklin Roosevelt's other more public strategy for restarting the New Deal remains controversial. He described it in an unusual fireside chat in June 1938 during which the President said he was speaking "as the head of the Democratic Party." That night FDR told listeners that "many Copperheads" who did not share his liberal principles were blocking reforms wanted by the great majority of the people. The President announced that he would campaign in primaries "in those few instances where there may be a clear-cut issue between candidates for a Democratic nomination involving these [liberal] principles." At the time, Roosevelt was already trying, without much success, to enlist liberal candidates to run in the primaries against conservative incumbents. In July FDR campaigned for key New Deal supporters such as Senator Barkley, and against a few of the most prominent Democratic opponents of the New Deal. In Barnesville, Georgia, while Democratic Senator Walter George sat on the platform listening, Roosevelt endorsed the Senator's primary opponent saying, "on most public questions he [George] and I do not speak the same language." FDR targeted five Southern Senators and Congressman O'Connor this kind of treatment, but only O'Connor was defeated.

FDR's effort to achieve more ideological consistency in the Democratic party failed. As the major political story of the 1938 primary season the President's so-called "purge" reinforced the conservative charge that FDR still harbored dictatorial ambitions. Conservatives repeated that charge in the

November election. Republicans also claimed that New Dealers were responsible for sit-downs and the CIO strike wave. New Deal supporters already on the defensive because of the recession, did not respond effectively. Many of them failed to hold their seats. Republicans picked up seven seats in the Senate and 75 members in the House, mostly at the expense of Democratic liberals.

The 1938 congressional elections closed the door on the New Deal. Although the Democratic Party controlled the new 76th Congress and its committees, a coalition of Republicans and just 50 conservative Democrats could vote down any administration bill in the House. President Roosevelt did win support for expanding social security benefits, and he did get congressional approval for a scaled-down Executive reorganization plan.[3] He also won approval for important liberal appointees including Frank Murphy as Attorney General and Felix Frankfurter and William O. Douglas to the Supreme Court. But most of the time New Deal opponents forced him into defending what had already been achieved in domestic policy, rather than allowing him to extend the New Deal.

Before the 76th Congress convened in January 1939, Vice-President Garner offered to act as liaison between the White House and the conservative Democrats on Capitol Hill. Garner advised FDR to moderate his attacks on "economic royalists" and "Copperheads," and to go along with some legislation desired by business organizations. In 1939–40, the President moved a bit in the direction Garner outlined, reluctantly accepting some pro-business measures such as repeal of the undistributed corporate profits tax. Under pressure from the AFL and congressional conservatives who wanted to amend the Wagner Act, FDR also changed the personnel of the NLRB so that it was no longer dominated by men who clearly favored the CIO's industrial organizing drive. And he signed into law bills that emerged from conservative congressional investigations. Cuts in work relief, termination of the Federal Theater Project, and the Hatch Act all fell into this category.[4]

Events overseas strongly influenced these domestic political developments. As war spread across Asia and Europe in these years a politics of fear arose in the United States, especially among conservative opponents of the New Deal. What is usually called "McCarthyism" – the particular form of witness-baiting associated with Senator Joseph McCarthy's investigations of the early 1950s – was actually first used to great effect by congressional conservatives against a host of New Deal agencies, New Deal officials, and the CIO in 1939–40. To counter the politics of fear, and to prepare the country for possible intervention in the world war, Franklin Roosevelt once again appealed for national unity to preserve democracy.

War overseas, and the threat that Nazi Germany might conquer Western Europe and Britain, presented Franklin Roosevelt with a whole new set of political challenges and opportunities. During his first term as President, FDR had concentrated on domestic affairs. His "Good Neighbor" renunciation of the use of force in the Caribbean and Latin American countries, and Secretary of State Cordell Hull's pursuit of more liberal trading arrangements with "most favored nations" were significant international initiatives. But Roosevelt had also gone along with isolationists in Congress who imposed prohibitions on American loans and trade with belligerent nations. Congress' fiscal conservatism and the Neutrality Acts of 1935–37 made it very difficult for FDR to pursue his preferred policy of sending aid to Britain when the war started in Europe. In 1939 Franklin Roosevelt put his plans for new reforms on the back burner. Turning away from the economic security issues that had so divided the country, he once again asked for the country to unite behind him as it faced a new and truly frightening national emergency.

World War II gave FDR the rare political opportunity for a second "rendezvous with destiny." It took all of his considerable political skills to slowly steer the country and the Congress towards intervention in a global conflict certain to be long, costly, and very bloody. In 1940 he was not really ready to relinquish the office which he loved, and he also feared conservative Democrats would nominate one of their own. So FDR decided to run for an unprecedented third term. In 1940 his victory margin over Republican challenger Wendell Wilkie was significantly smaller than his majority in 1936. Moreover, Democrats picked up just a few seats in Congress in 1940. But Roosevelt himself still retained the solid support of the ethnic and working class voters who wanted the right to economic security protected. The election of 1940 ratified what the New Deal had achieved; there would be no conservative counter-revolution any time soon. But neither would there be an opportunity to fulfill all the liberal promises of the New Deal. Nearly 60 years after he set down the agenda, Franklin Roosevelt's wartime "Economic Bill of Rights" remains a blueprint for future liberal reforms.

FURTHER READING

Primary Sources

Farley, James A. *Behind the Ballots: The Personal History of a Politician.* New York: Harcourt, Brace and Company, 1938.

Freedman, Max, ed. *Roosevelt & Frankfurter: Their Correspondence, 1928–1945.* Boston: Little, Brown and Company, 1967.

Ickes, Harold L. *The Secret Diary of Harold Ickes, Volume II: The Inside Struggle 1936–1939.* New York: Simon and Shuster, 1954.

Perkins, Frances. *The Roosevelt I Knew.* New York: Viking, 1946.

Eleanor Roosevelt. *This I Remember.* New York: Harper & Brothers, 1949.

Elliot Roosevelt ed. *F. D. R.: His Personal Letters 1928–1945.* New York: Duell, Sloan and Pearce, 1950.

Markowitz, Gerald and Rosner, David eds. *"Slaves of the Depression": Workers Letters about Life on the Job.* Ithaca: Cornell University Press, 1987.

Roosevelt, Franklin D. *The Public Papers and Addresses of Franklin D. Roosevelt, 1937 Volume: The Constitution Prevails.* New York: Macmillan, 1941.

Roosevelt, Franklin D. *The Public Papers and Addresses of Franklin D. Roosevelt, 1938 Volume: The Continuing Struggle for Liberalism.* New York: Macmillan, 1941.

Roosevelt, Franklin D. *The Public Papers and Addresses of Franklin D. Roosevelt, 1939 Volume: War – And Neutrality.* New York: Macmillan, 1941.

Simon, Rita James. *As We Saw the Thirties: Essays on Social and Political Movements of a Decade.* Urbana: University of Illinois Press, 1967.

Zinn, Howard ed. *New Deal Thought.* Indianapolis: Bobbs-Merrill, 1966.

Secondary Sources

Bernstein, Irving. *A Caring Society: The New Deal, The Worker, and the Great Depression*. Boston: Houghton Mifflin, 1985.

Bernstein, Irving. *Turbulent Years: A History of the American Worker, 1933–1941*. Boston: Houghton Mifflin, 1971.

Blum, John Morton. *From the Morgenthau Diaries: Years of Crisis, 1928–1938*. Boston: Houghton Mifflin, 1959.

Brinkley, Alan. *The End of Reform: New Deal Liberalism in Recession and War*. New York: Alfred A. Knopf, 1995.

Dallek, Robert. *Franklin D. Roosevelt and American Foreign Policy*. New York: Oxford University Press, 1979.

Dubofsky, Melvyn. *The State and Labor in Modern America*. Chapel Hill: University of North Carolina Press, 1994.

Egerton, John. *Speak Against the Day: The Generation before the Civil Rights Movement in the South*. Chapel Hill: University of North Carolina Press, 1994.

Fine, Sidney. *Sit-Down: The General Motors Strike of 1936–37*. Ann Arbor: University of Michigan Press, 1969.

Huthmacher, J. Joseph. *Senator Robert F. Wagner and the Rise of New Deal Liberalism*. New York: Atheneum, 1968.

Leuchtenburg, William E. *The Supreme Court Reborn: The Constitutional Revolution in the Age of Roosevelt*. New York: Oxford University Press, 1995.

Leuchtenburg, William E. *The FDR Years: On Roosevelt & His Legacy*. New York: Columbia University Press, 1995.

Patterson, James T. *Congressional Conservatism and the New Deal: The Growth of the Conservative Coalition in Congress, 1933–1939*. Lexington: University of Kentucky Press, 1967.

Sitkoff, Harvard. *A New Deal for Blacks: The Emergence of Civil Rights as a National Issue*. New York: Oxford University Press, 1978.

Zieger, Robert H. *The CIO, 1935–1955*. Chapel Hill: University of North Carolina Press, 1995.

Epilogue: The Legacy of the New Deal

"We are definitely in an era of building, the best kind of building – the building of great public projects for the benefit of the public and with the objective of building human happiness."
Franklin D. Roosevelt, Radio Address Delivered at Two Medicine Chalet, Glacier National Park, August 5, 1934

This book has treated the New Deal as a creative political response to the Great Depression. Some of the reforms initiated by Franklin Roosevelt's New Deal might well have been enacted under different circumstances, but we cannot know this for sure. What we do know is that the particular economic and political circumstances of the Great Depression allowed the Roosevelt administration to achieve the most significant liberal reform of the federal government in American history. For just a few short years in the mid-1930s, public faith in private enterprise and individualism was so shaken that liberals who believed government could do good things well had a unique opportunity to put their ideas into practice without significant conservative opposition. The New Deal's greatest successes – including its reversal of the terrifying downward economic spiral in 1933 and its establishment of greater economic security for all Americans in 1935 – insured that its economic reforms would remain secure for at least as long as most voters could remember the Great Depression.

The New Deal also created an enduring liberal nationalism. New Deal nationalism differed greatly from the "100% Americanism" that had flourished in the 1920s. It was premised on respect for cultural differences, not Anglo-Saxon racial superiority. Many New Dealers promoted the ideals of cultural pluralism, imbedding them in federal policies that reversed Washington's longstanding presumption of white supremacy. Perhaps the most striking reversal occurred in 1934 when Congress approved the Roosevelt administration's Indian Reorganization Act. For 50 years the federal government had tried to force Native Americans to live like white farmers. The so-called "Indian New Deal" of 1934 completely rejected this assimilationist policy goal. New Dealers restored tribal ownership of land and created the machinery for establishing tribal self-government. Although the original legislation was flawed and rejected by some of the tribes, the Roosevelt administration's advocacy of self-determination for Native Americans set a new course for federal Indian policy.

The New Deal created a political climate in which advocates of cultural pluralism could successfully challenge white supremacy. Judged by our current standards, Franklin Roosevelt and the New Deal may look woefully inadequate when it came to guaranteeing racial equality and the participation of minority groups in American life. But this judgment is unfair and distorted by present-mindedness. We must remember that white supremacy ruled in American politics until the New Deal. The New Deal did not completely overcome this entrenched white supremacy, but it did take significant first steps that undermined its legitimacy in national politics.

"He made concessions to the South . . . ," W. E. B. DuBois wrote in 1948,

> He was often ill-advised by [white] Southerners. But nevertheless, under no recent President have Negroes felt that they have received as much justice as under Franklin Roosevelt. I supported him all four terms.

So did almost every other African-American voter. Minority voters recognized that New Dealers were serious when they said that economic security should be a political right for all Americans. Most other Americans also recognized this commitment to racial equality, and many of them turned against the New Deal for just that reason. As a result, race issues once again began to play a major role in defining the country's political competition. The New Deal created the basis for this new, more democratic era in American politics by making racial equality a legitimate goal of public policy.

The New Deal clearly imbedded its liberal legacy in the nation's government and politics. It also imbedded its legacy in America's built environment. In January 1937, Henry Luce's new photo-magazine *Life* published a two-page view of the country titled "What President Roosevelt Did To The Map of The U.S. In Four Years With $6,500,000,000." Luce's mapmakers highlighted improvements in urban infrastructure, hydroelectric dams and water projects, construction of educational facilities, and new recreational areas. Their map of the United States included little drawings of New York's Triborough bridge and Midtown tunnel, Chicago's sewer plant, and the San Francisco Post Office. It shows the Norris, Fort Peck, and Grand Coulee dams; and the Humboldt and Los Angeles aqueducts. It also depicts public schools built in rural South Carolina and Fort Worth, Texas; dormitories at Texas Tech and the University of Minnesota; and the Roanoake Island restoration, Dinosaur Park, and Glacier Park's Trans-Mountain Highway. *Life*'s map was of course incomplete. No map its size could display the all of construction and restoration projects brought to fruition by the Roosevelt administration. Nonetheless, *Life*'s map presented a striking representation of an important fact; by 1937 the New Deal had become modern America's master builder.

Today, many Americans have a hard time imagining their federal government could have ever done so many things well. This was not the case in the 1930s. Although New Deal critics hammered away at the Roosevelt administration's spending programs, most Americans recognized what was being achieved. Poet Stephen Vincent Benet wrote in 1940,

> It's written in the water and the earth of the Tennessee Valley
> The contour-plowing that saves the dust-stricken land,
> And the lights coming on for the first time, on lonely farms.

Benet's poem testified to the fact that people in poor and lightly populated regions saw spectacular changes in their built environment during the 1930s. These regions of the United States were transformed by the New Deal as a matter of public policy. The Rocky Mountain and Pacific Coast states benefited most. Before the New Deal, the West was for the most part very sparsely populated and economically underdeveloped. The New Deal took income generated in the East and spent it in the West. The hydroelectric dams, water projects, irrigation canals, and roads built by the New Deal made possible the great expansion of population in West during and after World War II. TVA and other New Deal projects had a similar impact on the Southeast.

Public enterprise improved America in the 1930s. This New Deal achievement greatly disturbed conservatives. So did the New Deal's treatment of all labor, including unemployed labor, as dignified and creative. Nearly 20,000,000 Americans participated in federal work relief programs during the 1930s. You didn't have to live in the West or the Tennessee Valley to see the evidence of their creative labor. All across the United States, the streets, sidewalks, sewers, parks, schools, and other public buildings of almost everyone's hometown showed what these millions of men and women working for the FERA, CWA, WPA, and NYA could do. By now some of what they built has fallen into disrepair or disappeared altogether, but anyone anywhere in America can find the physical legacy of New Deal – whether it's a bridge or road, a Post Office mural or National Forest campground – still serving the nation as intended. For this New Deal legacy all Americans, regardless of their political orientation, can be grateful.

Appendix: A Partial Chronology of Civil Unrest and Financial Panic, the Winter of 1932–33

November 1932

11/5   A black man accused of assaulting a white girl escapes a lynch mob by surrendering to the local sheriff in Blythdale, Arkansas.

11/7   Klansmen attack 7,000 mostly black demonstrators at the Jefferson County Courthouse in Birmingham, Alabama after a speaker calls for racial equality.

A white mob in Clearwater, Florida whips W. D. Williams, a black advocate of equal relief for whites and African-Americans.

Police use tear gas to break up a Communist-led demonstration outside the Supreme Court as it ordered new trials in the *Scottsboro* case.

11/10   A bomb destroys the Birmingham, Alabama home of Owen Roper, an African-American.

Hundreds of whites chase Henry Campbell, a black man accused of murder, into a South Carolina swamp where Campbell is shot to death.

11/19   William House, an African-American arrested for insulting a white woman, is abducted from jail and lynched in Wisner, Louisiana.

11/21   In Cleveland mounted police injure a dozen people

while battling hundreds of demonstrators on the City Hall steps.

11/23   Police use clubs to break up a protest march to Chicago's Humboldt relief station injuring 14 women and children.

11/24   District police block taxis carrying the Children's Misery March to the White House and arrest the group's leaders and a black cab driver on charges of contributing to the delinquency of minors.

11/28   Tens of thousands attend rallies in 46 states at the beginning of the second National Hunger March. Police break up demonstrations in Birmingham, Alabama; Charlotte, North Carolina; and Chattanooga, Tennessee.

December 1932

12/2   Trenton, New Jersey workers stage a general strike when Hunger Marchers pass through downtown. In Wilmington, Delaware police use clubs and tear gas to drive the marchers out of the city.

12/3   500 hooded and armed Klansmen hold a "They Shall Not Pass" rally blocking one column of the Hunger March in Virginia.

12/4   1,200 District police confine and harass 3,000 hunger marchers for three days on a section of New York Avenue in Northeast Washington.

12/5   Heavily armed police surround the Capitol when the 72nd Congress opens its lame duck session in Washington.
        Masked vigilantes take six union organizers from jail in Vacaville, California, paint them red and whip them. Sheriff's deputies near Elkhorn, Wisconsin use machine guns and tear gas to evict farmer Max Cichon.

12/6   Vigilantes calling themselves "Minute Men" attack picket lines in the Vacaville fruit pickers' strike.

12/7   After protests by Senator Costigan and Congressmen

LaGuardia, Amlie, and Swing, police permit several thousand white and black Hunger Marchers to parade along a heavily guarded route to the Capitol.

In Clarendon, South Carolina, Moody Jackson, a black man, is moved from jail to save him from a lynch mob.

12/12 A three-month-old Oakland taxi strike erupts into fighting between strikers and strikebreaking vigilantes that leaves one man dead and one missing.

12/19 In Reeltown, Alabama, sheriff's deputies and white vigilantes shoot at least 17 African-Americans and beat many others including a 100-year-old man whom they dragged from his bed.

12/20 A black murder suspect is moved from a jail in Yuma, Arizona after crowd of whites threatened to lynch him.

January 1933

1/2 The President's Commission on Recent Social Trends warns there "can be no assurance" that "violent revolution" can be averted.

Rent strikes organized by a Communist-led Bronx Tenants' Emergency League in south Bronx spread to Manhattan and Queens; daily confrontations between thousands of pickets and police result.

Thousands of Iowa farmers stop foreclosure actions at the county courthouses in Harrison, Montgomery, and Linn counties.

1/4 Rival miners' unions fight a gun battle in Taylorville, Illinois. Two miners are killed and 14 wounded. State police arrest 18 men for murder.

Los Angeles police use tear gas and clubs to disperse thousands of demonstrators demanding "Work or Wages."

1/5 New York City (NYC) police disperse hundreds of demonstrators in front of the President-elect's Manhattan townhouse. Police also battle 2,000 demonstrators at an eviction in the Bronx.

The "Farmers' Council for Defense" takes over the courthouse in Le Mars, Iowa, slapping the local sheriff, and forcing a judge ask the governor for a foreclosure moratorium.

In Chicago, a white mob attacks the house of a black man who had moved into an all-white neighborhood.

1/7   A thousand farmers stop a resumption of foreclosure actions in Le Mars, Iowa.

Governor Rolf refuses to meet with over 1,000 delegates from California's Unemployed Councils.

Several thousand Hunger Marchers begin three days of disruptive demonstrations in Olympia, Washington.

1/12   A white mob flogs and kills Fell Jenkins, a black man, in Homer, Louisiana.

1/13   Thousands of Iowa farmers demonstrate, blocking sheriff's sales in Bedford and Holstein, and taking over a courthouse in Logan.

Thousands of unemployed demonstrators protesting racial discrimination in relief repeatedly charge police lines at the entrance to NYC's Emergency Work and Relief Bureau.

1/15   Fighting erupts during a Los Angeles City Council meeting when the police Red Squad tries to arrest people testifying against the deportation of alien radicals.

1/16   State police in Trenton, New Jersey defend the doors of the state capitol against hundreds of demonstrators trying to bring demands for adequate relief to the legislature.

1/21   Hundreds of cars carrying southeastern Minnesota farmers and businessmen slow traffic with motorcade to St. Paul, where they demand tax relief from Governor Olson.

500 farmers force Shelby, Nebraska's sheriff to accept a low bid from the property's owner at a tax auction.

NYC police break up a food riot at a Union Square restaurant after hundreds of unemployed people demanded free meals.

1/22   Over 1,000 farmers take over a courthouse in Willmar, Minnesota, preventing foreclosure actions.

In Pilger, Nebraska, hundreds of farmers threaten to lynch a sheriff unless he accepts the owner's $25 bid at a farm foreclosure sale.

1/23   6,000 workers strike four Briggs auto body plants in Detroit protesting wage cuts and a speedup.

1/24   1,000 farmers seize the Pocahantas, Iowa courthouse, forcing a judge to impose a moratorium on foreclosures.

In Overton, Nebraska, 200 farmers stop a tax auction by threatening to douse bidders in a horse tank.

1/25   City and state police club hundreds of demonstrators trying to reach the governor's office in Springfield, Illinois.

Two Chicago policeman are beaten unconscious during a food riot on the city's southside.

1/26   Street fighting between demonstrators and police spreads in Chicago.

The Associated Press reports mass demonstrations and courthouse takeovers by farmers in Idaho, South Dakota, Iowa, Wisconsin, and Ohio on this day.

Women from Illinois' coal fields stage a "peace march" in Springfield.

1/27   Six white policemen are severely beaten by hundreds of black demonstrators in Chicago.

Police battle 1,000 strikers at a Briggs plant gates in Detroit.

800 farmers compel an auctioneer to accept the owner's low bid for a farm near Bowling Green, Ohio.

In Idaho, a "United Farmers League" is formed; it threatens an armed march on the state capitol unless foreclosures and tax collections are suspended.

1/28   Hundreds of heavily armed police wearing military helmets prevent thousands of demonstrators from gathering in downtown Chicago.

Briggs' management offers concessions that ends the violent strike in Detroit.

1/31   Farmers take over the Howard City, Michigan court-
        house, stopping foreclosure proceedings.
        Police battle hundreds of demonstrators protesting on
        Sixth Street in Manhattan.

February 1933

2/1   Thousands of angry farmers force "penny sales" in
        Ivesdale, Illinois; Aurora, Nebraska; and Cherokee,
        Oklahoma.
        Massed farmers protest foreclosures in South Caroli-
        na's capital city.
        Georgia's Governor Talmadge negotiates a foreclos-
        ure moratorium with 15 mortgage lending companies.
        Thousands march through New York's garment dis-
        trict protesting inadequate relief.
2/2   In Clearwater, Florida a lynch mob wrecks the home
        of Reverend G. W. Brown while searching for W. D.
        Williams who had returned to see his family (see 11/7
        above).
2/3   Four men are shot when they try to run a roadblock
        put up by striking dairy farmers in Riverside, Iowa.
2/4   A farmer is shot dead while trying to run a Farm Holi-
        day roadblock near Jefferson, South Dakota.
        Over 1,000 farmers block a foreclosure sale in −22
        degree temperatures in Willmar, Minnesota.
        The governors of Minnesota, Ohio, Illinois, South
        Carolina, and Tennessee call for foreclosure morato-
        ria on this day.
2/6   100 farmers try to lynch a landlord in Anita, Iowa;
        the sheriff intervenes and arrests the landlord.
        Police in Chester, Pennsylvania use tear gas against
        demonstrators protesting evictions.
2/7   2,000 farmers in Bowling Green, Ohio force an auc-
        tioneer to accept the owner's low bid on his foreclosed
        farm.
2/8   Over 1,000 farmers, some armed with axe handles,

attack a bank representative near Ithaca, Michigan.
Over 700 farmers in Yorkville, Illinois pledge to use force if necessary to block foreclosures and evictions.
200 farmers in Reidsville, Georgia force a "penny sale" of an auctioned farm.

2/10   Idaho farmers calling themselves "Minute Men" use whips and tar and feathers to stop all foreclosure actions in the Twin Falls region.
Police club demonstrators outside reach relief offices in Pittsburgh.

2/11   An Unemployed Council demonstration is broken up by police in Richmond, Virginia and its African-American organizers are arrested.

2/13   Detroit's leading bankers urge Michigan's Governor Comstock to declare a bank holiday.
11 farmers are arrested during a foreclosure riot in Jefferson, Wisconsin.

2/14   Governor Comstock declares an eight-day bank holiday in Michigan.
Hundreds of demonstrators repeatedly charge police lines outside a NYC relief bureau.
Thousands of jobless people seize the 11-story county building in Seattle.
Police call up reserves to evict hundreds of demonstrators who had seized a Welfare Bureau station in Rochester, New York.

2/15   Guiseppe Zangara tries to kill Franklin D. Roosevelt in Miami (see Chapter 6).
Over 4,000 farmers march on the Nebraska State Capitol demanding an end to foreclosures.
5,000 demonstrators turn fire hoses on police trying to remove them from Seattle's county building; the police respond with tear gas and clubs.
Over 5,000 farmers march on the Indiana State Capitol demanding suspension of property tax collections.
7,000 demonstrators organized by the Unemployed Workers League march on the state capitol in Columbus, Ohio.

Farm groups and unemployed miners in Pennsylvania announce a march on the state capitol in Harrisburg.

2/16   In South Carolina, 16-year-old Will Sanders, an African-American, is arrested, arraigned, tried, convicted, and sentenced to death in one hour after being accused of murdering a white woman.

2/17   The governors of Iowa, South Dakota, and Wisconsin sign foreclosure moratoria into law; similar legislation is pending in six other states.

2/18   Thousands of farmers stop foreclosure sales in Kankakee, Illinois; Willmar, Minnesota, and Enid, Oklahoma.

Sheriff's deputies prevent hundreds of farmers from disrupting an auction sale in Fairmont, Minnesota.

Striking dairy farmers block roads, stop trucks, and dump milk in Wisconsin.

2/19   Roadblocks and milk dumping spread in Wisconsin.

Accused murderer Nelson Nash, a black man, is abducted from jail and lynched by a white mob in Ringgold, Louisiana.

In Aiken, South Carolina, George Jeter, a black man, is flogged to death by a white mob who accused Jeter of stealing bootleg liquor.

2/20   Michigan's legislature votes to give the governor power to close all banks in the state.

2/21   Thousands of farmers prevent foreclosures in three separate Idaho locations.

The Oklahoma, Texas, Arkansas, and Alabama legislatures all debate emergency foreclosure moratoria.

2/23   Michigan's bank holiday is extended indefinitely. A bank holiday is declared in neighboring Indiana.

Police battle over 1,000 demonstrators who had seized the City County Building in Salt Lake City.

100 sheriff's deputies disperse thousands of farmers who were demonstrating in Kankakee, Illinois.

Hundreds of farmers block auction sales in Fairmont, Minnesota.

Striking dairy farmers continue to block roads and

dump milk in Wisconsin.

2/24   Martial law is imposed on southern Illinois after rioting in the coalfields.

2/25   A bank holiday is declared in Maryland.
Protests against evictions, foreclosures, and inadequate relief continue; dairy strikes are begun in Pacific Northwest and the Northeast.

2/27   A bank holiday is imposed in Arkansas. For next 10 days the bank panic and the inauguration of the New Deal completely dominate the news.

2/28   State governments close banks in Ohio and Tennessee. Seventeen state legislatures consider limiting withdrawals or declaring bank holidays.

March 1933

3/1   Bank holidays are declared in Alabama and Louisiana; Kentucky and West Virginia leave the decision to close up to individual banks.

3/2   Bank holidays are imposed in California, Arizona, Oregon, Nevada, Mississippi, and Oklahoma. The District of Columbia and several states require 60-day notices for withdrawals from banks.

3/3   The governors of Georgia, Wisconsin, New Mexico, and Utah declare bank holidays; North Carolina, Virginia, and Wyoming restrict withdrawals.

3/4   New York and Illinois close the nation's largest banks. Unemployed Council and Unemployed Citizens League demonstrations are held in many cities. Police fight a pitched battle with protestors in Oakland, California.
Franklin D. Roosevelt is inaugurated President of the United States.

Notes

Notes to Chapter 1

1   The term "progressive" describes a political orientation that had emerged in response to the rise of big business and industrial cities. Progressives formed significant factions in both the Republican and Democratic parties. They believed government had a duty to remedy persistent economic and social problems.

2   Stock purchasers borrowed from brokers to buy particular issues. The stock purchased served as collateral for brokers' loans. These loans were known as call loans because brokers could demand full repayment at any time, and would do so whenever the price of stocks dropped. In 1929, brokers could loan up to ninety percent of the purchase price of a stock to their customers. The extensive use of these loans made this stock market highly vulnerable to panic selling.

3   The United States Census defined "rural" as any place with fewer than 2,500 inhabitants.

4   When the moratorium expired in mid-1932, war debt and reparations payments were not resumed. Only Finland ever fully repaid its war debt to the United States.

Notes to Chapter 2

1   These widely Bureau of Labor Statistics *estimates* of average annual unemployment were based on limited surveys of various local labor markets and reports made by labor unions and relief agencies. More accurate unemployment measures were developed after 1933.

2   Slow assets are investments such as real estate and mortgages that cannot be easily converted to cash, especially in a depressed economy.

3   "Liberal" was beginning to replace the older term "progressive" in the early 1930s. In those years, progressive Republicans and liberal Demo-

crats shared similar ideas about government reform and controlling big business.

Notes to Chapter 3

1   Almost 900,000 voters, 2.2 percent of the total, cast their ballots for the Socialist Party candidate, Norman Thomas.

Notes to Chapter 4

1   The Democratic convention had unambiguously endorsed the repeal of prohibition in 1932. During the campaign, Franklin Roosevelt hardly mentioned repeal but voters were well aware of the Democratic position on the issue. After the Democratic landslide in the election, Congress debated and passed the Twenty-first Amendment repealing prohibition. The amendment was sent to special state conventions in February 1933 and was ratified 10 months later.
2   Scrip was usually issued in the form of small bill-like sheets of paper on which was printed the issuer's promise to pay the bearer a specific amount at some future date.

Notes to Chapter 5

1   During bank holidays government officials and bankers tried to arrange loans that would allow weak institutions to meet the demands of depositors. They hoped these actions would encourage depositors to leave their funds in the banks.

Notes to Chapter 6

1   Anton Cermak's fight for life was front-page news along with reports of FDR's movements and the spreading bank panic. Cermak finally succumbed to his wounds on March 5th, the day after Roosevelt's inauguration.
2   This was the greatest volume of White House mail in American history. Franklin and Eleanor Roosevelt continued to receive an unprecedented numbers of letters: 15,000,000 by 1945. Hoover's mailroom had been staffed by a single person. FDR hired 70 people to insure that every letter received a signed reply.

Notes to Chapter 7

1 Life expectancy at birth increased from 61 to 64 years for whites during the 1930s. Life expectancy for blacks increased from 48 to 53 years.
2 FDR had asked Morgenthau to become acting Treasury Secretary in November 1933 when William Woodin took a leave of absence for health reasons. Morgenthau's position was regularized in January 1934 after Woodin failed to recover.

Notes to Chapter 8

1 The Court also struck down the 1934 Farm Mortgage Act, and it denied the President power to remove members of regulatory commissions.
2 The term "sick industry" described an older industry burdened by over-capacity spread over many firms. Unregulated sick industries were likely to produce fierce price competition, as well as wage-cutting and increased work loads (speed-ups and stretch-outs) for workers.

Notes to Chapter 9

1 Speculation that Long might run for President turned out to be moot. Huey Long was assassinated in Baton Rouge on September 8, 1935.

Notes to Chapter 10

1 See Chapter 7 for the fiscal ramifications of this proposal.
2 Each state, the District of Columbia, Puerto Rico, Hawaii, and New York City had a WPA administrative center. California was divided between WPA offices based in San Francisco and Los Angeles.
3 These challenges were resolved on May 24, 1937 when the Supreme Court ruled the social security was constitutional because it addressed problems which were "plainly national in area and dimension."
4 The federal government already taxed full estates before heirs received any shares. The inheritance tax was designed to tax what heirs received from estates as personal income.
5 The National Emergency Council was established in November 1933 to help FDR coordinate the activities of Cabinet departments and recently created New Deal agencies. It met every few weeks in 1934 as Roosevelt tried to use it to plan policy, but gradually became moribund in 1935.
6 In May the Supreme Court had invalidated the Guffey Bituminous Coal Conservation Act.

Notes to Chapter 11

1   Independent and minor party candidates won four Senate seats and 13
    places in the House in 1936. Most of these representatives supported
    New Deal reforms.
2   The amendments pushed the retirement age up to 75 years while limit-
    ing the President's power to expand the Court to just one additional
    judge per year.
3   The reorganization plan's most important feature was the establishment
    of the Executive Office of the President which included a staff of six
    presidential assistants.
4   The Hatch Act originated in an investigation of political influence in the
    WPA, and ended up a sweeping prohibition against any political activ-
    ity by federal employees.

Index

Hughes, Charles Evans, 130, 257, 260, 262
Hull, Cordell, 128, 282
Humboldt Aqueduct (Nevada), 287
Hundred Days (1933), 8, 136–47, 173, 194
  criticisms, 145–7
hunger *see* starvation
hunger marches, 108
Hutcheson, William, 204–5
Hyde Park (Manhattan), 122, 126, 204, 210, 271
hydroelectric power, 140, 196, 210, 271, 287, 288
  rural expansion, 221
  see also electricity

Ickes, Harold, 128, 138, 213, 218, 238–9, 276
  and oil industry, 189
  and Public Works Administration, 184, 187, 223
Idaho, delegations, 178
ideology, and political affiliations, 48–9
Il Duce *see* Mussolini, Benito
Illinois
  bank holidays, 119
  National Guard troops, 69
  poor relief, 68, 88
  relief programs, 227
  urban demonstrations, 108
Illinois Central Railroad, 110
IMF *see* International Monetary Fund (IMF)
immigration
  illegal, 65
  restrictions, 23, 65–7
Immigration and Naturalization Service, 65
Inauguration Day, 130
income *see* wages
Indian Reorganization Act (1934), 286

Indiana, urban demonstrations, 108
Indiana Harbor (Indiana), riots, 106
industrial production
  decline, 24
  investments, 151–2
  pricing policies, 155
industrial recovery, politics, 180–8
industrial relations
  and class conflict, 248–9
  crises, 247
industrialized nations, unemployment, 29
inflation, 162–3
  and recovery, 165
  see also deflation; reflation
insurance companies, collapse, 117
Interior Department, 219, 278
international economic relations, issues, 26–7
International Labor Office, studies, 26, 87
International Monetary Fund (IMF), 32
international monetary system, and Great Depression, 27
Interstate Commerce Commission, 189
Interstate Oil Compact, 189
investments
  industrial production, 151–2
  overseas, 25
Iowa, agrarian revolt, 102, 172–3
Issacs, Ben, 80
Italy
  fascism, 32
  gold payments, 30–1
  tariffs, 29

Jackson, Robert, 276
Japan
  assault on China, 9
  "Co-Prosperity Sphere", 32
  economic decline, 26

AMR237
48